COMPUTATIONAL INTELLIGENCE FOR PATIENT CARE

Blockchain, AI, and ML in Healthcare

COMPUTATIONAL INTELLIGENCE FOR PATIENT CARE

Blockchain, AI, and ML in Healthcare

Rishabha Malviya, PhD
Rishav Sharma, MPharm
Sathvik Belagodu Sridhar, PhD
Suraj Kumar, BPharm

APPLE ACADEMIC PRESS

First edition published 2026

Apple Academic Press Inc.
1265 Goldenrod Circle, NE,
Palm Bay, FL 32905 USA

760 Laurentian Drive, Unit 19,
Burlington, ON L7N 0A4, Canada

CRC Press
2385 NW Executive Center Drive,
Suite 320, Boca Raton FL 33431

4 Park Square, Milton Park,
Abingdon, Oxon, OX14 4RN, UK

Library and Archives Canada Cataloguing in Publication

CIP data on file with Canada Library and Archives

Library of Congress Cataloging-in-Publication Data

CIP data on file with US Library of Congress

ISBN: 978-1-779640-80-2 (hbk)
ISBN: 978-1-779640-81-9 (ebk)
DOI: 10.1201/9781779640819

About the Authors

Rishabha Malviya, PhD
Professor, Department of Pharmacy, School of Medical and Allied Sciences, Galgotias University, India; Galgotias Multi-Disciplinary Research & Development Cell (G-MRDC), Galgotias University, Greater Noida, U.P., India

Rishabha Malviya, PhD, has over 13 years of research experience and is presently working as Professor in the Department of Pharmacy, School of Medical and Allied Sciences, Galgotias University, Greater Noida, Uttar Pradesh, India. His areas of interest include formulation optimization, nanoformulation, targeted drug delivery, localized drug delivery, and characterization of natural polymers as pharmaceutical excipients. He has authored more than 150 research and review papers for national and international journals. He holds over 50 patents and has published many papers in reputed national and international journals, for which he received an outstanding reviewer award from Elsevier. He has edited 110 books (Wiley, Springer Nature, CRC Press/Taylor & Francis, Apple Academic Press, River Publisher, Lambert, and OMICS Publishing Group) and authored 87 book chapters. His name has been included in the World's Top 2% Scientists list by Elsevier BV and Stanford University. He is reviewer, editor, and editorial board member of more than 50 national and international journals. He was an invited author for the magazine *Atlas of Science* as well as a pharma magazine dealing with B2B industry, *Ingredient South Asia.* He completed his BPharm from Uttar Pradesh Technical University and MPharm (Pharmaceutics) from Gautam Buddha Technical University, Lucknow, Uttar Pradesh, India. His PhD (Pharmacy) work was in novel formulation development techniques.

Rishav Sharma, MPharm
Scientist, F&D Department, Aculife HealthCare Pvt Ltd. (Nirma Group), Ahmedabad, Gujarat, India

Rishav Sharma, MPharm, is currently working as Scientist in F&D department of Aculife HealthCare Pvt Ltd. (Nirma Group), Ahmedabad, Gujarat, India. He has authored two books and eight book chapters with reputed international publishers. He has published 15 SCI/ Scopus manuscripts with reputed international publishers and attended more than 10 national and international conferences. He has completed his BPharm from the Kanpur Institute of Technology and Pharmacy, Kanpur, Uttar Pradesh, India, and MPharm from Galgotias University, Greater Noida, Uttar Pradesh, India.

Sathvik Belagodu Sridhar, PhD
Associate Dean and Professor, Department of Pharmacy, RAK Medical and Health Sciences University, Ras Al Khaimah, United Arab Emirates

Sathvik Belagodu Sridhar, PhD is currently working as an Associate Dean and Professor at RAK College of Pharmacy (RAKCOP), RAK Medical and Health Sciences University located in Ras Al Khaimah, United Arab Emirates. Dr. Sathvik completed his PhD in Clinical Pharmacy from Rajiv Gandhi University of Health Sciences, Bangalore, India. He received an FIP fellowship for higher training in renal clinical pharmacy at the Royal Adelaide Hospital and Queen Elizabeth Hospital in Adelaide, South Australia. Dr. Sathvik has worked as an Assistant Professor and Clinical Pharmacist at JSS College of Pharmacy and JSS Medical College Hospital, Mysore, India, for eight years and later joined International Medical University (IMU), Malaysia, as a Senior Lecturer in the Department of Pharmacy Practice from 2008 to 2010. Dr. Sridhar joined as an Assistant Professor in the Department of Clinical Pharmacy at RAK College of Pharmacy, RAK Medical, and Health Sciences University in 2010 and worked as a Professor and Chairperson of the Department of Clinical Pharmacy and Pharmacology from 2018 to 2023. Dr. Sridhar has been honored with a prestigious teacher award by the Society of Pharmaceutical Education & Research (SPER). He has also received training in pharmacovigilance at the Uppsala Monitoring Centre in Uppsala, Sweden. Dr. Sridhar has 25 years of teaching experience and practicing clinical pharmacy in India, Malaysia, and the UAE.

His research interests include medication safety, pharmacovigilance, pharmacoepidemiology, and renal and psychiatry clinical pharmacy. Dr. Sridhar has more than 75 research papers published in reputable national and international journals, along with book chapters. He has presented more than 75 research papers at numerous national and international conferences and has been honored with many awards. He also serves as a reviewer for various national and international pharmacy practice-related journals.

Suraj Kumar, BPharm
Assistant Professor, Pragya College of Pharmaceutical Sciences, Gaya, Bihar, India; Department of Pharmacy, School of Medical and Allied Sciences, Galgotias University, India

Suraj Kumar completed BPharm from SRM University, Chengalpattu, Tamil Nadu, India, and MPharm from Galgotias University, Greater Noida, Uttar Pradesh, India. Currently, he is working as an Assistant Professor at the Pragya College of Pharmaceutical Sciences, Gaya, Bihar, India. He has attended more than 10 international and national conferences. He has published more than 10 SCI-indexed publications with reputed international publishers including Elsevier, Wiley, and Bentham Science, with a 40 cumulative impact factor. He has published eight book chapters, and one book is under consideration for publication.

Contents

Abbreviations

AD	Alzheimer's disease
AF	atrial fibrillation
AI	artificial intelligence
AI-ECG	artificial intelligence-enhanced echocardiogram
ALL	ambient aided living
AMD	age-related macular degeneration
ANN	artificial neural network
AREDS	age-dependent ocular disease investigation
ARPANET	Antidepressant Response Prediction Network
AS	aortic stenosis
ASD	autism spectrum disorder
AUC	area under the curve
BBB	blood–brain barrier
BCT	blockchain technology
BMI	body mass index
CAD	coronary artery disease
CAS	Computer-Assisted Surgery
CBR	case-based reasoning
CCTA	coronary artery disease computed tomographic angiogram
CDR	cup-to-disc ratio
CDSS	cardiovascular disease decision support system
CGM	continuous glucose monitoring
CHD	congenital heart disease
CMR	cardiac magnetic resonance imaging
CNN	convolutional neural network
CNS	central nervous system
CNV	choroidal neovascularization
CRT	cardiac resynchronization therapy
CT	computed tomography
CVD	cardiovascular disease
DC	dilated cardiomyopathy
DCNN	deep convolutional neural network
DDCS	digital drug control system
DL	deep learning
DMO	diabetic macular edema
DNN	deep neural network

DPoS	delegated proof of stake
DR	diabetic retinopathy
DTI	drug–target interactions
ECA	embodied conversational agents
ECG	electrocardiogram
EEG	electroencephalogram
EF	ejection fraction
EGFRs	epidermal growth factor receptors
EHR	electronic health record
EHT	endocrine hypertension
EMR	electronic medical record
FFR	fractionated flow reserve
FHIR	fast healthcare interoperability resources
fUS	functional ultrasound
GDPR	General Data Protection Regulation
GHMS	general health monitoring system
GSM	General Smart Monitoring
HAR	activity recognition of humans
HCM	hypertrophic cardiomyopathy
HDAC	histone deacetylase
HF	heart failure
HTS	high-throughput screening
IoMT	Internet of Medical Things
IOP	intraocular pressure
IoT	Internet of Things
KNN	K-nearest neighbor
LID	levodopa-induced dyskinesia
LVEF	left ventricle ejection fraction
MBF	myocardial blood flow
m-health	mobile-health
MHMS	mobile health monitoring system
MID	medical imaging and image diagnostics
ML	machine learning
MMMER	Medication Management and Medication Error Reduction
MPI	myocardial perfusion imaging
MPR	myocardial perfusion reserve
MR	mixed reality
MRI	magnetic resonance imaging
NLP	natural language processing
NN	neural network
OCT	optical coherence tomography
ONH	optic nerve head

PA	primary estrogenic deficiency
PD	Parkinson's disease
PHM	patient health monitoring
PHT	primary arterial hypertension
PoC	proof of capacity
PoS	proof of stake
PoW	proof of work
QSAR	quantitatively structure-activity relationship
RAS	robot-assisted surgery
RASS	robotic-assisted surgical system
RGN	recurring geometric shape network
RHMS	remote health monitoring system
ROP	retinopathy of prematurity
RP	recurrent partitioning
SHM	smart health monitoring
SOM	self-organizing maps
SPECT	single-photon emission computed tomography
SVM	support vector machine
TL	transfer learning
VF	visual field
VF	ventricular fibrillation
VNA	virtual nurse assistants
WHMS	wearable health monitoring system
WHO	World Health Organization

Foreword

This book, *Computational Intelligence for Patient Care: Blockchain, AI, and ML in Healthcare,* explores the role of revolutionary technologies and their use in healthcare. The book, authored by Dr. Rishabha Malviya and team, explores the potential of blockchain technology in securing electronic health records (EHRs), in enhancing clinical research, and for detecting medical fraud. It also discusses the synergy between blockchain and big data, highlighting the role of these technologies that can work together to create robust, efficient, and secure healthcare systems.

The role of artificial intelligence (AI) is highlighted for its ability to improve patient outcomes via smart health monitoring systems and remote monitoring technologies. The extensive investigation of the role of AI in the management of diabetes and cardiovascular disease demonstrates the potential for personalized therapy and improved diagnostic reliability. The book also offers insights concerning various technologies, covering both the advantages and disadvantages.

The book explains that AI-powered diagnostic and therapeutic solutions are revolutionizing patient care in specialized domains like cardiovascular health and ophthalmology. The growth of AI and machine learning (ML) in drug discovery, particularly for the central nervous system, demonstrates the potential for game-changing advances in drug development. The book explores the technicalities of applying AI and ML to discover new drug targets and create treatments for neurological illnesses.

The regulatory landscape has been managed with precision, providing a thorough overview of the issues and duties that regulators face. This topic is critical for determining the future of AI integration in healthcare and ensuring that these technologies are used ethically and effectively.

The book provides an in-depth overview of computational intelligence and its applications in healthcare, emphasizing its transformational power.

The authors have compiled a resource that is both informative and visionary, emphasizing the revolutionary power of computational technology. The book will be an invaluable resource for those looking to use technology to improve patient care and healthcare outcomes, showing computational intelligence's transformative potential in this field.
Happy Reading and Best Wishes!

—Dr. Dhruv Galgotia
CEO, Galgotias University,
Greater Noida, Uttar Pradesh, India

Preface

This book, *Computational Intelligence for Patient Care: Blockchain, AI, and ML in Healthcare,* explores the revolutionizing applications of blockchain, artificial intelligence (AI), and machine learning (ML) in healthcare systems. With unparalleled potential to improve patient outcomes, strengthen data security, and streamline operations, the book attempts to close the gap between cutting-edge computational approaches and real-world healthcare applications. The book is divided into 10 chapters, each of which focuses on a crucial area of healthcare-related computational intelligence.

The first chapter of the book provides an overview of blockchain technology and its uses in the healthcare industry, highlighting its potential for clinical research, medical fraud detection, and electronic health records (EHRs). The book further explores the use of blockchain technology in the creation of digital healthcare systems, emphasizing the benefits of combining big data with blockchain technology while also going over institutional considerations and security issues.

Furthermore, the book discusses the use of AI in healthcare, covering topics such as telemedicine's development, AI-assisted remote monitoring, and smart health monitoring systems. Additionally, the book explores AI's inclusive approach to disease management, management of chronic illnesses, accuracy of diagnoses, and personalized therapy. The book also covers the development of AI and ML in CNS drug discovery, emphasizing novel uses of these technologies in the development of pharmaceuticals for neurological disorders.

The last chapter discusses the regulatory landscape, including the problems and duties of regulators in regulating the integration of AI in healthcare, as well as insights into future regulatory policies.

CHAPTER 1

Blockchain: A Distributed Ledger Technology for Patient Care

ABSTRACT

The administration of data, banking, food science, the Internet of Things, and cybersecurity is just a few of the businesses and professions that benefit from blockchain technology. Even healthcare and brain research have shown a growing interest in blockchain technology. There has been an incredible uptick in curiosity about how blockchain technology may be put to use to improve the delivery of trustworthy healthcare data management. In addition, blockchain is transforming conventional healthcare methods to more trustworthy means, allowing for more precise diagnosis and more efficient treatment thanks to the secure sharing of patient data. Blockchain has the potential to be a technology that aids in providing tailored, authentic, and secure healthcare in the future by centralizing all of a patient's up-to-date clinical data and presenting it in a modern, safe healthcare environment. In this chapter, investigators examine the recent and ongoing changes brought about by the introduction of blockchain technology to the healthcare industry. Investigators also talk about the blockchain's potential uses, as well as its current limitations and potential in the future.

1.1 INTRODUCTION

A sector that relies heavily on data is the healthcare clinical arena because of the sheer volume of data that is constantly being created, retrieved, and disseminated. Due to the significance of preserving the confidentiality

Computational Intelligence for Patient Care: Blockchain, AI, and ML in Healthcare.
Rishabha Malviya, Rishav Sharma, Sathvik Belagodu Sridhar, and Suraj Kumar (Authors)

DOI: 10.1201/9781779640819-1

of individual records, keeping and sharing this amount of data present many challenges [1]. The healthcare business and clinical settings require diagnosis and International Classification of Diseases for Mortality and Morbidity data exchange. By utilizing the information-sharing mechanism, doctors can easily transmit their patients' medical records to the appropriate authority for prompt follow-up. To guarantee that all parties involved in a patient's treatment have accurate and up-to-date information, primary care physicians and other specialists must be able to securely and promptly share their patients' clinical data. Conversely, telemedicine and electronic health care are rapidly expanding fields in which patients' medical records are electronically transmitted to a remote doctor for a second opinion. The patient's information is transmitted in these two types of online clinical settings or by real-time online monitoring in the medical industry, sometimes known as "store-and-forward technology" (such as telemonitoring, telemetry, and the like) [2, 3]. Patients can receive second opinion from specialists anywhere in the world thanks to these virtual clinics. Since patient information is often highly sensitive, protecting its confidentiality is a top priority in all therapeutic settings. Supporting healthy and relevant clinical communications, especially about remote patient cases, necessitates the capacity for reliable, secure, and scalable data sharing. Clinical communication is aided by the secure and reliable transfer of information when experts in other fields weigh in with their recommendations or confirmations, enhancing the quality of both diagnosis and treatment [4–6]. Furthermore, numerous interoperability issues are constantly being confronted in this field. Clinical data transmission between hospitals and universities, for example, can be extremely difficult to do safely and securely. Clinical data exchanges of this nature necessitate substantial, trustworthy, and healthy engagement among the entities involved. Patient matching algorithms, ethical standards, and government regulations are all complex, and they all add another layer of difficulty to process all the potential stumbling hurdles, as is the private and sensitive nature of clinical data. All of these key concerns need to be resolved peacefully before there can be a meaningful exchange of clinical data [7]. Researchers have been working hard over the past few years to develop Internet of Things, artificial intelligence (AI), machine learning (ML), and computer vision applications that can aid clinicians in the detection and management of persistent health problems. There has been a significant uptick in the study of how blockchain can be put to use in fields including neuroimaging, healthcare data distribution, and brain modeling and simulation [8–10]. A blockchain is the natural evolution of the internet's peer-to-peer system. In essence, it is a structure for multifield, peer-to-peer integrated networks that use distributed consensus methods to address the problems with data consistency that have plagued traditional approaches to distributed databases. There are six main characteristics of the blockchain: decentralization, transparency, immutability, privacy, anonymity, and open-source development (as described in Table 1.1).

TABLE 1.1 Features Essential to Blockchain Technology

Vital Components	Specifying Function
Decentralized	Access to the database is granted to all network users without restriction. Multiple platforms are available for accessing, monitoring, storing, and updating the data
Transparent	Those interested in accessing the data may see exactly what is being recorded and kept on the blockchain, and the data can be easily updated as needed. Blockchain, because of its immutable nature, may be able to stop data from being corrupted or stolen
Immutable	Once the data has been recorded, it is locked away permanently and cannot be easily changed unless more than 51% of the nodes are controlled by the same party
Autonomy	Each node in the blockchain system has its secure means of accessing, transferring, storing, and updating the data, making it reliable and immune to tampering from third parties
Open Source	By design, blockchain technology is open source, so anyone with network access can study it. This unparalleled adaptability allows not only for public record searching but also the creation of a wide range of useful future applications
Anonymity	Individuals' identities are concealed during data transfers between nodes, making the system more secure and trustworthy

Each new transaction must be validated by a member of this network. The immutability of a blockchain increases as each transaction within the computer in the network checks every new block to make sure it is valid. Blockchain has the potential to be a technology that aids in tailored, dependable, and secure healthcare in the future by compiling all relevant clinical information about a patient in real time and displaying it as part of a modern, risk-free healthcare system [11].

1.2 RELATED WORK

Several studies have shown that blockchain technology (BCT) could facilitate better healthcare data interchange and other diagnostic applications. An example of such a system is the healthcare data gateway technique described by Yue et al. [12], which suggests keeping track of each patient's clinical data in a private blockchain. In this individualized healthcare model, patients have access to a blockchain (a centralized database system with restricted access control only entitled to authorized or specified users) containing their whole medical history and a summary of their treatment. Similarly, Griggs et al. [13] used an ethereum-based private blockchain to eliminate the drawbacks of remote patient monitoring and ensure the secure distribution of medical sensors. Their blockchain-based approach may pave the way for trustworthy real-time remote monitoring, allowing doctors to keep tabs on their patients' health from afar while keeping a secure and up-to-date medical record. Ivan et al. also showed how to create encryption using a public blockchain (a distributed database technology that permits unrestricted access by everyone on the network), which is a step in the direction of safe health data storage [14]. A blockchain-based electronic health record (EHR) is used in this method created by making the encrypted healthcare data publicly available (personal health record). By using their method, patients will have complete control over their medical records, including the freedom to see, edit, and share their information with any healthcare provider of their choosing. Similarly, Chen et al. [15] cloud computing and distributed ledger technologies (blockchain) were offered as a means of organizing and disseminating patients' medical records. Therefore, the proposed method may be employed for the safekeeping and transmission of private patient medical records. The proposed solution is novel since it does not involve any intermediaries in the handling of patients' sensitive medical data. Using parallel processing and simulated medical networks, Wang et al. [16] have introduced a blockchain structure for diagnosing patients' health conditions. The proposed method utilizes parallel executions and computational trials to evaluate the current state, diagnosis, and treatment process of the patient, thereby informing clinical decision-making. Real-world and simulation tests have been conducted on the proposed technique and simulated healthcare environments to determine its efficacy in making correct diagnoses and providing appropriate therapy. BloCHIE was created by Jiang et al. and is the first blockchain-based healthcare data exchange platform [17]. The proposed system assesses data sharing needs in healthcare, not only for individual health records and electronic medical files but also for other types of information. Using blockchain with several data sources, they integrated verification both on- and off-chain procedures into the platform to ensure it met users' needs for anonymity and transparency. Using BCT, confidentiality, privacy, and transparency in data exchange between clinicians and healthcare providers can be improved. The same principle was used in [18], which proposed an innovative and organized architecture using BCT to secure patient data, solve pressing data security problems, and introduce the technology across a whole healthcare network. The fields of biomedical study and clinical practice also show enormous promise for BCT. Before beginning a clinical trial or examination, all consents, protocols, and designs could be digitally signed using BCT and kept permanently in one central location. In this approach, the public would have access to information that is timely, accurate, protected, and safeguarded from unauthorized use. In contrast, smart contracts might be implemented, reproduced, and ultimately executed throughout the various clinical trial phases to ensure transparency and candor (if followed and validated correctly). For the remote diagnosis and treatment of malignant tumors, Shubbar introduced a blockchain-based telemonitoring healthcare infrastructure [19]. The suggested protocol is predicated on the use of smart contracts and distributed ledger technology (blockchain) both of which can be widely deployed to ensure the integrity and confidentiality of patient information in healthcare settings, other healthcare facilities, as well as in patients' own homes. To help patients get the dermatological care they need, DermoNet was developed as a blockchain-based solution for use in a teledermatology monitoring system. In contrast, the Proactive Aging [20] platform uses BCT to promote healthy aging and active participation in life for older adults. It is important to note that there are situations where BCT is ideally suited such as in protracted medical treatment processes including those associated with chronic diseases (such as cancer), surgical procedures, and aging. Furthermore, DNA data saved on blockchain may allow pharmaceutical businesses, medication producers, and biomedical researchers to perform cutting-edge multinational research at the genomic level. One can look to the future and predict that blockchain will be one of the developing technologies of any time, given the worldwide rise in the popularity of ICTs. As a result, it is reasonable to anticipate that BCT will advance, extend, and acquire new avenues at a quicker rate in the years to come [20].

1.3 APPLICATION

While BCT's early development was motivated by its obvious financial and cryptocurrency uses, the technology is finding increasing applicability in other domains, including biology [10]. Due to its ability to stabilize and protect the dataset with which users can engage via various sorts of transactions, BCT is showing promise in medicine, genomics, telemedicine, telemonitoring, e-health, neuroscience, and personalized healthcare applications (as depicted in the model, shown in Figure 1.1).

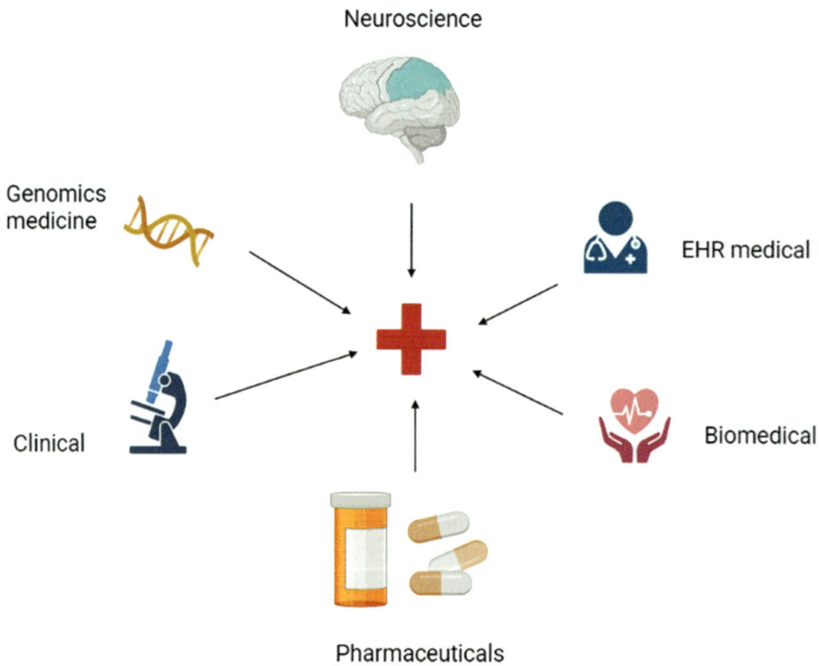

FIGURE 1.1 Applications of blockchain technology in healthcare.

Source: Adapted from Ref. [56]

Below, the investigator looks at a few sectors of healthcare and medicine where BCT shows very promising results.

1.4 BLOCKCHAIN FOR EHRS

The need to digitize medical health records has skyrocketed over the past decade since doing so facilitates easier gaining access to and exchanging information, thus laying the groundwork for more sound and swifter decision-making. This holds especially true for medical centers and equipment. Today, electronic medical records (EMRs) are the primary application of the use of blockchain in medical care (as shown in Figure 1.2).

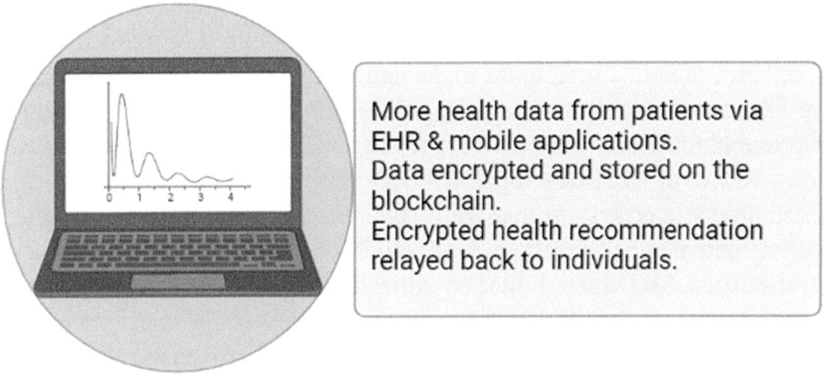

FIGURE 1.2 Schematic illustration of the interactions between preventative care, blockchain technology, and mobile health applications.

Source: Adapted from Ref. [56]

Conversely, EHRs were not meant to handle a patient's entire medical history across multiple institutions; consequently, as patients move from one provider's care to another, their records often end up dispersed across multiple EHR systems, making it difficult for them to retrieve information from their past data [21–23]. Many scholars have proposed using BCT to manage EHRs, citing the urgent need for a novel approach to promote patient engagement with their medical records, both current and historical. MedRec is a prototype that uses the benefits of the blockchain to handle issues such as authentication, privacy, and the reliability of data transfers. Built on top of a decentralized database management system, it will allow patients to easily share and access their medical records across all of their care providers and facilities [24]. It is not necessary to adjust to using "MedRec," nor does it save any medical records. The patient, who is ultimately responsible for the record's location, is given guidance as to where the data can be transferred and a unique identifier is recorded on a blockchain.

The seal ensures that a copy of the record in its original form was purchased. Also, it shifts the burden of ownership from the company to the individual patient, which can be seen as both a burden and a source of power. The purpose of administration associations is to serve as patient agents for those patients who would rather have someone else handle their information. Many of today's separate patient entrances have complicated designs, add extra work, and include different UIs across facilities. Architecture for medical research and evaluation features a user interface for better, more long-lasting access to healthcare records as they are transferred between facilities. Medical records that have been compromised in terms of threat to privacy, data integrity, audit trails, and loss of control over data tracing are all serious problems that arise while implementing EHR, making it impossible for healthcare providers to share data. Because of these restrictions, Xia et al. [25] developed MeDShare, a platform built on top of a distributed ledger system that facilitates private transactions and medical records between organizations with which one cannot establish a reliable level of trust. MeDShare might be utilized by healthcare providers, hospitals, and research facilities in the cloud to safely exchange and store patient information and EHRs, while also improving data provenance, providing individual audit control, and reducing the risk of data loss. EHRs include private and vital information about patients and are routinely shared among doctors, radiologists, nurses, pharmacists, and researchers to improve patient care and speed up recovery after treatment. This highly sensitive patient information poses serious risks to patient health and to keeping an accurate medical history when it is stored, transmitted, and distributed among multiple entities. Chronic illness patients' protracted experiences with diagnosis, care, and recovery (such as cancer and HIV) can increase the prevalence of such hazards. As a result, keeping a current medical history is crucial for providing appropriate care. To circumvent these regulations, Dubovitskaya et al. [26] devised a blockchain-based system for organizing, storing, and exchanging electronic medical records of cancer patients. They settled on a private blockchain network for the safe transfer, storage, and management of patient data. Each of these systems can be utilized to put BCT into action into use in clinical settings, allowing for more convenient and secure access to patient records and data. The Estonian blockchain-based project for healthcare records is another historical benchmark. The Estonian government's 2016 proposal to protect the privacy of millions of medical records while making them easily accessible to healthcare professionals and insurance helped propel the country to the forefront of BCT [27]. Patients' confidence in BCT to ensure the integrity of their healthcare records may be driving its rapid adoption around the world. It is possible to immediately flag and recognize across the blockchain every attempt at access or modification. This aids in the prevention of identity theft and the discovery of criminal acts like the widespread forging or tampering of medical records. Furthermore, valid medical care records will be considerably simpler to analyze and exchange. A patient's visit typically gets fast attention from the majority of their providers. Without the need for time-consuming pharmaceutical compromise forms, appropriate patient-caring algorithms can quickly and efficiently adapt medication bugs, hypersensitivities, and drug remedies across all blockchain records. As a result, BCT will lead to improved patient access, medical record management [28], clinical information validation promptly, higher levels of security, and more streamlined care delivery [29].

1.5 BLOCKCHAIN IN CLINICAL RESEARCH

Clinical trials can face a variety of challenges such as those related to patient enrollment [29], information security [30], confidentiality [31], veracity [32], and utility. Since blockchain represents the future generation of the internet, it is well positioned to offer workable answers to these issues. Researchers in the healthcare sector are attempting to find solutions to these problems by employing BCT [31, 32]. Together, blockchain, AI, and ML will soon disrupt the healthcare industry.

When integrated with preexisting clinic-based data management systems, ethereum's smart contract functionality on the blockchain can improve efficiency and accuracy. Discovering efficient means of boosting patient enrollment was the primary focus of this study. Results demonstrated that ethereum led to faster transactions than bitcoin, hence the study's conclusion recommended using the ethereum blockchain to facilitate transparent data management in clinical trials. This has led to blockchain being used for patient enrollment in clinical trials. Mehdi Benchoufi [33, 34] did supplementary research: patient-informed consent is now collected in a method that is safe, publically verifiable, and unfalsifiable thanks to a newly established system. When designing the workflow, they turned to BCT.

1.5.1 BLOCKCHAIN IN MEDICAL FRAUD DETECTION

Pharmaceutical supply chain management is only one area where blockchain is showing its worth in the healthcare sector. Because of the increasing complexity of healthcare supply chains, reliable supply chain management is of paramount importance in this sector. This is because patient's health is directly tied to the integrity of the healthcare supply chain [35]. Since supply chains involve many different parties and people, they are susceptible to fraud and have many potential entry points. Blockchain provides a trustworthy platform with enhanced data transparency and product traceability that can do away with the problem and, in certain situations, forestall fraud from happening. This makes it difficult to manipulate blockchain [36]; blockchain data with only a smart contract can verify and update.

1.5.2 BLOCKCHAIN IN NEUROSCIENCE

The field of neuroscience is included in the increasing amount of coverage given to blockchain applications in the media and academic research [37]. The goal of today's neural technologies is to create a new norm in which people do not need to physically interact with their environments to command their devices and their data. These neural devices may someday be able to decode a person's thoughts from their brain activity and use that information to control external devices. Multiple sensors, computing processors, and a wireless link make it possible for neural interface devices to read and analyze brain signals. They detect brainwaves, decode them, and send the information to the machinery they are in charge of. This is accomplished through a single gadget worn on the head that performs all of these functions. On the neural interface, complex algorithms and large data will utilize the blockchain philosophy to record mental processes. Companies such as Neurogress have revealed their intentions to implement BCT. The firm, which was established in 2017 and has its headquarters in Geneva, focuses on developing neural-control technologies that will enable people to command intelligent robot arms, drones, smart home appliances, and virtual reality gadgets. These technologies are now under development. In order to improve its accuracy in reading brain activity, Neurogress's control system depends on ML, which requires retaining

90% of brain data. The inventors have devised a method to educate about the performance of AI. Therefore, the capacity to store for the organization is "exabytes" (1 exabyte = 1 billion gigabytes) of storage capacity that is required for "big data of user brain activity." According to the company, blockchain "effectively tackles information privacy and security issues"; thus, it's no surprise that Neurogress intends to implement it. Because of the distributed ledger technology used by blockchain, user information is "immune to hacker attacks" and is, therefore, more secure. In addition, when it comes to "possible consumers of the Neurogress platform services," the Neurogress system is "open and transparent" thanks to BCT. Personal information provided in the system will be safe and secure due to the ease with which unusual behavior may be identified. Undoubtedly, one of the numerous possible benefits of BCT, which is a type of information technology, is the potential to facilitate brain augmentation, brain stimulation, and brain-like mental processes. Keeping all that data from a fully digitized human brain in one place is a challenge, and when something like this occurs, BCT is used again. It has been proposed that mind files, the data components of unique thought chains, be stored in a distributed file system where previous versions can be recovered. A computer is a computing system with input, processing, and output; the blockchain way of thinking is recommended because it has various properties that can benefit AI, human augmentation, and the possibility of combining the two. To verify the integrity of a distributed ledger and its original creator, blockchain permits a network of computers to "high five" each other at regular intervals marked by a timestamp [12, 13]. If a designer were to start from scratch and design a brain, this sort of trust mechanism may help neural networks distinguish between the subjective and objective aspects of an experience to store and retrieve relevant information more reliably and accurately. Safely constructing a quantified-self data commons for humans is made possible by multifactor verification based on one's mental chain, realized as a blockchain. This type of data commons dismantles organizational barriers to data while allowing people to retain control over the information they share and the reason they share it, whether for profit or personal reasons. In the future, with the help of an improved variant of this technology in which multiple observers witness the same event from unique vantage points, the investigator could piece together their accounts to form a more objective picture of what occurred in that instant. The potential for subjectively seeing from another person's perspective and the possibility of creating virtual reproductions of prior experiences are two exciting possibilities that could be unlocked through this [14, 15]. If the researcher could more easily tie specific feelings and events to specific memories, the investigator could include sensory data in the blockchain of the future (i.e., sight, smell, and so forth). There are already plans to develop the necessary technology. Soon, wearable electronics, the current state of brain and nerve implants, biofeedback imaging, and any other sensors that allow for a multifactor fingerprint distinct to a given human's record of temporal experience may make it possible for us to begin storing sensory experiences. Studies on how to enhance decision-making, learning, memory, and rehabilitation protocols can all make use of these technologies as a springboard.

1.5.3 BLOCKCHAIN TECHNOLOGY FOR THE PHARMACEUTICAL INDUSTRY AND RESEARCH STUDIES

When it comes to providing healthcare, the pharmaceutical industry is not only rapidly expanding but also a forerunner. The pharmaceutical industry plays a vital role in guaranteeing the quality of consumer-facing pharmaceuticals and medical supplies and paving the way for the development of novel, potentially life-saving treatments. The pharmaceutical industry not only helps evaluate [28] and process safe pharmaceuticals but also helps patients recover from their illnesses more quickly. Drug manufacturers often have trouble keeping accurate records of where their products are, which can put patients in danger if counterfeiters can undermine manufacturing or sneak in fake pharmaceuticals. In light of this, falsified medications are a major problem worldwide, especially in underdeveloped regions. When it comes to assessing, keeping an eye on, and checking up on the manufacturing of cutting-edge medications, blockchain may be an ideal technology for use in both manufacturing and R&D. Hyperledger [38], a research organization, recently started a project to check and combat the creation of counterfeit medicines utilizing BCT as a primary tool. Globally, but especially in developing nations, the use of digital technology to monitor, assess, and assure the entire process of manufacturing and supplying pharmaceutical pharmaceuticals is urgently needed to ensure the efficient distribution of safe and legal medicines to those who need them. Therefore, a digital drug control system (DDCS)

[39] may be an effective long-term strategy for combating the sale of imitation drugs. Big pharmaceutical companies, including Sanofi, Pfizer, and Amgen, have launched a pilot program to inspect and evaluate new medications utilizing blockchain-based distributed ledger technology (DDCS) [40]. Besides enhancing counterfeit pharmaceuticals' traceability [41], the safety of the distribution network for pharmaceuticals [42], and the assurance of high-quality medication for patients, this helps prevent the spread of dangerous drugs [39]. Blockchain might be used to track the manufacturing and placement of drugs at any given moment. Table 1.2 provides a summary of applications of BCT to help progress healthcare and medical research.

TABLE 1.2 Integrating Blockchain into the Healthcare Industry

Implementation	Brief Overview
Electronic health records	The security of an electronic health record is stored on an approved blockchain's distributed ledger with no tampering from humans at any time along the process (from data creation to data retrieval)
Clinical research	Blockchain creates a distributed, impenetrable data storage system, paving way to conceivable future partnerships in the field of medical investigation. By doing this, researchers can safely share data
Medical fraud detection	Because of its immutability, blockchain technology can aid in the discovery of fraudulent transactions, prohibiting any alterations or duplicates to the deal, and ultimately permitting a safe and open exchange of information
Neuroscience research	As a new technological development, blockchain has many potential uses shortly, including brain hacking, brain stimulation, and brain analysis. If designers are ever going to be able to fully digitize the human brain, investigators would need a way to store all of that data, and that is where blockchain technology comes in
Pharmaceutical industry and research	Blockchain's ability to track transactions in minute detail allows it to monitor the entirety of a process, where the medicine comes from, how it is made, and what goes into making it which are all part of the pharmaceutical supply chain; ownership is often checked at each level to prevent forgery and theft of merchandise

1.6 CHALLENGES

As a promising new technology, blockchain is quickly gaining traction across industries [43] because of its many useful features [44] and promising prospects [45]. However, there are problems with this technology that need fixing (as depicted in Figure 1.3). Some of the more significant ones are covered below.

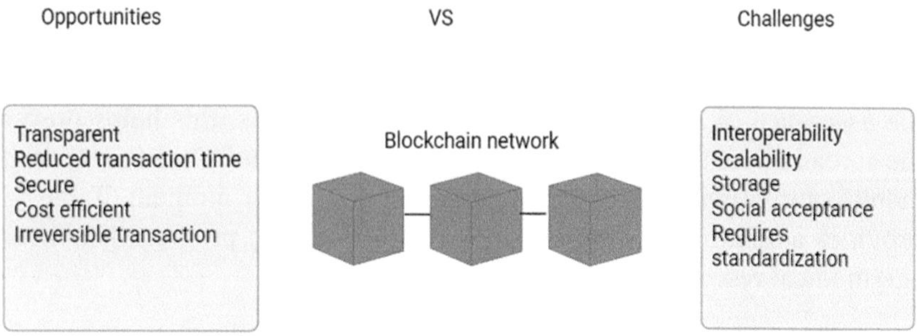

FIGURE 1.3 Possibilities and problems with healthcare blockchains.
Source: Adapted from Ref. [56]

1.6.1 INFORMATION DISCRETION AND SAFETY

The primary issue is, first and foremost, keeping information secret and private [46]. A trusted third party is not necessary while conducting a transaction, thanks to the use of blockchain-based applications [44]. Blockchain's distributed ledger technology means that the community as a whole may attest to the accuracy of its records instead of relying on any one entity to do so.

Consequently, due to the data's exposed design [47], it may be at risk of being compromised. Since all nodes may see what information is being sent by any one node, privacy is compromised. The onus of authorizing another person's access to a patient's information and/or medical history falls on the patient, who must instead designate one or more representatives. This representative can now grant access to a group of people who will all be viewing the same patient's details, which might result in a massive data breach endangering one's privacy and safety. The receivers will only be able to access partial or incomplete data if high-security methods are applied to the data, which will cause transfer difficulties between blocks. In addition, a 51% attack [48] is a type of security vulnerability that can occur on blockchain networks. Collective mining power that owns more than 50% of a blockchain's blocks can launch a majority control attack. Miners gain control over the network and can block further transactions if they choose not to approve them. Coindesk [49] reports that five cryptocurrencies have fallen prey to this attack in recent weeks. The information contained in a patient's record may also be too private to be stored on a public ledger [50].

1.6.2 MANAGING STORAGE CAPACITY

The administration of storage space is another difficulty in this area. Because of its narrow focus, BCT does not require large amounts of storage space to record and process transactions [51]. As technology grew and expanded into new areas, including healthcare, new storage difficulties were plain to see. Data processing is a constant challenge in the healthcare industry. In a blockchain, all nodes will have access to the same data about every patient, including their medical history, lab results, and even MRI scans and X-rays will require a lot of room in the closet [52, 53]. Furthermore, because of the transactional nature of blockchain applications, the underlying databases tend to grow quickly. As databases grow larger, it takes longer to look up and retrieve records, making them inappropriate for certain sorts of transactions. This emphasizes the importance of scalability and robustness in a blockchain solution [54].

1.6.3 INTEROPERABILITY ISSUES

Interoperability [46] is another problem plaguing BCT, which refers to the inability to interact between blockchain from different providers and services in an appropriate manner. Since this is a problem, information cannot be shared as effectively as possible [55].

1.6.4 INTEROPERABILITY ISSUES

For the time being, as BCT is still in its infancy, there will undoubtedly be standard obstacles on the path toward medical and healthcare applications that put it to use in the real world. A good example of this is the necessity to have several internationally ratified standards that have been thoroughly verified and validated. The quantity, type of data, and organization of the information that is distributed between blockchain applications might all be evaluated with the use of these set standards. These norms will act as both checks and balances on the information being exchanged and a degree of safety in and of itself.

1.6.5 SOCIAL CHALLENGES

In addition to the aforementioned technological obstacles, societal barriers, such as a change in culture that BCT must overcome, are significant. It is never simple to accept and use a new technology that stands in stark contrast to the way things have always been done. There is still a long way to go until the medical industry completely accepts digital technologies, particularly ones such as blockchain, which has not been tested in therapeutic applications. This is one of the many challenges facing the industry. It will take some time and effort to persuade doctors to abandon paper in favor of digital tools. The health sector's slow adoption of this technology and the accompanying policies have led to a general lack of confidence in digital tools [54, 55]. Researchers cannot yet call it a feasible and universal solution for all concerns in healthcare because of all of these challenges and obstacles [44]. Researcher used a SWOT analysis to dig deeper into the advantages, disadvantages, chances, and obstacles that BCT faces in the medical field (as depicted in Figure 1.4). The SWOT analysis is a tool for assessing the advantages, disadvantages, opportunities, and threats facing a business.

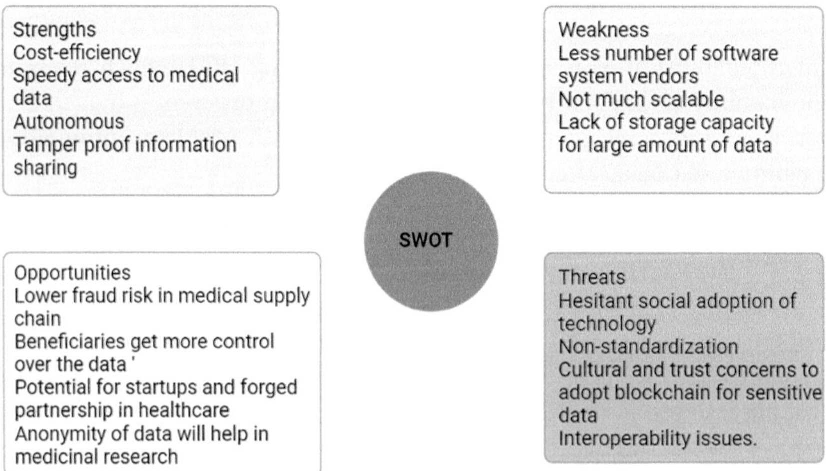

FIGURE 1.4 Healthcare blockchain SWOT analysis.

Source: Adapted from Ref. [56]

1.7 FUTURE PERSPECTIVES

The medical field stands to gain significantly resulting from the utilization of blockchain systemization. Medical research hopes to benefit from BCT in a similar vein to how the internet transformed healthcare and introduced telemedicine in the past by cutting down on the expenses associated with monitoring, configuring, and maintaining a centralized server for the data, as well as the administration responsible for monitoring medical data. Because the whole collection of data is immediately available, the use of distributed ledger begins immediately after a patient enrolls in a research study that is publicly accessible on the ledger blockchain in healthcare contexts which would considerably cut the amount of time that is spent processing information. The doctor would not have to second guess the patient's condition because they will be able to see the patient's real-time, genuine, authentic, and quality source-documented data in being truthful about their medical history. Because the information is public, patients can feel comfortable seeking a second opinion from a specialist if they so want. People will be able to locate and connect with others who are dealing with the same medical ailments through the use of patient records that have been saved on a blockchain, which will improve their health and give them the emotional and psychological fortitude to persevere in the face of adversity. Patients will retain complete authority over their information and will be able to choose which parties are given access to it. In 2016, at a book launch, Richie Etwaru coined the term "Freedom-as-a-Service" to describe the future.

1.8 CONCLUSION

Despite healthcare's occasional lag behind other industries in adopting technological advances, the possibility for data integrity may provide an incentive to embrace BCT in the healthcare industry. Many potential considerations may arise when using a blockchain to manage EHRs. The benefits of using smart contracts in healthcare have been discussed, and this has swung public opinion in their favor. If they were put into practice, personalized treatment plans might be considered, thanks to the immutable chain of blocks generated by smart contracts, which will not compromise existing clinical frameworks that are already in place. Convergent clinical systems will prohibit the central parent system from producing a clone by utilizing blockchain-based smart contracts. One way in which BCT can be useful to scientists is by providing immutable, time-stamped versions of research. Researchers can have a permanent record of their findings if they use a blockchain to document their work, much like how patients can control their data via smart contracts. Blockchain is a critical tool in the vast pharmaceutical market.

KEYWORDS

- **blockchain**
- **healthcare**
- **biomedical**
- **data-sharing**
- **medicine**

REFERENCES

1. Griebel L, Prokosch HU, Köpcke F, Toddenroth D, Christoph J, Leb I, Engel I, Sedlmayr M. 2015. A scoping review of cloud computing in healthcare. *BMC Med Inform Decis Mak. 15*, 17.
2. Houston MS, Myers JD, Levens SP, McEvoy MT, Smith SA, Khandheria BK, Shen WK, Torchia ME, Berry DJ. 1999. Clinical consultations using store-and-forward telemedicine technology. In *Mayo Clinic Proceedings;* Elsevier: Rochester, MN, USA, Volume 74.
3. Bhatti A, Siyal AA, Mehdi A, Shah H, Kumar H, Bohyo MA. 2018, February. Development of cost-effective tele-monitoring system for remote area patients. In *Proceedings of the 2018 IEEE International Conference on Engineering and Emerging Technologies (ICEET)*, Lahore, Pakistan.
4. Castaneda C, Nalley K, Mannion C, Bhattacharyya P, Blake P, Pecora A, Goy A, Suh KS. 2015. Clinical decision support systems for improving diagnostic accuracy and achieving precision medicine. *J Clin Bioinform. 5*, 4.
5. Zhang P, White J, Schmidt DC, Lenz G, Rosenbloom ST. 2018. Fhirchain: Applying blockchain to securely and scalably share clinical data. *Comput Struct Biotechnol J. 16*, 267–278.
6. Berman M, Fenaughty A. 2005. Technology and managed care: Patient benefits of telemedicine in a rural health care network. *Health Econ. 14*, 559–573.
7. Downing NL, Adler-Milstein J, Palma JP, Lane S, Eisenberg M, Sharp C, Longhurst CA. 2017. Health information exchange policies of 11 diverse health systems and the associated impact on volume of exchange. *J Am Med Inform Assoc. 24*, 113–122.

8. Azaria A, Ekblaw A, Vieira T, Lippman A. 2016, August. MedRec: Using blockchain for medical data access and permission management. In *Proceedings of the 2nd International Conference on Open and Big Data (OBD 16),* Vienna, Austria (pp. 25–30).
9. Zhang J, Xue N, Huang X. 2016. A secure system for pervasive social network based healthcare. *IEEE Access 4*, 9239–9250.
10. Kuo T-T, Kim H, Ohno-Machado L. 2017. Blockchain distributed ledger technologies for biomedical and health care applications. *J Am Med Inform Assoc. 24*, 1211–1220.
11. Angraal S, Krumholz HM, Schulz WL. 2017. Blockchain technology: Applications in health care. *Circ Cardiovasc Qual Outcomes 10*, e003800.
12. Yue X, Wang H, Jin D, Li M, Jiang W. 2016. Healthcare data gateways: Found healthcare intelligence on Blockchain with novel privacy risk control. *J Med Syst. 40*, 218.
13. Griggs KN, Ossipova O, Kohlios CP, Baccarini AN, Howson EA, Hayajneh T. 2018. Healthcare blockchain system using smart contracts for secure automated remote patient monitoring. *J Med Syst. 42*, 130.
14. Ivan D. 2016. Moving toward a blockchain-based method for the secure storage of patient records. In *ONC/NIST Use of Blockchain for Healthcare and Research Workshop; ONC/NIST: Gaithersburg, MD, USA.*
15. Chen Y, Ding S, Xu Z, Zheng H, Yang S. 2018. Blockchain-based medical records secure storage and medical service framework. *J Med Syst. 43*, 5.
16. Wang S, Wang J, Wang X, Qiu T, Yuan Y, Ouyang L, Guo Y, Wang FY. 2018. Blockchain-powered parallel healthcare systems based on the ACP approach. *IEEE Trans Comput Soc Syst. 99*, 1–9.
17. Jiang S, Cao J, Wu H, Yang Y, Ma M, He J. 2018, June. Blochie: A blockchain-based platform for healthcare information exchange. In *Proceedings of the 2018 IEEE International Conference on Smart Computing (SMARTCOMP),* Taormina, Italy.
18. Cyran MA. 2018. Blockchain as a Foundation for Sharing Healthcare Data. Blockchain in Healthcare Today. Blockchain Healthc. Today.
19. Shubbar S. 2017. *Ultrasound Medical Imaging Systems Using Telemedicine and Blockchain for Remote Monitoring of Responses to Neoadjuvant Chemotherapy in Women's Breast Cancer: Concept and Implementation.* Master's Thesis, Kent State University, Kent, OH, USA.
20. Ianculescu M, Stanciu A, Bica O, Neagu G. 2017. Innovative, adapted online services that can support the active, healthy and independent living of ageing people. *A Case Study. Int J Econ Manag Syst. 2*, 321–329.
21. Mandl KD, Markwell D, MacDonald R, Szolovits P, Kohane IS. 2001. Public Standards and Patients' Control: How to keep electronic medical records accessible but private. *BMJ 322*, 283–287.
22. Brandon RM, Podhorzer M, Pollak TH. 1991. Premiums without benefits: Waste and inefficiency in the commercial health insurance industry. *Int J Health Serv. 21*, 265–283.
23. Gorman L. 2006. The history of health care costs and health insurance. *Wisconsin Policy Res Inst Rep. 19*, 1–31.
24. Ekblaw A, Azaria A, Halamka JD, Lippman A. 2016, August. A case study for blockchain in healthcare: "MedRec" prototype for electronic health records and

medical research data. In *Proceedings of the IEEE Open and Big Data Conference,* Vienna, Austria; Volume 13.
25. Xia Q, Sifah EB, Asamoah KO, Gao J, Du X, Guizani M. 2017. MeDShare: Trustless medical data sharing among cloud service providers via blockchain. *IEEE Access 5*, 14757–14767.
26. Dubovitskaya A, Xu Z, Ryu S, Schumacher M, Wang F. 2017. Secure and trustable electronic medical records sharing using blockchain. In *AMIA Annual Symposium Proceedings; American Medical Informatics Association,* Washington, DC, USA (p. 650), Volume 2017.
27. Heston T. 2017. A case study in blockchain health care innovation. *Int J Curr Res.* 9, 60587–60588.
28. Mettler M. 2016, September. Blockchain technology in healthcare: The revolution starts here. In *Proceedings of the 2016 IEEE 18th International Conference on e-Health Networking, Applications and Services (Healthcom)*, Munich, Germany.
29. How Blockchain Will Revolutionise Clinical Trials. 2018 June. Available online: https://pharmaphorum. com/views-and-analysis/how-blockchain-will-revolutionise-clinical-trials-clinical-trials/ (Accessed November 20, 2018).
30. Moe Alsumidaie, Blockchain Concepts Emerge in Clinical Trials, Applied Clinical Trials. May 2018. Available online: http://www.appliedclinicaltrialsonline.com/blockchain-concepts-emerge-clinical-trials (Accessed October 15, 2018).
31. Nugent T, Upton D, Cimpoesu M. 2016. Improving data transparency in clinical trials using blockchain smart contracts. *F1000Research 5*, 2541.
32. Buterin V. 2014. *A Next-generation Smart Contract and Decentralized Application Platform*. White paper; Ethereum foundation (Stiftung Ethereum): Zug, Switzerland.
33. Wood G. 2014. *Ethereum: A Secure Decentralised Generalised Transaction Ledger*. Yellow paper; Ethereum foundation (Stiftung Ethereum): Zug, Switzerland.
34. Benchoufi M, Porcher R, Ravaud P. 2017. Blockchain protocols in clinical trials: Transparency and traceability of consent. *F1000Research 6*, 66.
35. Kevin AC, Breeden EA, Davidson C, Mackey TK. 2018. Leveraging blockchain technology to enhance supply chain management in healthcare: An exploration of challenges and opportunities in the health supply chain. *Blockchain Healthc. Today*.
36. Mauri R. 2017, July. Blockchain for fraud prevention: Industry use cases. Available online: https://www.ibm.com/blogs/blockchain/2017/07/blockchain-for-fraud-prevention-industry-use-cases/ (Accessed October 16, 2018).
37. Swan M. 2015. Blockchain thinking: The brain as a decentralized autonomous corporation. *IEEE Technol Soc Mag. 34*, 41–52.
38. Taylor P. 2016, April. Applying blockchain technology to medicine traceability. Available online: https://www.securingindustry.com/pharmaceuticals/applying-blockchain-technology-to-medicinetraceability/s40/a2766/ (Accessed October 16, 2018).
39. Plotnikov V, Kuznetsova V. 2018. The prospects for the use of digital technology "Blockchain" in the pharmaceutical market. In *MATEC Web of Conferences; EDP Sciences*, London, UK, Volume 193.
40. Markov A. Use of blockchain in pharmaceutics and medicine. Available online: https://miningbitcoinguide. com/technology/blokchejn-v-meditsine/ (Accessed October 16, 2018).

41. Sylim P, Liu F, Marcelo A, Fontelo P. 2018. Blockchain technology for detecting falsified and substandard drugs in distribution: Pharmaceutical supply chain intervention. *JMIR Res Protoc. 7*, e10163.
42. Trujllo G, Guillermo C. 2018. *The Role of Blockchain in the Pharmaceutical Industry Supply Chain as a Tool for Reducing the Flow of Counterfeit Drugs*. PhD Thesis, Dublin Business School, Dublin, Ireland.
43. Shae Z, Tsai JJ. 2017, June. On the design of a blockchain platform for clinical trial and precision medicine. In *Proceedings of the 2017 IEEE 37th International Conference on Distributed Computing Systems (ICDCS)*, Atlanta, GA, USA.
44. Alhadhrami Z, Alghfeli S, Alghfeli M, Abedlla JA, Shuaib K. 2017, November. Introducing blockchains for healthcare. In *Proceedings of the 2017 IEEE International Conference on Electrical and Computing Technologies and Applications (ICECTA)*, Ras Al Khaimah, UAE.
45. Fernández-Caramés TM, Fraga-Lamas P. 2018. A review on the use of blockchain for the Internet of Things. *IEEE Access 6*, 32979–33001.
46. Kuo T-T, Hsu C-N, Ohno-Machado L. ModelChain: Decentralized privacy-preserving healthcare predictive modeling framework on private blockchain networks. arXiv 2016, arXiv:1802.01746.
47. Zheng Z, Xie S, Dai H, Chen X, Wang H. 2017, June. An overview of blockchain technology: Architecture, consensus, and future trends. In *Proceedings of the 2017 IEEE International Congress on Big Data (BigData Congress)*, Honolulu, HI, USA.
48. Investopedia "Blockchains". Available online: https://www.investopedia.com/terms/1/51-attack.asp (Accessed October 20, 2018).
49. Hertig A. 2018, June. Blockchain's once-feared 51 percent attack is now becoming regular. Available online: https://www.coindesk.com/blockchains-feared-51-attack-now-becoming-regular/ (Accessed October 20, 2018).
50. Linn LA, Koo MB. 2016. Blockchain for health data and its potential use in health it and health care related research. In *ONC/NIST Use of Blockchain for Healthcare and Research Workshop; ONC/NIST*, Gaithersburg, MD, USA.
51. Esposito C, De Santis A, Tortora G, Chang H, Choo KK. 2018. Blockchain: A panacea for healthcare cloud-based data security and privacy? *IEEE Cloud Comput. 5*, 31–37.
52. Bennett B. 2017. Blockchain HIE overview: A framework for healthcare interoperability. *Telehealth Med. Today 2*.
53. Pirtle C, Ehrenfeld J. 2018. Blockchain for healthcare: The next generation of medical records? *J Med Syst. 42*, 172.
54. McKinlay J. 2016. *Blockchain: Background Challenges and Legal Issues*. DLA Piper Publications: London, UK.
55. Boulos MN, Wilson JT, Clauson KA. 2018. Geospatial blockchain: Promises, challenges, and scenarios in health and healthcare. *Int J Health Geogr. 17*(1), 25.
56. Siyal, Asad & Junejo, Aisha & Zawish, Muhammad & Ahmed, Kainat & Khalil, Aiman & Soursou, Georgia. (2019). Applications of Blockchain Technology in Medicine and Healthcare: Challenges and Future Perspectives. Cryptography. 3. 3. 10.3390/cryptography3010003.

CHAPTER 2

Development of Digital Healthcare with Blockchain: Prospects for Patient Care

ABSTRACT

The existing strategy utilized to collect patient information has to be reexamined in light of the rising number of documented incidences of security breaches that jeopardize individual privacy. Based on the experience with bitcoin and the blockchain technology it uses, researchers know that there are methods for encrypting such data. In this chapter, investigators discuss the problems associated with the current methods for managing individual health data and offer a new method for facilitating the exchange of such data between different institutions. When the information is made available to researchers, the solution will be found to boost clinical efficiency and research. Providers, hospitals and clinics, insurers, and consumers would all benefit from the blockchain-based system solution that has been offered. Individuals or patients would retain all rights to their data at all times. To solve this problem, the designer proposes using a private blockchain system, in which all participants are predetermined and mutually trusted, to ensure the confidentiality and integrity of the data.

2.1 INTRODUCTION

What designers mean by "big data" is datasets that are so enormous and complex that conventional database and software tools have a hard time keeping up with them. Researchers contribute data to the healthcare system every time they interact with the system, whether it is by visiting

Computational Intelligence for Patient Care: Blockchain, AI, and ML in Healthcare.
Rishabha Malviya, Rishav Sharma, Sathvik Belagodu Sridhar, and Suraj Kumar (Authors)

DOI: 10.1201/9781779640819-2

their primary care physician, seeing a specialist, visiting the emergency room, or undergoing surgery. Furthermore, the availability of wearables and other IoT devices has led to a dramatic increase in the rate at which data is being generated. The information given by healthcare providers is then used by insurance companies to determine payment. This information is presented in a variety of formats; it is no longer limited to traditional forms such as basic patient data [1, 2]. Every one of us has encountered the common practice of medical professionals keeping detailed records on each patient. They have us sign a document saying the investigator understands their privacy policy, but their actual security measures are inadequate. Several high-profile cases of patient data theft or loss have been reported in the news recently [3, 4]. There is a high priority on safeguarding sensitive health information since hackers target this industry. The failure to secure medical documents might result in costly legal action and adversely affect patient treatment. The high cost of implementing adequate security measures increases the risk that just minimal precautions will be taken. The question of who owns and who shares medical records is also contentious. Reports, pictures, movies, and data are all part of the medical record, and this information may be organized or unorganized [5, 6]. Compatibility concerns may also arise since they may be provided in a variety of formats that are exclusive to a given provider's system. The doctors have absolute discretion over whether or not they share a patient's records with anyone, even the patient themselves [7]. The validity of the resulting documents may also be an issue because of concerns over whether or not the information placed into the file has been altered, deleted, or otherwise destroyed. Access to a patient's medical record by a specialist may be necessary on occasion. Accessing this data quickly and efficiently could mean the difference between life and death. The patient should have the ability to decide who has access to their medical records, and those records should be consistent and portable across healthcare facilities [8, 9]. In this chapter, the researcher examines two options for managing patients' health data and for facilitating its exchange across different facilities. If the solution can get the data into the hands of researchers, it will boost clinical efficiency and lead to more studies being conducted. Providers, hospitals and clinics, insurers, and consumers would all benefit from the blockchain-based system solution that has been offered. For the answer, the researcher assumes a few things [10–12]. First, there is value for every node in this network to receive data from other nodes. Second, the patient has control over who gets access to their information and when, and third, the information is secure and auditable, so all parties feel comfortable sharing it [13–15]. A decentralized peer-to-peer network built on blockchain technology has the potential to address all of these concerns. Our goal in writing this chapter is to offer a blockchain-based solution that will enable healthcare stakeholders to collaborate and share data, thereby lowering overall healthcare costs and improving a variety of other metrics, including the timeliness and quality of patient care by allowing different providers to pool the information they keep separately in their health record systems (Figure 2.1).

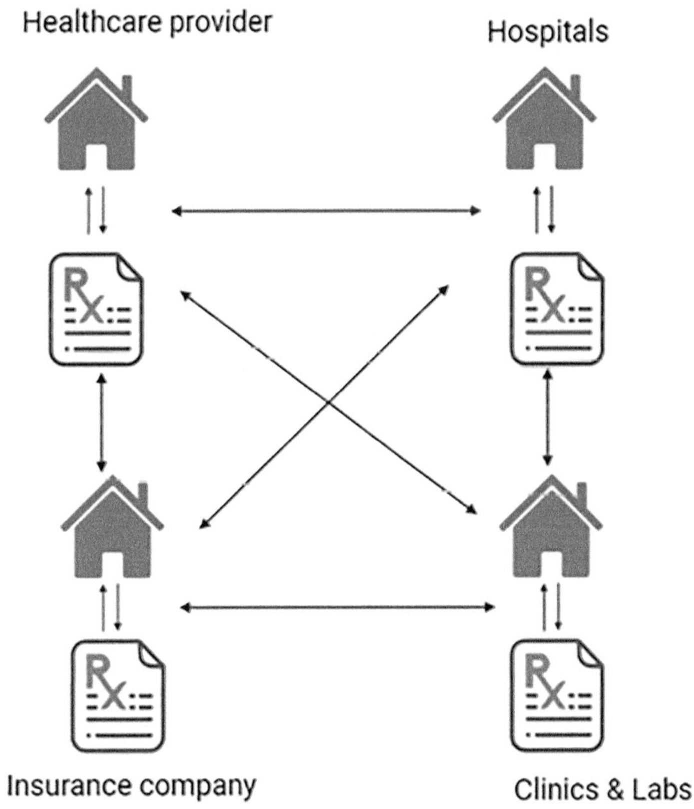

FIGURE 2.1 Members of the healthcare blockchain.

2.2 INSTITUTIONAL ASPECTS OF THE BLOCKCHAIN

2.2.1 DECENTRALIZED

Access to the database is granted to everyone who is currently online. Data may be accessed, monitored, stored, or updated by more than one system at a time.

2.2.2 TRANSPARENT

Potential users benefit from the immutability and accessibility of data stored in a blockchain. The immutability of blockchains should protect information from being corrupted or stolen.

2.2.3 IMMUTABLE

Records, once stored, cannot be easily altered without control of more than 51% of the node at once.

2.2.4 AUTONOMY

Every node in the blockchain network may independently and securely access, transmit, store, and update all of the network's data without having to rely on or even communicate with any other nodes.

2.2.5 OPEN SOURCE

The open source is intended to be available to anybody with network access, and this is what blockchain technology aims to achieve. This unparalleled adaptability facilitates not only public document evaluation but also the creation of a plethora of near-term applications.

2.2.6 ANONYMITY

A more secure and trustworthy system results from the fact that users' identities are concealed when data is sent from one node to another.

Organizations invest heavily in information systems and data transfers, which necessitates constant upkeep and backups. It can be costly and time-consuming for participants to extract data and send it to a third party that has requested the data before they can begin sharing it. The solution investigator gives can be useful. Providers, hospitals, clinics, insurers, and patients are all part of the solution implemented with blockchain technology. Individuals or patients would retain all rights to their data at all times. A private blockchain system, in which all participants are well known and dependable, is proposed as a means of resolving these issues [16, 17].

2.3 BLOCKCHAIN AND BIG DATA IN HEALTHCARE

In a world where incredible technical advancements are occurring, healthcare transformation has emerged as a top priority. Modern healthcare data management systems are centralized, which could cause problems in the event of a widespread power outage or other catastrophic incident. In recent years, blockchain technology has skyrocketed in popularity as a potential solution to numerous healthcare data management issues. There has been a lot of excitement around the prospect of using blockchain to transmit confidential medical records. Many of the most pressing problems in healthcare data management today could be mitigated or even eliminated with the help of blockchain technology. This includes issues such as patient consent, data ownership, information governance, data auditing, privacy, security, traceability, immutability, flexible access, and the reconciliation of conflicting changes from multiple sources [18–20].

2.3.1 UTILIZING BLOCKCHAIN TECHNOLOGY

In the blockchain, a block is a collection of connected transactions that have been permanently recorded. A blockchain is made up of many of these blocks connected. The size of the blockchain grows proportionally with the volume of transactions. Genesis chain refers to the very first chain in a blockchain. A hash, which is essentially a digital fingerprint, is included in each block to identify the transaction as being one and only. A hash to the previous block is also sent. As can be seen in Figure 2.2, only the genesis block is devoid of a pointer to the previous block [13, 14].

A block's contents are protected by its hash, which is calculated using data from the previous block. Data tampering is indicated if the hash can no longer be confirmed because of changes to the contents. Data on a blockchain is immutable because of this tamper-proofing; information included within a block can never be altered [21, 22].

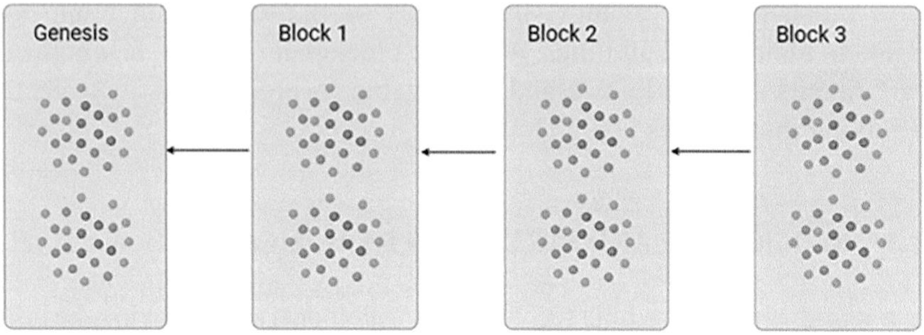

FIGURE 2.2 Example of blockchain.

2.3.2 BLOCKCHAIN FEATURES

Distributed ledger systems, or blockchains, have several useful properties.

2.3.2.1 CENTRALIZED DATABASE

A ledger is a shared, unchangeable record of business transactions that can be accessed by all parties involved. The consensus ledger is the only reliable record of transactions. As a result of replication, every member of the network possesses a replicated copy of the ledger. Permissions can be set up in the ledger to ensure that users only have access to the data to which they have been granted access [23].

2.3.2.2 PERMISSION

Permissions can be set on a blockchain. Permissioned blockchains give users granular control over who can view which aspects of a transaction by assigning digital identities to each user and enforcing restrictions based on those identities. Organizations can now meet the requirements of laws like HIPAA, which govern data privacy. When conducting a transaction with a counterparty, for instance, all relevant information is visible to both parties. There is a record of the transaction that can be seen by a third party, but they do not have access to any of the information contained within. Digital certificates can be used to give an auditor access to the transaction data once they join the network. The blockchain network can be set up to work with a certification body to confirm the validity of a digital certificate, which can be used to establish the identity of a user or party [24, 25].

2.3.2.3 CONSENSUS

A consensus method aids in making sure that the next block in the chain is the only truth, and stops the influential third of the chain's forking parties, from exchanging information. For a transaction to be irrevocably added to the blockchain, consensus must be reached. Three consensus methods exist:

- Tolerance for byzantine faults practice
- The evidence of stake
- Evidence of stake assignment

2.3.2.4 DIGITALLY SIGNED, OR "SMART," AGREEMENTS

Smart contracts are digital agreements or protocols that specify the terms of a financial or business transaction and are maintained on a distributed ledger (blockchain) and carried out mechanically during a transaction. Let us pretend for a moment that they ordered pizza online and the company promises it will come at the door within 30 min. If the delivery does not come within 30 min, the smart contract can be programmed to automatically return some of the payment to the customer via the blockchain. Financial contracts that stipulate payment by a certain date, as well as travel insurance policies that pay out automatically in the event of certain occurrences (such as a flight being delayed for longer than a predetermined amount of time), can benefit greatly from this type of contract [26, 27]. The healthcare industry may have finally found its savior in blockchain technology, presuming it is properly implemented and used in a wide variety of contexts. The applications of blockchain technology are indicated in Figure 2.3.

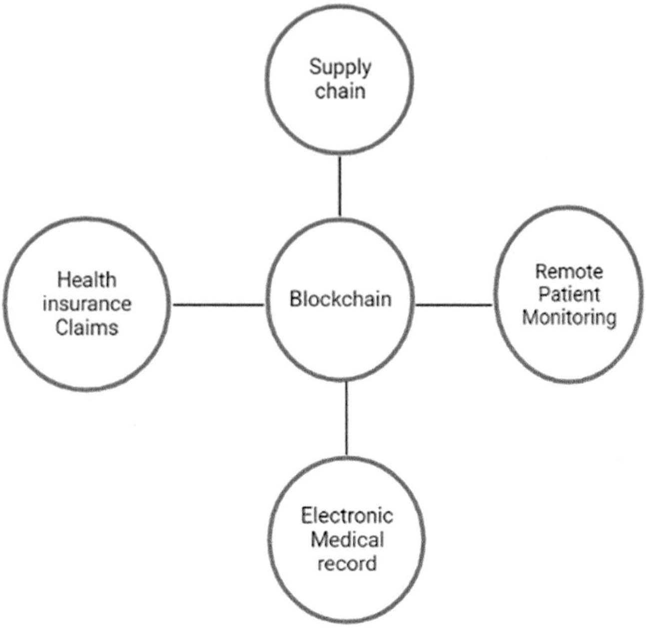

FIGURE 2.3 Schematic illustration of blockchain technology applications in the health industry.

2.4 BLOCKCHAIN TYPES

Even though blockchain technology was initially created for the bitcoin currency, its potential has recently been recognized by several previously unanticipated sectors. Currency's public bitcoin concept may impose unnecessary limits or act as a barrier to entry for some industries. Many other kinds of blockchains might be employed, each with its own set of advantages and drawbacks, depending on the situation and the nature of the business. Public and private blockchains are the two most common types [28, 29].

2.4.1 CONSORTIUM

Between the two extremes of public and private blockchains exists the consortium blockchain. It is a cross between public and private blockchains, with neither the low-trust entity model of the former nor the high-trust entity model of the latter. When it comes to privacy and efficiency, private blockchains can be advantageous; nevertheless, a consortium platform avoids providing sole power to any one organization. One of the benefits of private blockchains are their increased efficiency and anonymity can be realized on a consortium platform without granting sole authority to any one entity. Typically, a consortium has a governing body that ensures its smooth operation [30, 31].

2.4.1.1 BIG DATA IN HEALTHCARE

The healthcare industry is undergoing profound changes as a result of the explosion in the volume of data collected over the past several years. In addition, developments in technology have simplified the process of gathering and analyzing information from various sources such as healthcare providers, health insurers, hospitals, and labs. Doctors used to rely on their discretion when deciding on a course of therapy, but that has changed in recent years as the field shifts toward one that is more evidence-based. As part of this revised strategy, clinical data will be reviewed and treatment decisions will be based on the best available evidence. When compared with industries such as banking and retail, healthcare has been slow to adopt big data. By analyzing large amounts of patient data, healthcare providers can better foresee outbreaks, treat illnesses more effectively, increase the standard of living for patients, and reduce the number of needless deaths [32, 33]. There have been a plethora of fitness tracker wearables released in recent years, including the Fitbit, Samsung Gear Fit, and Jawbone. Soon, researchers will be able to provide the doctors with this information, which is going to help doctors incorporate it into their diagnosis when they are consulted by investigators with a medical issue. As more information is gathered, clinicians will be able to recommend a course of therapy based on the experiences of others who have a similar set of circumstances, genetic makeup, and way of life. At the moment, large amounts of medical data are kept in isolated databases across many medical institutions. To put all this information to good use in the future, it will need to be shared [34, 35].

2.4.1.2 SECURITY AND PRIVACY OF MEDICAL DATA

Who should have ownership of a patient's medical information—the doctor or the patient? Physicians assert that patients do not have any legal right to their records because they contain the doctors' professional opinions about the patient and are not theirs to keep. But the patient's record and lab results are personal information that should be kept confidential. The medical record belongs to neither the doctor nor the patient. Medical professionals often argue that patients should not have access to their records since they contain the doctors' professional judgments regarding the patient's health. However, the patient's record and lab results are personal information that should remain with the patient; there is no reason for anybody else to claim ownership over them. Owning one's medical records is governed by a patchwork of state laws in the United States, with 30 states having no laws that define custody of records, 19 states that explicitly grant ownership to hospitals or doctors, and New Hampshire that explicitly grants ownership to patients. The medical records department of the hospital is where the patient in Utah must go to get their information, which can take a long time if the department is busy. Internet portals are used by many systems to grant users confined access to data [36, 37]. Huge amounts of data are being collected and stored each year, and this trend is expected to continue. The revelation of such details may attract unwelcome attention. New security breaches are discovered or published nearly every day, making cybercrime a major social and political issue. The government, healthcare companies, and patients all bear astronomical financial and reputational consequences as a result of these breaches. Data security issues affect organizations of all sizes, from small businesses to large governments. Health insurance providers Anthem Blue Cross and Blue Shield, Community Health Services, and Advocate Medical Group have all been targets of high-profile, privately led attacks in recent years. No one knows for sure if the HIPAA Privacy Rule has enhanced awareness of whether it has bolstered individual privacy rights, significance of health information privacy, and patient's role in that process. Investigators are entitled to the same privacy protections and rights as patients when it comes to their medical records.

2.5 BLOCKCHAIN TECHNOLOGY FOR HEALTHCARE SECURITY AND PRIVACY

A distributed ledger like blockchain may record and verify transactions with the agreement of all participants (as depicted in Figure 2.4) transparently and permanently. The system relies on the idea of a central, unchangeable ledger to record and verify every occurrence. Data in modern ledger systems is stored in convenient locations such as an EHR database, a health IT data warehouse, or an HIE repository. It is very uncommon for providers, patients, and researchers to experience frustration due to data silos and interoperability challenges caused by the fact that each of these systems has a unique design and can produce and store data in a format that is only available to it. Contrarily, a blockchain requires each user, or node, to maintain a copy of the ledger at all times. The security is improved and the possibility of an illegal change is decreased since every modification is checked against every node and must be allowed [37].

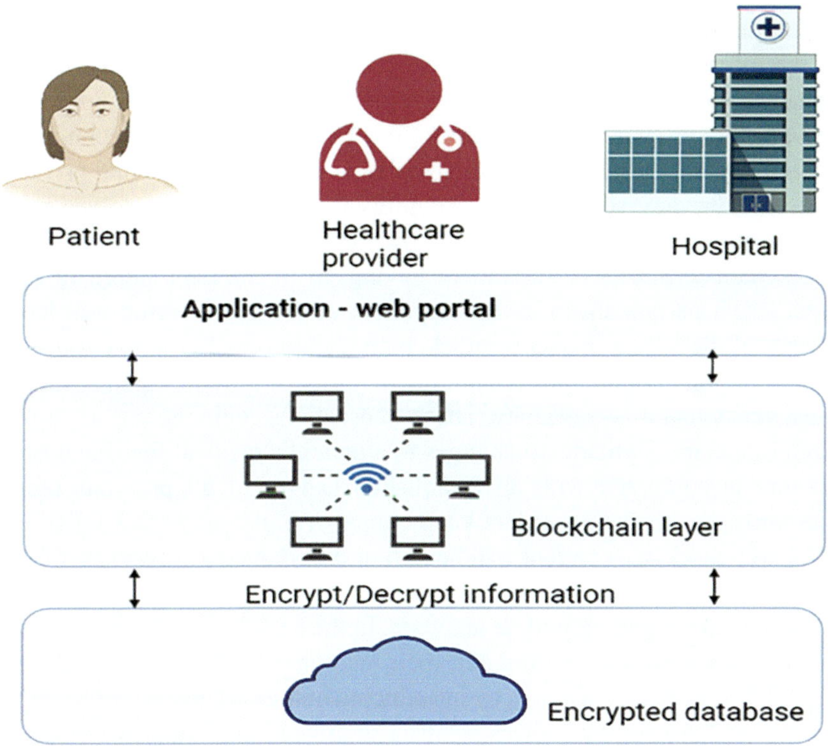

FIGURE 2.4 Tiered approach.

Blockchain will offer the healthcare business the verification it needs, and it is reliable for all involved. While a central repository is responsible for storing the data, all users of the blockchain share responsibility for ensuring its security. The number of people who can access a healthcare blockchain is restricted to only those who need to see it, such as the patient, their doctor, any hospitals they visit, and possibly the patient's family. As there are no central data aggregators, this method of working together will solve several problems now plaguing the healthcare sector [37]. There are no trust difficulties when sharing a patient's record via the blockchain method because all participants are known and authorized in advance. As if the problems with data harmonization were not enough, the healthcare industry also has serious privacy and security flaws. Data in the healthcare industry is highly sensitive and private, and this data is currently housed in a centralized database. Like a bank vault, only those who are authorized to do so and possess the necessary means of doing so can gain access to the data stored inside. Unfortunately, once a hacker has the key, all of the information is theirs to use as they like. Increasing reports of PHI breaches indicate that the healthcare industry has to rethink its approach to data storage, sharing, and security [38]. The blockchain, the technology behind bitcoin, has the potential to resolve healthcare security and privacy concerns. Privacy, security, and scalability issues could all be solved with private and hybrid blockchains. But how can investigators choose the right blockchain technology? Instead of having all of the data stored in one place, each participant in each component of the hybrid setup will have a copy of the ledger thanks to blockchain technology. For a new transaction to be added to the blockchain, the majority of the participating nodes must verify that it is legitimate. These transactions could include anything from monetary payments to changes to a patient's medical file. Each new activity is compared with an established history of all previous ones. Currently, healthcare providers keep copies of a patient's record that are not cross-checked. A patient will have four different sets of records if they visit four different doctors, each of which may contain inaccuracies and about which the patient will be unaware. In the healthcare system, patients can use blockchain to see and edit their records if they find any inaccuracies. It also increases security by introducing numerous, instead of a single source for sensitive data, checkpoints. The protection of sensitive medical information will also be greatly enhanced by blockchain technology. Patients who use blockchain can now accept or refuse access to their data, giving them more power over who has access to and can make changes to their information. In this instance, the patient, who is the rightful owner of the data, will have more influence over how it is used [39]. While the decentralized data architecture utilized by health information exchanges is comparable, blockchain technology differs from other types of technology due to the validation process of competition. The accuracy of data being shared between hospitals and other institutions is now impossible for patients and their doctors to check. In contrast, those who take part in a blockchain will know without a doubt that the data has been verified. Another advantage is that patients can visit a new expert without having to gather their documents from other doctors. Blockchain technology allows for the ledger to be made accessible to the new specialist thanks to blockchain technology. Finally, patients can reap the benefits of the concept that there is a central repository of data that can be instantly disseminated to all parties involved and does not necessitate time-consuming, laborious data reconciliation [40].

2.6 BLOCKCHAIN-BASED FIXES

2.6.1 QUICK RESOURCES FOR HEALTHCARE INTEROPERABILITY

To facilitate the exchange of electronic health records (EHRs), a new standard is emerging, that is fast healthcare interoperability resources (FHIR) [15]. Data formats, elements, and publicly accessible application programming interfaces are all included in FHIR. As a result, investigators should expect to see more widespread adoption of cloud computing, medical device integration, mobile applications, and adaptive treatment plans. Data elements in EHRs can now be independently stored as resources in the FHIR. There are a variety of uses for resources, including distinguishing between doctors and patients and highlighting typical clinical tasks. Data from a wide variety of sources can be made available through FHIR modules. Health-related material, drug administration records, diagnostic tests, and financial data are used in billing and claims processing, for instance. A new standard called FHIR offers a historical record of ownership and origin as well as audit trails, making it suited for use in blockchain entries; thus, researchers are adopting it to facilitate communication between various parties. Blockchain technology is combined with EHRs to provide a three-wheeled solution. However, there is currently no all-encompassing answer to the problem of patient data sharing and access. Since blockchain is already set up to allow for safe transactions, it may be used to bring disparate technologies together. Patient information is encrypted so that only authorized parties can access it. There are three potential channels for data exchange inside an EHR system. The "push" setting is the default. Push refers to the transmission of information between healthcare providers. A physician uses an email program named "Direct." On the other hand, there are difficulties along this path. Let us pretend investigators were visiting a remote town or city where there is no nearby access to medical treatment. However, if the designer receives an emergency, patient health records are stuck even though it urgently requires the information at the previous hospital until that establishment agrees to release it. In addition, it cannot guarantee that the data will be kept safe and sound. The sensitivity of email is also considered [16]. The "pull" mode is the alternative one. If the investigator transfers to another hospital in the same area, the new facility can seek medical records from the previous facility. But it is not quite as simple as it seems. There would not be a common approval process, so depending on how they communicate with the old hospital, the new hospital may or may not be able to receive the data "View" is the third available mode. Healthcare provider networks may have numerous doctors and other staff members accessing records, but there is no consistent standard for data safety during transmission. As an alternative, medical personnel at one facility may use email to securely transmit the medical records to those at another facility. In the case of a hospital, a hacker with access to the system may potentially request patient information without having to verify their identity or provide any sort of certification. Blockchain can store all the data and provide a transparent audit trail of who recorded what and when. An investigator can handle the responsibility of authorizing access for each medical service provider. The current model, in which healthcare providers act as gatekeepers for their patient's health records by facilitating data entry, transfer, and access control on an individual basis, is problematic. Instead, providers need only add new patient information and other updates to their health database, which can then be linked to the immutable blockchain. For starters, blockchain EHR will merely facilitate HIPAA compliance and immediate access to accurate historical information for all providers. Researchers do not need to wait for access to medical records when they could potentially save lives in a crisis. Investigators could avoid doing that by using blockchain technology [10].

2.6.2 SMART CONTRACTS

The term "smart contract" refers to a certain type of computer code able to aid in, carry out, and enforce the blockchain-based agreement negotiation or implementation technology. The system is fully automated and can function as a substitute for or supplement a signed legal document. Researchers will heavily rely on smart contracts to put the solution into practice to regulate who may view which documents, set parameters for when and how access can be revoked, and more. They can be used to streamline the process through which doctors, patients, and insurers agree to share medical records and financial data [19, 20].

2.6.3 BLOCKCHAIN FOR HEALTHCARE TRANSACTIONS

Blockchain technology is used as a strategy to create a dependable distributed system fit for storing sensitive medical records. Users may control who has access to their data and when through a web interface, where they can also perform other critical tasks like viewing activity logs. Because they are controlling their private information, rather than handing it over to a third party, individuals will have greater assurance that their data is secure and private. As a bonus, they can connect you with a third party if you need it. Due to the variety of options, picking a blockchain platform is not simple. Either ethereum or Hyperledger, another blockchain app platform currently in development by the Linux Foundation, would work for the application investigator was proposing. The benefit of Hyperledger is that it aims to build a trustworthy distributed ledger from blockchain technology without the need for proof of work or proof of stake protocols. Because of its practicality, it is quickly overtaking alternative blockchain implementation. The application layer would be the foundation, functioning as a control panel for managing things such as user accounts and reports [12, 13]. The blockchain's private implementation would be accessible via the application layer. The second layer is called the blockchain layer, and it is where blockchain nodes only communicate with other nodes, the application layer, key authoring entities, databases, and other nodes. The ability to generate new public/private key pairs for use in the blockchain is possessed by authoring resources. All electronically protected health information is kept in an encrypted database as the third layer.

Before being sent to the database, a medical record created by a healthcare facility or provider would be encrypted. When data is written to a database, a link to the relevant health record and the user's identifier are both recorded in the blockchain. Patients will be notified that their records have been updated. In addition to external sources, the patient can contribute information received from various wearable sensors. The patient will have complete access to this information regardless of where they are in the globe and will have the ability to decide how and with whom they share it. A web portal gives the user insight into who has viewed their blockchain and when. Those that need access to the patient's records can be granted permission through the portal. Users will have a fine-grained say over who can see their data and for how long. Just by granting access to his medical records, the patient can easily switch to a new doctor. Data in the database is encrypted at rest, but upon receiving a request, the database decrypts the data and re-encrypts it using the requestor's public key. This data can be encrypted using the requester's private key. Several crucial components, including identifying data and a transaction log, come together to form an individual blockchain block. Those utilizing the private blockchain networks share data, and the contents of the blocks reflect who owns the data and what permissions each member has to use it. Data pointers to the database, rights to see certain documents, and participant relationships are all recorded using smart contracts in a decentralized medical record. The data record is not stored in the block. You may get to the real data by following the data pointer back to the database [16]. Using a private blockchain, investigators propose a system where various healthcare providers, labs, and hospitals may all communicate with one another and share information on a patient's visit [17]. All of a patient's health records and data acquired throughout their lifetime will be recorded in the blockchain, together with details about the data format and storage location. Each block's worth of transactions would include the user's unique identification, as well as details about the health record's storage location, the data format, and the transaction timestamp.

2.6.4 ADVANTAGE OF BLOCKCHAIN OVER CURRENT SYSTEMS

Multiple positive outcomes for the healthcare sector can be expected from the proposed strategy. Anyone involved in healthcare, including patients, doctors, researchers, and others, will have instantaneous access to up-to-date, accurate data thanks to blockchain technology. Now, either centralized electronic medical records systems or paper files are used to keep patient information at doctors' offices. It may take a few days, or maybe a week, to get access to this data. Many stakeholders in the healthcare business, including providers, patients, and researchers, stand to benefit from a blockchain solution [41]. Researchers in healthcare need access to large amounts of patient data to advance the knowledge of diseases, create new treatments more quickly, and personalize treatment strategies for each patient based on their genetic makeup. Due to its decentralized structure, a blockchain would provide a more complete picture of patient populations by including data from a wider range of locations and ethnicities. It has the potential to track a person's health status for their whole life. If data stored on a blockchain were instantly accessible, it would greatly enhance healthcare coordination and would be particularly useful in emergencies. Researchers and public health workers will be able to detect potentially dangerous diseases much more quickly with this tool. The time it takes to identify an outbreak and stop it is reduced. When both the healthcare professional and the patient have access to the same data, they can work together to make an informed decision about the most effective course of therapy. Health data breaches will be reduced and care coordination will be simplified thanks to the implementation of blockchain [42].

2.7 CONCLUSION

The exponential growth of big data in healthcare presents several challenges for providers, researchers, and patients, but these can potentially be overcome with the help of blockchain technology. The healthcare industry may be able to fix many of its problems sooner than predicted if it can figure out how to adopt this strategy. While some have speculated that blockchain technology could transform the way designer share healthcare data, others have warned that despite the technology's hype, the difficulties and the data and realities of healthcare may be insurmountable. More practical applications are required to assess the potential value of blockchain technology, the potential impact of its deployment, and the extent to which the technology is just hype.

KEYWORDS

- **blockchain**
- **big data**
- **healthcare**
- **patent data**
- **privacy**

REFERENCES

1. Who Owns Medical Records: 50 State Comparison. 2015. Health information and the law. *George Washington University Hirsh Health Law and Policy Program*. August 20, 2015.
2. Bhuiyan M, Wang G, Tian W, Rahman M, Wu J. 2017 December. *Content-Centric Event-Insensitive Big Data Reduction in Internet of Things*. IEEE GLOBECOM 2017: Singapore.
3. Son J, Park J, Oh H, Bhuiyan M, Hur J, Kang K. 2017. Privacy-preserving electrocardiogram monitoring for intelligent arrhythmia detection. *Sensors 17*(6), 1360, https://doi.org/10.3390/s17061360
4. Wang T, Bhuiyan MA, Wang G, Rahman M, Wu J, Cao J. Big data reduction for smart city's critical infrastructural health monitoring. *IEEE Commun Mag (COMMAG) 56*(3), 128–133.
5. Bhuiyan M, Zaman M, Wang G, Wang T, Wu J. 2017 August. Privacy-protected data collection in wireless medical sensor networks. In *The 12th International Conference on Networking, Architect and Storage (NAS 2017)*, Shenzhen, China.
6. Rahman F, Bhuiyan M, Ahamed S. 2017. A privacy preserving framework for RFID based healthcare systems. *Future Generat Comput Syst. 72*, 339–352.
7. Luo E, Bhuiyan MA, Wang G, Rahman M, Wu J, Atiquzzaman M. 2018. PrivacyProtector: Privacy-protected patient data collection in iot-based healthcare systems. *IEEE Commun Mag (COMMAG) 56*(2), 163–168.
8. Kenneth M, Markwell D, MacDonald R, Szolovits P, Kohane I. 2001. Public Standards and Patients' Control: How to keep electronic medical records accessible but private. *BMJ 322*(7281), 283–287.
9. Wood, G. 2014. Ethereum: A secure decentralised generalised transaction ledger. Ethereum Project Yellow Paper (2014).
10. Ekblaw A, Azaria A, Halamka J, Lippman M. 2016. A case study for blockchain in healthcare: MedRec" prototype for electronic health records and medical research data. https://www.media.mit.edu/publications/medrecwhitepaper/

11. Yue X, Wang H, Jin D, Li M, Jiang W. 2016. Healthcare data gateways: Found healthcare intelligence on blockchain with novel privacy risk control. *J Med Syst. 40*(10), 218.
12. Tak P, Liu S. Medical record system using blockchain, big data and tokenization https://hbr.org/2014/12/why-health-care-may-finally-beready-for-big-data
13. Zillner S, Neururer S. Big data in the health sector. In Cavanillas J, Curry E, Wahlster W. (Eds.), *New Horizons for a Data-Driven Economy*. Springer: Cham.
14. Miles P. 2017. *Blockchain: The Complete Guide to Understanding Blockchain Technology*. CreateSpace Independent Publishing Platform.
15. Fast Healthcare Interoperability Resources (FHIR). https://www.hl7.org/fhir/overview.html
16. Narayanan B. *Bitcoin and Cryptocurrency Technologies*. Princeton University Press: Princeton.
17. Tran T, Rahman M, Bhuiyan M, Kubota A, Kiyomoto S, Omote K. 2017. Optimizing share size in efficient and robust secret sharing scheme for big data. *IEEE Transactions Big Data*, https://doi.org/10.1109/TBDATA.2017.27080
18. Leeming G, Ainsworth J, Clifton DA. 2019. Blockchain in health care: Hype, trust, and digital health. *Lancet 393*(10190), 2476–2477.
19. Balicer RD, Afek A. 2017. Digital health nation: Israel's global big data innovation hub. *Lancet 389*(10088), 2451–2453.
20. Mettler M. 2016 Sep. Blockchain technology in healthcare: The revolution starts here. In *2016 IEEE 18th International Conference on e-health Networking, Applications and Services (Healthcom)* (pp. 1–3). IEEE.
21. Srivastava S, Singh SV, Singh RB, Shukla HK. 2021. Digital transformation of healthcare: A blockchain study. *Int J Innovative Sci Engineer Technol. 8*(5), 414–425.
22. Novikov SP, Kazakov OD, Kulagina NA, Azarenko NY. 2018 Sep. Blockchain and smart contracts in a decentralized health infrastructure. In *2018 IEEE International Conference Quality Management, Transport and Information Security, Information Technologies (IT&QM&IS)* (pp. 697–703). IEEE.
23. Ilinca D. 2020. Applying blockchain and artificial intelligence to digital health. In *Digital Health Entrepreneurship* (pp. 83–101).
24. Yu P, Lu S, Hanes E, Chen Y. 2022. The role of blockchain technology in harnessing the sustainability of chinese digital finance. In *Blockchain Technologies for Sustainable Development in Smart Cities* (pp. 155–186). IGI Global.
25. Muminova E, Honkeldiyeva G, Kurpayanidi K, Akhunova S, Hamdamova S. 2020. Features of introducing blockchain technology in digital economy developing conditions in Uzbekistan. In *E3S Web of Conferences* (Vol. 159, p. 04023). EDP Sciences.
26. Razzaq A, Mohsan SA, Ghayyur SA, Al-Kahtani N, Alkahtani HK, Mostafa SM. 2022 Dec. Blockchain in healthcare: A decentralized platform for digital health passport of COVID-19 based on vaccination and immunity certificates. In *Healthcare* (Vol. 10, No. 12, p. 2453). MDPI.
27. Jat AS, Grønli TM. 2022 Aug. Blockchain for cybersecure healthcare. In *Mobile Web and Intelligent Information Systems: 18th International Conference, MobiWIS 2022,* Rome, Italy, *August 22–24, 2022, Proceedings* (pp. 106–117). Cham: Springer International Publishing.

28. Bennacer SA, Aaroud A, Sabiri K, Rguibi MA, Cherradi B. 2022. Design and implementation of a New Blockchain-based digital health passport: A Moroccan case study. *Inform Med Unlocked 35*, 101125.
29. Ichikawa D, Kashiyama M, Ueno T. 2017. Tamper-resistant mobile health using blockchain technology. *JMIR mHealth uHealth 5*(7), e7938.
30. Fatima N, Agarwal P, Sohail SS. 2022. Security and privacy issues of blockchain technology in health care—A review. In *ICT Analysis and Applications* (pp. 193–201).
31. Mohanta BK, Jena D, Panda SS, Sobhanayak S. 2019. Blockchain technology: A survey on applications and security privacy challenges. *Internet of Things. 8*, 100107.
32. Esposito C, De Santis A, Tortora G, Chang H, Choo KK. 2018. Blockchain: A panacea for healthcare cloud-based data security and privacy. *IEEE Cloud Comput. 5*(1), 31–37.
33. Yoon HJ. 2019. Blockchain technology and healthcare. *Healthc Inform Res. 25*(2), 59–60.
34. Saha A, Amin R, Kunal S, Vollala S, Dwivedi SK. 2019. Review on Blockchain technology based medical healthcare system with privacy issues. *Secur Privacy 2*(5), e83.
35. Patil P, Sangeetha M, Bhaskar V. 2021. Blockchain for IoT access control, security and privacy: A review. *Wirel Pers Commun. 117*, 1815–1834.
36. Mohanta BK, Jena D, Ramasubbareddy S, Daneshmand M, Gandomi AH. 2020. Addressing security and privacy issues of IoT using blockchain technology. *IEEE Internet of Things J. 8*(2), 881–888.
37. Manu MR, Musthafa N, Balamurugan B, Chauhan R. 2020. Blockchain components and concept. In *Blockchain Technology and Applications* (pp. 21–50). Auerbach Publications.
38. Qureshi A, Megías Jiménez D. 2020. Blockchain-based multimedia content protection: Review and open challenges. *Appl Sci. 11*(1), 1.
39. Ranjan N, Kumar S, Jain A. 2021. Apply and analyse several blockchain techniques in IoT and big data sector. In *Blockchain for Information Security and Privacy* (pp. 19–42). Auerbach Publications.
40. Rao UP, Shukla PK, Trivedi C, Gupta S, Shibeshi ZS (Eds.), 2021. *Blockchain for Information Security and Privacy*. CRC Press.
41. Yu S. *Using a Group Decision Method to Judge the Value of Blockchain for an Enterprise in Supply Chain* (Doctoral dissertation, University of Missouri—Columbia).
42. Kumari M, Gupta M, Ved C. 2021. Blockchain in pharmaceutical sector. In *Applications of Blockchain in Healthcare* (pp. 199–220).

CHAPTER 3

Improvement of Patient Outcomes with AI

ABSTRACT

Rapid progress is being made in the study of artificial intelligence (AI) in healthcare, with promising applications already being shown in several areas of medicine. However, only a small number of these methods have been successfully implemented in actual clinical settings so far. This chapter delves into the primary difficulties and restrictions of AI in healthcare, as well as the measures needed to bring these potentially game-changing technologies out of the lab and into actual use. Dataset shift, accidental fitting of confounders, unexpected discriminating bias, the difficulties of generalization to new populations, and the unanticipated negative repercussions of new algorithms on health outcomes are all threats that developers of AI algorithms must keep an eye on. This chapter suggests that in the future, healthcare AI may use technology to analyze a patient's health and issue an alert if it detects a decline. So that AI can aid in the treatment of specific disorders and take into account the patient's perspective, researchers require large-scale patient-reported outcome databases.

3.1 INTRODUCTION

In recent years, healthcare technology has grown quickly. It is ready for any significant changes. There are almost infinite ways to utilize technologies to deploy more reliable, efficient, and impactful treatments at just the right time in the treatment of a patient, from infectious diseases and cancer to

Computational Intelligence for Patient Care: Blockchain, AI, and ML in Healthcare.
Rishabha Malviya, Rishav Sharma, Sathvik Belagodu Sridhar, and Suraj Kumar (Authors)

DOI: 10.1201/9781779640819-3

radiology and risk evaluation. Chronic diseases including cardiovascular disease (CVD), diabetes, and Alzheimer's have become more prevalent, and by 2030, 66% of deaths will be attributed to these conditions. Technology is used in telehealth, which includes virtual healthcare, to enhance communication between medical professionals, clinics, and patients. Electronic communication technology enables clinics, physicians, and patients to communicate, track, and follow up on care plans, allowing for the greatest possible virtual involvement during medical treatment. According to the World Health Organization, technology may now be used to carry out treatments, undertake preoperative planning, and remotely monitor outcomes [1]. To prevent situations when a patient's life is in danger, it is essential to regularly monitor those who have chronic diseases. This decade has seen the rise of the Internet of Things (IoT), which has been heralded as ushering in a new age of global connection for ordinary objects. Remote health monitoring technologies [2, 3], parking management [4], smart homes [5], smart cities [6], smart environments [7], industrial sites [8], and agricultural areas [9], among others. IoT may be used to manage healthcare by monitoring environmental and physiological parameters. Since they have a straightforward structure, IoT systems are becoming more significant in real-time applications. To analyze data in real time, the IoT links computers to the Internet through sensors and networks [10, 11]. The traditional adage "Health is Wealth" has been proven true in modern times as well. Poor and unhealthy life quality has been brought on by a hectic lifestyle, rising pollution levels, and the emergence of epidemic and pandemic illnesses. More than 90% of the population has recently been shown to have been exposed to a contaminated environment [12]. Most people now live impoverished lifestyles as a result of the industrial revolution and population increase. Monitoring, enhancing, and promoting a healthy lifestyle are thus required. The development of affordable sensors and devices for real-time monitoring and data gathering has been made possible by industry 5.0 and 5G communications technologies [13]. In Figure 3.1, the SHM's applications are shown.

3.2 INTERNET OF MEDICAL THINGS (IOMT)

The IoMT is a key component of smart health monitoring (SHM) in the IoT world [14]. The idea of interconnecting electronic devices on a network to

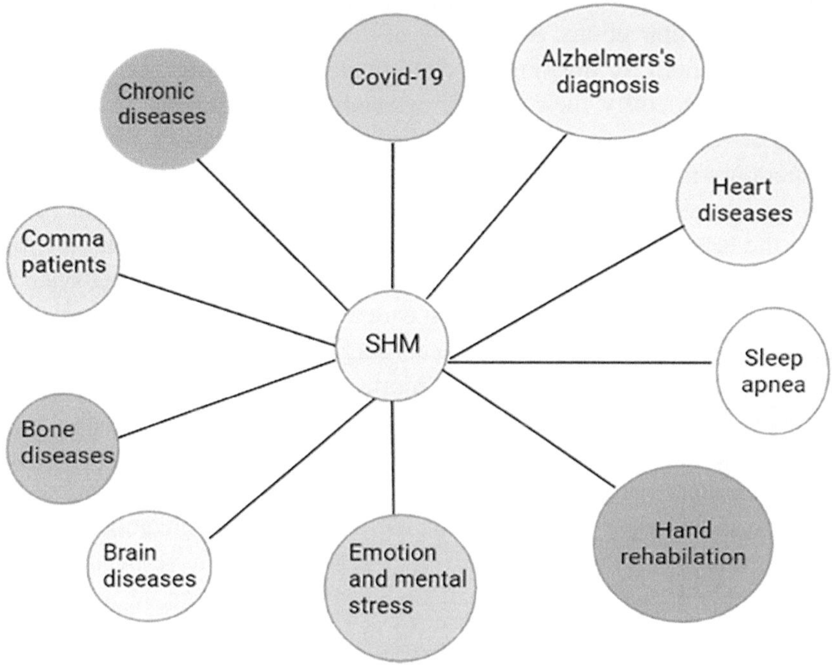

FIGURE 3.1 Benefits and applications of SHM.

facilitate data interchange for a particular area of application is where the IoT notion first emerged. The "IoMT" is a network of interconnected electronic devices specifically designed for use in the medical field. Examples include systems for remote and telemedicine care, disease detection, anomaly detection, patient monitoring, conditioning and screening, and medical nursing and rehabilitation. IoT and SHM are additions to hospital medical systems that allow patients to be treated with complete accuracy and care, unlike old approaches. In the past few decades, technological advancements have largely focused on improving human safety and decreasing the cost of inspections. There are many different new methods, such as SHM and General Smart Monitoring (GSM), where IoMT may help reduce direct and indirect expenses as well as nondistinctive evolution like electrical resistivity, ultrasonic surface waves, and ground penetrating radar approaches, to mention a few. IoTs are a collection of diverse electrical and wireless devices that are all linked to one another, exchange patient data for analysis and diagnosis, and also serve as a repository for patient data [15]. Several sensors and gadgets capture patient data via wireless connections. At the core of these, SHM is a development in the medical field for tracking the conditions of patients (especially coma patients), to identify their body movements by employing IoTs accelerometer (body movement measuring device and sensors), eye blinker, temperature measuring devices, and so on. The elderly and patients with chronic illnesses may benefit from these remote monitoring gadgets [16]. Over the last several decades, there has been a sharp rise in the number of elderly and chronic patients that need a remote health monitoring system (RHMS). Hospitalization and patient care are increasing globally with the arrival of an increase in patients. According to a poll, 770,000 Americans die each year, or a daily increase in mortality [17]. This is brought on by improper medicine use, delayed therapy, and wrong dose, among other things. The load on staff and other medical professionals is lessened in these situations thanks to SHM models [2, 18, 19]. Different sorts of stakeholders, including physicians, patients, and other organizations, make up the smart healthcare system. Even a few hospitals have begun using intelligent beds that can assess patients' conditions without the assistance of a nurse. These beds are quite good in helping coma and chronically sick patients identify, track, analyze, and react to their activities [20]. To attain a healthy lifestyle and real-time monitoring of routine and unique medical activities, IoMT is crucial in creating a healthy environment. In the emergence of the COVID-19 pandemic, SHM and IoTs have shown their importance. Different SHM models and smart gadgets played a significant part in preventing social gatherings and rust at the hospitals two years ago when the WHO proclaimed COVID-19 a pandemic when social distance became an essential condition and instances of COVID-19 were bursting forth [21, 22]. This assisted in controlling individuals with other disorders as well. In this case, as well as other areas like schools, workplaces, banks, and other government and nongovernment services, cell phones are the most useful tool. In hospitals, SHM plays a crucial function, such as when physicians treat patients at home. Patients with COVID, over a wireless telecommunications network, a patient and a doctor may communicate and exchange information and prescriptions [23]. Where access to medical facilities via road or rail is very difficult, the medications were bought online and delivered using drones and guided vehicles from remote places. Remote patient condition monitoring in real-time is possible with SHM. Currently, everyone chooses teleconsultation and online appointments over hospital visits, medical shops, and public gathering programs where there is a higher probability of interpersonal dialog [21]. This is because the COVID-19 epidemic has been mostly contained in most nations. The new developing technology, known as SHM, is discussed in the current review study. The current study includes information on the many SHM components, subclasses, and the functions of deep learning (DL) and artificial intelligence (AI) in managing the healthcare data produced by SHM. The fundamental technologies integrated into SHM for the security and privacy of patient and doctor confidential data are then reviewed, along with a few specific case studies where SHM played a significant role, with final thoughts and future implications for SHM technologies in society and daily life. Figure 3.2 displays the real-time systems for IoT applications.

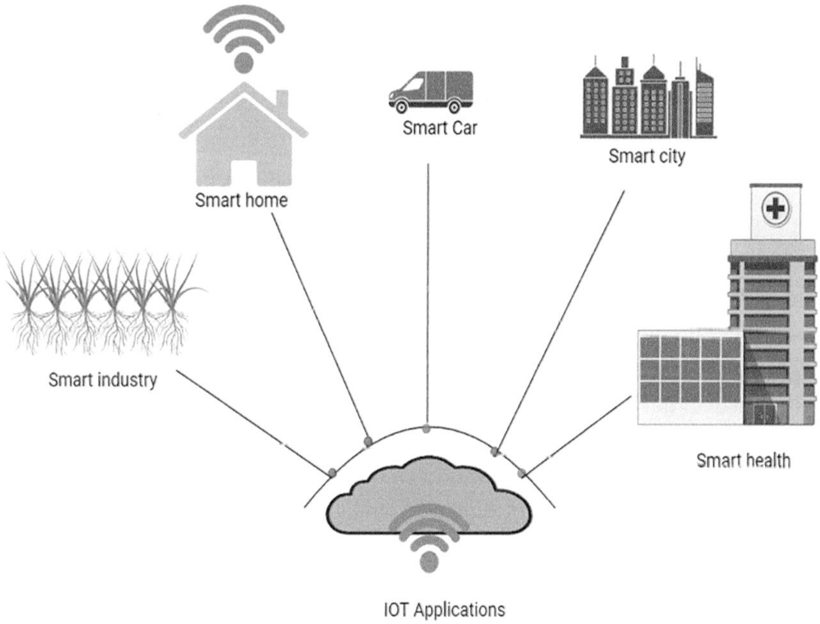

FIGURE 3.2 IoT applications in daily life.

3.3 FEATURES OF SHM AND IOMT

SHM systems provide many important benefits, including the ability for doctors to remotely monitor patients' conditions in real time and the reduction of needless hospital visits. These devices prevent hackers from accessing the data they create. These technologies serve to address the issue of the rising expense of healthcare, which is a significant advancement in the medical industry. IoMTs and SHM will continue to play a significant part in the overall development and expansion as a result of people's growing expectations for and beliefs in the sophistication of technology and digitalization. In the medical field, SHM is a cutting-edge technology that may be utilized to remotely regulate medical facilities to save the lives of vital patients experiencing heart attacks, asthma attacks, diabetic patients, etc. Regressive analysis and computation are required for the data produced by IoMT and SHM devices to allow for the convergence of numerous conclusions. Multiple objectives may be accomplished with the use of data analysis and calculation, including preventing the spread of certain illnesses, monitoring people's health in the future, preventing chronic diseases, and preventing patient fatalities [23]. The study of healthcare data requires the use of DL and AI [24]. There are several frameworks and suggested architects for the analysis of healthcare data in the SHM network that are available in the public domain [25–27].

3.4 ROLE OF DL AND AI IN SHM

The subfields of machine learning (ML) known as DL and transfer learning (TL) deal with large amounts of data that have been successfully verified on a variety of platforms through the use of multiple layers to gather useful data that is gradually used to extract higher level information from previous data. Through the collection of hidden data using staked blocks of layers of the DL skeleton, DL provides useful information. In a variety of fields, including research, SHM, telemedicine, and so on, DL models are employed [28]. Although the TL is a crucial component of the learning apparatus that humans use when they have gained knowledge from prior experiences, it poses difficulties for researchers and engineers when conducting experiments. Figure 3.3 displays the association between DL, ML, and TL.

The use of DL in SHM networks has several benefits. A large amount of data may be collected with the aid of DL models, which provide reliable and effective information. Reduce crucial case reporting delays as much as possible, and facilitate quick and simple diagnosis. Computational learning

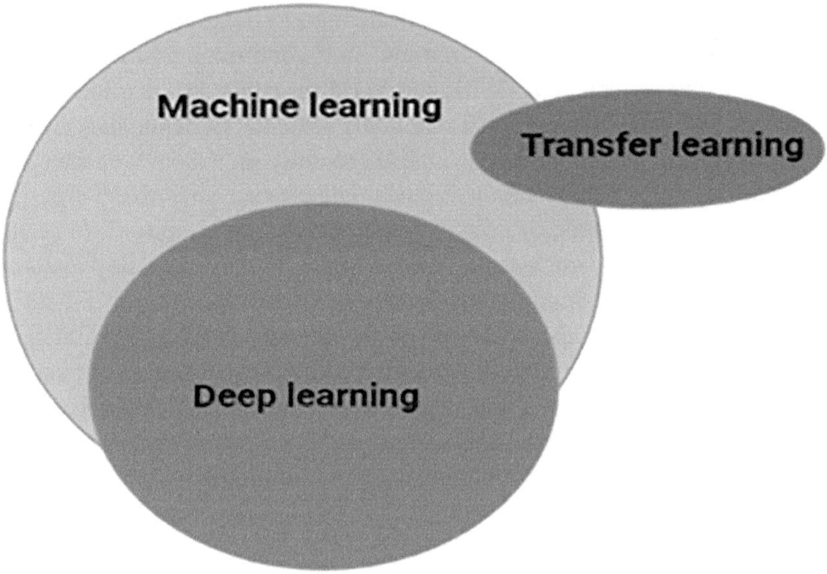

FIGURE 3.3 Relation of deep learning, machine learning, and transfer learning.

systems, SHM, IoTs, and knowledgeable doctors with the ability to identify patients' current conditions in real-time and have accurate knowledge or predictions of their future conditions and anomalies of diabetes, Alzheimer's diseases, general diseases, cancer, respiratory illness, and so on. By using certain applications, such as Happify, mood kit, and Wysa, to mention a few, SHM is useful in the early diagnosis of COVID-19, Alzheimer's illnesses, and other serious disorders [29]. Data integration, data security, and other scenarios have also included the improvisation of DL. The outcomes of AI are based on the data utilized in ML, which is applied to the applications of ML algorithms and software in healthcare systems. In essence, the games are where this is found. Convolutional neural networks, a form of artificial neural networks used for the viewing of pictures like those from X-rays, magnetic resonance imagings (MRIs), and ultrasounds, among others, are the foundation of DL models. By examining the genes, DL makes it simple to identify common disorders like Turner's syndrome, hemophilia, sickle cell anemia, and others, and this allows physicians to develop future therapies as well as new medications [25, 26]. In order for physicians to determine a patient's status, DL and ML can identify both normal and aberrant patient data. Advancements in IoMT hardware and software, the utilization of the graphics processing unit for deep neural network training, and minimizing time exploitation. By using several IoT, GSM, and SHM modules, DL is effective for gathering in-depth information about many essential patients, particularly coma sufferers. DL is also used to analyze medical data from wearable and medical devices, such as smart watches, pulse oximeters, blood pressure monitors, thermometers, eye blinkers, computed tomography (CT) scans, X-ray pictures, MRI, ultrasound images, and so on. The primary goals of real-time health data monitoring are the prevention of chronic illnesses, trauma cases, and disease outbreaks in certain states and nations, as well as the maintenance of a healthy lifestyle [10]. Recent research has shown that DL-based frameworks can record real-time data of coma patients. In contrast to conventional techniques, the IoMT and medical devices provide patients with a wire-free means of communication that also saves time and energy. The next section provides a discussion of several SHM elements and subclasses.

3.5 STRUCTURAL OF IOTM AND SHM

These devices may be broken down into numerous subparts based on a variety of factors, including:

1. Based on the exchange of health-related data or information between phones, that is, between patients and physicians.
2. Publisher
3. Broker
4. Subscriber

Blood pressure, environmental elegance, blood sugar level, and other parameters are included in the publishers' arrangement of linked sensors and patients' records. The broker may store the data in the cloud and gets the data or information from the publisher. The last is a subscriber, which is used to continually monitor data collected from a publisher and may be seen or recognized by smart devices such as Android smartphones, computers, tablets, wearable technology, and so on. According to parameter ranges for either one or more parameters, SHM may be divided into the following subgroups.

- RHMS
- MHMS (mobile health monitoring system)
- WHMS (wearable health monitoring system)
- GHMS (general health monitoring system)

The RHMS, which covers a wide range of symptoms, may be used in both homes and hospitals and can transfer data to or from a place. Mobile phones, smartphones, laptops, and pocket personal computers are all utilized in the MHMS as the primary processing station. In contrast, wearable technology such as digital watches, wristbands, eye blinkers, oximeters, pulse trackers, and so on, collects relevant data and original health data. by archiving and studying real-time data. In the previous 10 years, medical technology has evolved significantly. GHMS keeps track of general illnesses and is crucial in the current world. By doing this, hospitalizations for common illnesses are reduced [16, 17]. People may now address their health issues by utilizing online medical services and other internet resources since they are more conscious of their health nowadays. Utilizing a variety of medical apps accessible across various platforms, they may also discover the pertinent hospitals and doctor-related information on the internet (such as mobile or smart watches). The necessary elements for designing medical IoTs generally are:

1. Data acquisition
2. Communication gateway and
3. Server

The IoTs have three levels to properly gather data. Body sensors and wearable technology are included in the device layer. The fog layer, where data is partially processed, and cloud layers, which store all data or information using powerful computing power, are the next three levels. Utilizing powerful computing resources, the semiprocessed data from the fog layer is transformed into pertinent information and used to accomplish many intended tasks. A particularly cost-effective way to provide medical services is via the cloud, which also functions as an on-demand service [4, 5]. The first step in gathering all of a patient's data is called data acquisition, and it involves employing wearable and wireless sensors, two categories of smart health equipment. One example of a wireless sensor is a raspberry pi with cameras. Other examples include microphones, smartphones, and smart cameras. The most useful applications for these sensors include smart homes for independent elders, respiratory rate and cardiac rate measurement using air matter sensors, toilet seats integrated with the ECG monitor, cardiac, beat, and respiratory monitors, smart beds by using pillows with sensors, magnetic switches, and many more [10]. The WHMS and GHMS categories include wearable technology, which includes digital watches, clothing, fitness tracker bands, and other items. Wearable technology connects to other devices to capture a wide range of data. In specific situations, a smart vest is used to measure physiological parameters like the electrocardiogram (ECG) without the need for skin-contacting gel, the galvanic skin response, the body temperature, and blood pressure. It also aids in determining cardiac output by using an echo-Doppler, which is used to evaluate and improve the performance of athletes and people with disabilities [17]. For several common chronic conditions including Parkinson's disease, Alzheimer's disease, dementia, and so on, SHM and IoTs are thought to be particularly helpful. Nearly 25 million individuals worldwide experience the symptoms of dementia, the most prevalent chronic condition. Memory loss, trouble making decisions and solving problems, sadness, and worry are all classic signs of dementia. Dementia has a variety of disorders as causes and triggers. The most frequent causes are Parkinson's and Alzheimer's disorders. The SHM plays a crucial role in these situations, which is a fantastic accomplishment in the medical field [30]. However, there is always a chance that people and groups would abuse the data produced by IoMT to further their interests. The researchers have significant difficulty with the SHM system's data security. Figure 3.4 illustrates the categorization of SHM.

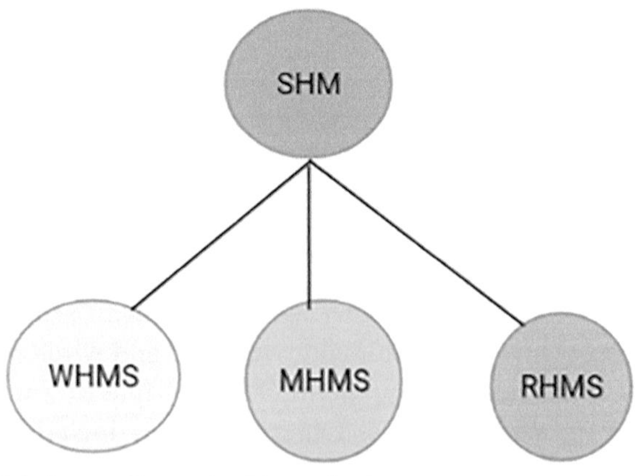

FIGURE 3.4 Subclasses of smart health monitoring.

3.6 DATA SECURITY IN SHM

Big data or health data refers to the information produced by IoMT and SHM networks. High computing resources and data storage capacity are needed to handle this healthcare data. The answer to managing healthcare data in the cloud is cloud computing and cloud storage. However, the majority of this information is kept private from the patient. The main issues in SHM are data security and privacy. It is best to prevent certain users, people, and organizations from misusing this sensitive data for their advantage. Physical security, authentication, network security, computer security, and storage security are all components of data security. More people use encoding and decoding methods, genetic algorithms, data encryption, and cryptography. Trust is a constant problem, hence the majority of security and privacy frameworks allow third parties. Recently, secure data exchange technology in the financial and banking industries has received attention thanks to blockchain and the Interplanetary file system [31–34]. Blockchain is made up of data sets in the form of blocks linked by chains, where each block includes several transactions. The addition of a new block to the chain includes the whole public ledger of transaction history, and new blocks are verified using cryptographic techniques. Blockchain is a strong and highly secure method of data transmission since it includes a time stamp and the value of the preceding block's block hash. Currently, production, management, logistics, and medical services have all effectively used blockchain technology. Many frameworks have proven successful in medical healthcare services and SHM networks and are accessible in the public domain [35–37].

3.7 LIMITATIONS OF SHM AND IOMT

These SHM and medical IoT devices have several drawbacks, such as heterogeneous data gathered by many types of sensors that are prone to mistakes that make it difficult to interpret or diagnose the patient's conditions. Wearable sensors may irritate people, especially youngsters, hence wireless sensors are preferred [36]. Due to the vulnerability of personal patient data, security concerns cannot be ignored. Fraudulence is also a topic of discussion when employing IoT healthcare systems. In essence, smart medical systems are better for chronic patients than traditional medical treatment. IoMT devices rely on battery power and/or constant electricity, both of which are unavailable in distant areas. Figure 3.5 presents significant difficulties. Real-time monitoring necessitates a quick and dependable network connection, both of which are challenging to get in distant areas and on low-powered devices. Since these restrictions are not just a result of new technologies, they may be controlled by progress in science and technology [34].

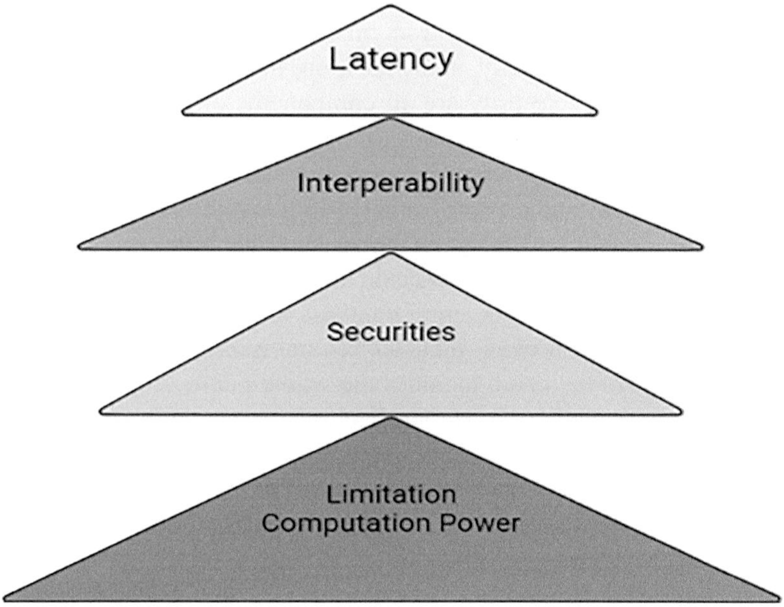

FIGURE 3.5 Challenges in SHM.

3.8 REMOTE MONITORING AND DIGITAL HEALTH TOOLS IN CVD MANAGEMENT

The COVID-19 epidemic has sped up medical innovation, with telemedicine being widely used practically instantly. For decades, perhaps centuries, the majority of doctor–patient interactions took place in person, with patients making regular visits to their physicians' offices. But now it is different [38]. Amid this health crisis, remote consultation and monitoring through mobile-health (m-health) technologies and wearables became necessary to substitute for (or at least supplement) the conventional in-person contact between patients and doctors. Many nations enacted speedy changes to their reimbursement policies to facilitate this digital transition. To what extent healthcare will return to business as usual once the pandemic has been contained, or whether it will continue to embrace the challenges and opportunities presented by the elimination of the requirement for the physical proximity of patients, data collection, and decision-making, remains to be seen.

3.9 REMOTE CARDIOVASCULAR MONITORING

Data collection from people with or at risk for CVD may be done easily through the Internet thanks to recent technological advances. Symptoms, body mass index, levels of physical activity (PA), pulse rate (HR), HR regularity, heart sounds (HRS), respiratory rate (RR), RR interval (RR interval), ECG, oxygen saturation, and quality of sleep may all expanding into this category of technology are wearables like watches and patches [39]. Innovations in point-of-care diagnostics have also helped improve the capacity to manage patients outside of hospitals. Cardiovascular implanted electronic devices (like a defibrillator) may offer almost constant streams of information on various physiological factors to patients with heart failure or a history of failed sudden cardiac death. Supporting the identification of persons with or at risk for clinically relevant events might be either conventional or ML methods. Remote monitoring data may help speed up preventative clinical measures including reinforcing patient adherence to prescriptions, adjusting drug treatment, or doing early clinical face-to-face reviews. Medication delivery services (like Amazon's PillPack) sent directly to patients' homes help to complete the cycle from monitoring to therapy. An increasing number of patients are actively participating in their health management via the use of patient-facing interfaces, such as smart-phone applications. The future may be dominated by self-management, with little involvement from the healthcare team, as more people resort to digital health resources for their healthcare needs. Health policymakers are optimistic about this individualized approach since it has the potential to improve people's health and reduce the overall cost of healthcare.

3.10 OPPORTUNITIES AND CHALLENGES

When it comes to patient outcomes, remote monitoring is useless unless it also affects patient treatment or behavior. Patients with type 1 diabetes mellitus may use patch technology for continuous blood-sugar monitoring in conjunction with a wearable insulin pump as an example of a closed-loop system that monitors and treats patients remotely. It has been suggested that using a smartphone app to aid in clinical decision-making with easy home blood pressure monitoring might lead to better blood pressure control [40]. Furthermore, digital technologies may aid in cardiac rehabilitation by providing patients with gamification and feedback on their real behaviors as they progress toward better health, all from the comfort of their own homes [41]. Things are not as bright as they seem. It has been challenging to consistently show the extra benefit of remote monitoring in terms of improved outcomes [42] for complicated illnesses like heart failure. However, after the events of COVID-19, people are now having a different conversation about the utility of remote monitoring, with greater emphasis placed on the benefits that come from patients not having to travel or otherwise inconvenienced by the process, and on the decreased need for social contact as a result. Getting the same effects as standard treatment can be good enough. The amount of data that might be useful for clinical decision-making is expected to increase by an order of magnitude in the future, necessitating the use of AI to augment human intellect. More clinical input is critically needed in conversations about the ethics of using AI in medicine[43].

3.11 CALL FOR ACTION

In order to maintain its competitiveness in a future that will (by necessity and design) become increasingly digital, the entire healthcare ecosystem, which comprises a wide range of stakeholders, must embrace digital transformation. According to a 2019 ESC member poll, the majority of cardiologists are only "somewhat" acquainted with digital health technologies, while many have no experience at all with m-health tools or wearables [44]. As the COVID-19 pandemic has proven, when the need is evident, regulatory and liability problems do not seem to be insurmountable [45]. As the world becomes more digital, employment changes, and new roles arise, the industry must invest more in the training and development of healthcare professionals [46]. Even though digital literacy is alarmingly low even in wealthy countries, it is crucial to continue to educate the general public about its importance.

Although electronic medical records (EMRs) are crucial to a digitally integrated strategy that records all data for clinical management, they are typically constructed without meaningful clinical involvement, leading to wasteful processes. When patients and physicians try to come to mutual conclusions based on all available information, the difficulty of combining data from nontraditional sources (such as wearables or apps) might cause a rift. Political pressure to deliver on investment and show the potential benefit of digital technology, while also protecting people from damage, adds complexity to already difficult regulatory concerns. Concerns about data protection and obtaining necessary permissions online are complex. The Food and Drug Administration in the United States has established a Digital Health Center of Excellence with the mission to "empower stakeholders to enhance healthcare by supporting responsible and high-quality digital health innovation." The new Medical Device Regulations in the European Union are projected to raise entry hurdles for digital technology, thus many companies are trying to have their products classified as "health and lifestyle" products rather than medical devices. Authorities responsible for reimbursement will likely face challenges. They want to help people have access to useful innovations at affordable (or at least manageable) prices. Developers of new technologies sometimes assume that tiny pilot studies will be enough to convince payers to cover the cost of their creations without any more convincing evidence of the technology's benefit. The National Institute for Health and Care Excellence in England has outlined a new strategy, one that requires a more proportional amount of information to be gathered concerning the cost and potential risks and benefits of technology within a patient pathway [47]. "Big Tech" creates a lot of gadgets catering to the affluent. This may harm the "digital divide," which means that fewer people who do not have access to resources like high-speed Internet and personal computers will be able to reap the benefits of innovation. In locations where getting to a doctor is difficult owing to distance, transportation issues, or a shortage of medical professionals, applications for smartphones may be a lifesaver. Access to smartphones is almost ubiquitous among youth but varies among age groups in many nations. To effectively promote digital literacy, including the adoption of evidence-based digital redesign and innovation, professional medical organizations must serve as conduits for meaningful interaction with other relevant stakeholders.

3.12 TEMPORAL DISPLACEMENT OF CARE

Patients with autoimmune and chronic conditions, most often those affecting the heart and kidneys (such as arrhythmia, high blood pressure, diabetes, and other cardiac-related difficulties), are central to the development of the premises of temporal displacement of care [48]. According to the theory of temporal displacement of care, the time it takes to get treatment may be replaced by the use of cutting-edge, sensor-enabled smart devices that can communicate vital data in real-time with a distributed group of healthcare providers. Therefore, it is both desired and practicable for a medical practitioner to intervene quickly in potentially lethal or life-threatening circumstances. AI-enabled IoT smart health systems are set to revolutionize the medical industry, trackers opportunities arise where previously unimaginable data allow for analytical processes to be carried out [49]. Considering the analytics that are embedded, such as supervised situations of emergency may be learned to handle via unsupervised learning expected with worrisome results for both the patient and the doctor. This case, for instance, is the genesis of time, and the importance of healthcare organizations generating services through facilitating. By combining state-of-the-art infrastructure with intelligent devices, via layers of combining analytics with information technology. To ensure the smooth running of healthcare facilities and make sure it is up to par, a hospital or clinic has to be provided with hardware and software for processing, analytics, precise data, and other information, and so on, element, therapeutic category, cost, and repercussions quantified. Information processing by use of neural "currents" infrastructure necessitates that information be made, gathered, and spread around, which fosters more collaboration amongst participants [50].

3.13 SENSOR ENABLED IOT-BASED DEVICES

There are a variety of connected gadgets on the market now that can monitor health and upload data to the internet. Users who have downloaded the mobile app and logged in with their credentials may see their fitness, step, run, bike, and sleep tracking stats [51]. In addition to continuous heart rate and blood pressure monitoring including ECG in higher variants with fall detection alarms, users of certain high-variant smart devices will also receive notifications about female health status, stress conditions, and guided meditation during stress conditions [52], fitness tracking, and evening exercise based on the day's calorie burnt [52], when there is a drastic shift in vitals, as shown by the appearance of new, unexpected patterns [52, 53]. These smart gadgets may continuously monitor oxygen saturation levels and alert users promptly if the percentage falls below 95% [52], in addition to monitoring the heart, blood pressure, activity, sleep, and female health. Diabetes and other metabolic problems may also be treated with the help of modern technology. To monitor diabetes, patients might use daily routine tests that require them to prick their fingers and read the blood sugar level on a fresh strip each day. The treatment, however, is both expensive and uncomfortable. However, the problem may be imaginatively addressed with the aid of smart technologies. Smart glucometers eliminate the need for frequent finger-pricking and the use of fresh needles or strips by allowing users to save their blood-sugar readings in the device's memory [54].

3.14 AI

The practitioner lacks confidence that the treatment will be successful for the patient because of the unreliability of the emergency room and doctor–patient communication owing to a lack of necessary knowledge about illness and drugs. Since these trials include small sample sizes, the studies are repeated, and the results are considered to be simply averages, even if half of the medications and therapies utilized by healthcare professionals have no effectiveness or viability impacts on the participants. Assuming physicians are incompetent only because they may not have all the information they need to provide a precise treatment plan is a dangerous assumption to make. Though much of the medical treatment they provide is enhanced with the far-fetched goal of incorporating AI. In the future of healthcare, doctors will have access to more sophisticated systems, technologies, and intelligence. With the help of AI, medical technology might be used as a second pair of eyes in the operating room. Huge volumes of information are created by the healthcare industry every day thanks to electronic health record (EHR) and EMR from in-patient data. Data on outpatients may also be acquired in real-time with the aid of smart healthcare systems and devices, allowing for the execution of ML algorithms and analytics grounded on AI [55]. The health industry now has access to more comprehensive data, which, when fed into multiple machine-learning algorithms, may help hospitals and clinics better predict and comprehend their patients' immediate and future care requirements. It would be challenging for a physician to compare and contrast the results of several patients' tests and the symptoms they're experiencing. Due to the sheer volume of samples, it will be challenging for doctors to make accurate diagnoses. When presented with a bewildering array of devices and DL algorithms, the selection of the ideal option must be made [56]. These tools have the potential to manage successfully with lower mistake rates and greater accuracy than the Technicians of the laboratory. Data acquired from EHRs, EMRs, and IoT enabled sensor-based smart wearables may be managed by AI learning algorithms over time, allowing for the prediction of a result [57]. AI devices are capable of human-level cognition, human-level movement, and supercomputer-level performance [58]. It improves the timeliness and accuracy of disease diagnosis. Patients and their current doctors may use a patient's clinical history to better understand the patient's risk for developing certain illnesses, as well as to guide how to manage any existing disorders and what additional evidence may be necessary for long-term health maintenance [59].

3.15 SMART HEALTHCARE SYSTEMS

Wearables, the IoT, and mobile Internet are just a few examples of the cutting-edge technologies used in "Smart Healthcare," which is defined as "a health service infrastructure that uses innovative, modern, and advanced technologies to remotely access knowledge, link individuals, materials, and organizations relevant to healthcare," and intelligently respond to and meet the needs of patients [60]. In other words, smart healthcare is a trend that utilizes cutting-edge technologies to better "connect to the patients," "manage availability," and "enhance medical procedures." The development of low-cost personal ICT technologies like laptops, PCs, and mobile phones has resulted in a leapfrog solution that enables large-data remote patient monitoring [61]. This has increased people's interest in and knowledge of healthcare wearable devices and mobile app-based monitoring systems that placed patients, physicists, and smart wearable healthcare devices have played a vital role in spreading awareness of and support for these innovations. including medical facilities like hospitals, on a single network enabling seamless, real-time to get to [62]. For example, in cardiac monitoring smart systems, which keep tabs on things like a patient's pulse, blood oxygen levels, and ECG [53], a cloud-based, IoT-enabled wearable device is constantly generating data, which is then stored; meanwhile, an AI algorithm uses supervised learning to uncover previously unseen patterns in the data. Which transforms the system into a smart one capable of accurately predicting falls or other unwelcome occurrences in real-time.

3.16 SHM

Compatibility for sensors IoT-based smart gadgets that include AI pose a threat to the status quo of healthcare delivery and administration by providing early warnings of impending problems. AI systems for arrhythmia, for instance, notice trends by keeping a running record of the heart's activity over time and using supervised learning to conclude it. In the future, when there is a noticeable shift in the pattern, it will alert users to a potential disturbance in their heart rhythm and advise them to see a doctor [53]. Indicators of stress are shown on the Samsung Active Watch 2 when the AI system detects a sudden, substantial shift in the user's heart rate and breathing pattern, and the user is prompted to engage in guided meditation via the Samsung Health mobile app [52]. Also, the conventional approach to health monitoring is transformed and improved upon by the combination of sensor-enabled data and AI. Wearable healthcare systems equipped with AI-enabled smart sensors will not only allow users to keep records of daily activities and physiological symptoms but will also aid medical professionals in making quick but precise decisions regarding the future course of treatment for in-patients. AI and analytics performed on huge lab data and IPD papers using supervised learning based on prior patient experiences aid intensivists and physicians in defining a clear course of therapy, hence reducing hospital stay and readmission rates [63].

3.17 CARE SERVICE ORCHESTRATION

Industry 4.0 is ushering in a new digital age, and with it comes the disruption of many industries, including healthcare, as machines and instruments become interconnected via the use of sensors. Today, hospitals are one of the most important parts of the healthcare system, as they offer diagnostic and treatment services for both acute and chronic conditions, including consultations, admissions, critical care, ambulatory services, laboratory tests, CT scans, radiology tests, radiations, and much more. However, in the not-too-distant future [64], hospitals will lose their significance and become a minor component of a vast healthcare ecosystem. The healthcare industry is fragmenting, leading to independent yet interconnected service silos. Hospitals, for instance, will have patients requiring major surgery and patients in critical care, but people requiring consultation, laboratory testing, radiology services, and ambulatory care will soon no longer be at the hospital. The current state of disjointed labor requires a new approach based on the notion of orchestration, in which individuals carry out their particular tasks in a coordinated fashion. Care service orchestration can be defined as the extent to which real-time digital technology is used to foster an inviting atmosphere in which users are more likely to interact positively [65]. This is accomplished by facilitating the growth and synchronous exchange of knowledge and service flow throughout the mechanism linking interactive stakeholders. Healthcare workers and administrators may present a more holistic picture of the system as a whole thanks to the integrative approach used by care service orchestration. This involves linking decentralized systems to a standardized, linked network. It may then use this for something called a "visual board." When many facilities are networked together, all of the advantages of each may be used for the greater good of the network as a whole. The foundation of care service orchestration is the idea that all parts, upstream and downstream, must work in harmony with one another. In which information may be sent without any hitches, making it possible for doctors to act quickly [65, 66]. From the perspective of healthcare organizations, doctors and nurses require the maximum possible degree of integration at all levels (as it is so important to exchange and distribute information). Understanding of current therapeutic advances, procedures, hospital capacity, necessary diagnostic tests (in pathology, radiology, etc.), and patient feedback to provide excellent care [67].

3.18 CONCLUSION

It is difficult to ensure the timely and secure implementation of AI research into systems that have been clinically evaluated and are adequately controlled for the benefit of all. It is crucial to conduct thorough clinical evaluations using metrics that are easily understood by physicians and which, ideally, extend beyond measurements of technical accuracy to incorporate quality of care and patient outcomes. There is still a need for more research into (1) identifying themes of algorithmic bias and unfairness and devising mitigations to address them, (2) reducing brittleness and improving generalizability, and (3) developing approaches for improved interpretability of ML predictions. If these objectives are met, they will have a profound impact on patient care. Recent developments in AI hold great promise for enhancing medical treatment. However, the successful use of research methods in clinical settings represents uncharted territory for clinical and ML studies. Clinically applicable performance metrics that extend beyond measures of technical accuracy are needed to ensure that AI systems are safe and effective. These metrics should consider the impact of AI on the quality of care, the variability of healthcare professionals, the efficiency and productivity of clinical practice, and most importantly, patient outcomes. To facilitate the comparison of different algorithms, it is necessary to curate independent datasets that are typical of prospective target populations, paying close attention to signals of potential bias and fitting to unintended confounders. Developers of AI tools need to be aware of the algorithms they create and the potential unexpected repercussions they may have on the world at large. The future acceptance and safety of algorithms will depend on continued work to improve their interpretability and to comprehend human-algorithm interactions, as well as the development of smart regulatory frameworks.

KEYWORDS

- **artificial intelligence**
- **patient monitoring**
- **healthcare**
- **medicine**

REFERENCES

1. Perumal K, Manohar M. 2017. A survey on internet of things: Case studies, applications, and future directions. In *Internet of Things: Novel Advances and Envisioned Applications* (pp. 281–297). Springer: Cham.

2. Rahaman A, Islam MM, Islam MR, Sadi MS, Nooruddin S. 2019. Developing IoT based smart health monitoring systems: A review. *Rev. d'Intelligence Artif. 33*(6), 435–440.
3. Islam SR. 2015. Kyung-sup Kwak the Internet of Things for health care: A comprehensive survey. *IEEE Access 3*, 678–708.
4. Lin T, Rivano H, Le Mouël F. 2017. A survey of smart parking solutions. *IEEE Trans Intell Trans Syst. 18*(12), 3229–3253.
5. Zualkernan IA, Rashid M, Gupta R, Alikarar M. 2017. A smart home energy management system using IoT and big data analytics approach. *IEEE Trans Consum Electron. 63*, 426–434.
6. Zanella A, Bui N, Castellani A, Vangelista L, Zorzi M. 2014. Internet of things for smart cities. *IEEE Internet Things J. 1*(1), 22–32.
7. Mois G, Folea S, Sanislav T. 2017. Analysis of three IoT-based wireless sensors for environmental monitoring. *IEEE Trans Instrum Meas. 66*(8), 2056–2064.
8. Chen B, Wan J, Shu L, Li P, Mukherjee M, Yin B. 2017. Smart factory of industry 4.0: Key technologies, application case, and challenges. *IEEE Access 6*, 6505–6519.
9. Ayaz M, Ammad-Uddin M, Sharif Z, Mansour A, Aggoune EHM. 2019. Internet-of-Things (IoT)-based smart agriculture: Toward making the fields talk. *IEEE Access 7*, 129551–129583.
10. Hasan M, Islam MM, Zarif MII, Hashem MMA. 2019. Attack and anomaly detection in iot sensors in iot sites using machine learning approaches. *Internet Things 7*, 100059.
11. Nooruddin S, Islam MM, Sharna FA. 2020. An IoT based device-type invariant fall detection system. *Internet Things 9*, 100130.
12. Dhimal M, Chirico F, Bista B, Sharma S, Chalise B, Dhimal ML, Ilesanmi OS, Trucillo P, Sofia D. 2021. Impact of air pollution on global burden of disease in 2019. *Processes 9*(10), 1719.
13. Tabaa M, Monteiro F, Bensag H, Dandache A. 2020. Green Industrial Internet of Things from a smart industry perspectives. *Energy Rep. 6*, 430–446.
14. De Michele R, Furini M. 2019, September. Iot healthcare: Benefits, issues and challenges. In *Proceedings of the 5th EAI International Conference on Smart Objects and Technologies for Social Good* (pp. 160–164).
15. Haricha K, Khiat A, Issaoui Y, Bahnasse A, Ouajji H. 2020. Towards smart manufucturing: Implementation and benefits. *Procedia Comput Sci. 177*, 639–644.
16. Portnoy JM, Pandya A, Waller M, Elliott T. 2020. Telemedicine and emerging technologies for health care in allergy/immunology. *J Allergy Clin Immun. 145*(2), 445–454.
17. Baig MM, Gholamhosseini H. 2013. Smart health monitoring systems: An overview of design and modeling. *J Med Syst. 37*(2), 1–14.
18. Albahri AS, Albahri OS, Zaidan AA, Zaidan BB, Hashim M, Alsalem MA, Mohsin AH, Mohammed KI, Alamoodi AH, Enaizan O, Nidhal S. 2019. Based multiple heterogeneous wearable sensors: A smart real-time health monitoring structured for hospitals distributor. *IEEE Access 7*, 37269–37323.
19. Hassanalieragh M, Page A, Soyata T, Sharma G, Aktas M, Mateos G, Kantarci B, Andreescu S. 2015, June. Health monitoring and management using Internet-of-Things

(IoT) sensing with cloud-based processing: Opportunities and challenges. In *2015 IEEE International Conference on Services Computing* (pp. 285–292). IEEE.
20. García-Magariño I, Lacuesta R, Lloret J. 2017. Agent-based simulation of smart beds with internet-of-things for exploring big data analytics. *IEEE Access 6*, 366–379.
21. Vedaei SS, Fotovvat A, Mohebbian MR, Rahman GM, Wahid KA, Babyn P, Marateb HR, Mansourian M, Sami R. 2020. COVID-SAFE: An IoT-based system for automated health monitoring and surveillance in post-pandemic life. *IEEE Access 8*, 188538.
22. Taiwo O, Ezugwu AE. 2020. Smart healthcare support for remote patient monitoring during covid-19 quarantine. *Inform Med Unlocked 20*, 100428.
23. Carter D, Kolencik J, Cug J. 2021. Smart Internet of Things-enabled mobile-based health monitoring systems and medical big data in COVID-19 telemedicine. *Am J Med Res. 8*(1), 20–30.
24. Azimi M, Eslamlou AD, Pekcan G. 2020. Data-driven structural health monitoring and damage detection through deep learning: State-of-the-art review. *Sensors 20*(10), 2778.
25. Jang HJ, Cho KO. 2019. Applications of deep learning for the analysis of medical data. *Arch Pharm Res. 42*(6), 492–504.
26. Yue L, Tian D, Chen W, Han X, Yin M. 2020. Deep learning for heterogeneous medical data analysis. *World Wide Web. 23*(5), 2715–2737.
27. Ravì D, Wong C, Deligianni F, Berthelot M, Andreu-Perez J, Lo B, Yang GZ. 2016. Deep learning for health informatics. *IEEE J Biomed Health Inform. 21*(1), 4–21.
28. Cai L, Gao J, Zhao D. 2020. A review of the application of deep learning in medical image classification and segmentation. *Ann Transl Med. 8*(11), 713.
29. Stamate C, Magoulas GD, Küppers S, Nomikou E, Daskalopoulos I, Luchini MU, Moussouri T, Roussos G. 2017 March. Deep learning Parkinson's from smartphone data. In *2017 IEEE International Conference on Pervasive Computing and Communications (PerCom)* (pp. 31–40). IEEE.
30. Wang L, Sha L, Lakin JR, Bynum J, Bates DW, Hong P, Zhou L. 2019. Development and validation of a deep learning algorithm for mortality prediction in selecting patients with dementia for earlier palliative care interventions. *JAMA Netw Open 2*(7), e196972–e196972.
31. Ratta P, Kaur A, Sharma S, Shabaz M, Dhiman G. 2021. Application of blockchain and internet of things in healthcare and medical sector: Applications, challenges, and future perspectives. *J Food Qual. 2021*.
32. Bhola J, Soni S, Cheema GK. 2019 March. Recent trends for security applications in wireless sensor networks—A technical review. In *2019 6th International Conference on Computing for Sustainable Global Development (INDIACom)* (pp. 707–712). IEEE.
33. Bhola J, Soni S, Cheema GK. 2020. Genetic algorithm based optimized leach protocol for energy efficient wireless sensor networks. *J Ambient Intell Humaniz Comput. 11*(3), 1281–1288.
34. Kumar A, Jagota V, Shawl RQ, Sharma V, Sargam K, Shabaz M, Khan MT, Rabani B, Gandhi S. 2021. Wire EDM process parameter optimization for D2 steel. *Mater Today Proc. 37*, 2478–2482.

35. Pham HL, Tran TH, Nakashima Y. 2018, December. A secure remote healthcare system for hospital using blockchain smart contract. In *2018 IEEE Globecom Workshops (GC Wkshps)* (pp. 1–6). IEEE.
36. Griggs KN, Ossipova O, Kohlios CP, Baccarini AN, Howson EA, Hayajneh T. 2018. Healthcare blockchain system using smart contracts for secure automated remote patient monitoring. *J Med Syst. 42*(7), 1–7.
37. Antwi M, Adnane A, Ahmad F, Hussain R, urRehman MH, Kerrache CA. 2021. The case of hyperledger fabric as a blockchain solution for healthcare applications. *Blockchain: Res Appl. 2*(1), 100012
38. Mueller B. 2020. *Telemedicine Arrives in the UK:'10 Years of Change in One Week'. The New York Times.*
39. Krittanawong C, Rogers AJ, Johnson KW, Wang Z, Turakhia MP, Halperin JL, Narayan SM. 2021. Integration of novel monitoring devices with machine learning technology for scalable cardiovascular management. *Nat Rev Cardiol. 18*(2), 75–91.
40. McManus RJ, Little P, Stuart B, Morton K, Raftery J, Kelly J, Bradbury K, Zhang J, Zhu S, Murray E, May CR. 2021. Home and Online Management and Evaluation of Blood Pressure (HOME BP) using a digital intervention in poorly controlled hypertension: Randomised controlled trial. *BMJ 372*, m4858.
41. Subedi N, Rawstorn JC, Gao L, Koorts H, Maddison R. 2020. Implementation of telerehabilitation interventions for the self-management of cardiovascular disease: Systematic review. *JMIR MHealth UHealth 8*(11), e17957.
42. Klersy C, Boriani G, De Silvestri A, Mairesse GH, Braunschweig F, Scotti V, Balduini A, Cowie MR, Leyva F, Health Economics Committee of the European Heart Rhythm Association. 2016. Effect of telemonitoring of cardiac implantable electronic devices on healthcare utilization: A meta-analysis of randomized controlled trials in patients with heart failure. *Eur J Heart Fail. 18*(2), 195–204.
43. Arnold MH. 2021. Teasing out artificial intelligence in medicine: An ethical critique of artificial intelligence and machine learning in medicine. *J Bioethical Inq. 18*(1), 121–139.
44. Asteggiano R, Cowie MR, Richter D, Christodorescu R, Guasti L, Ferrini M. 2021. Survey on e-health knowledge and usage in general cardiology of the Council of Cardiology Practice and the Digital Health Committee. *Eur Heart J-Digital Health 2*(2), 342–347.
45. Frederix I, Caiani EG, Dendale P, Anker S, Bax J, Böhm A, Cowie M, Crawford J, De Groot N, Dilaveris P, Hansen T. 2019. ESC e-Cardiology working group position paper: Overcoming challenges in digital health implementation in cardiovascular medicine. *Eur J Prevent Cardiol. 26*(11), 1166–1177.
46. Topol E. 2019. *The Topol Review: Preparing the Healthcare Workforce to Deliver the Digital Future* (p. 103). Health Education England. https://topol. hee. nhs. uk/wp-content/uploads/HEE-Topol-Review-2019. pdf.
47. National Institute for Health and Care Excellence. 2019. Evidence standards framework for digital health technologies.
48. Thompson S, Whitaker J, Kohli R, Jones C. 2019. Chronic disease management: How IT and analytics create healthcare value through the temporal displacement of care. *MIS Quarterly, Forthcoming.*

49. Bhatt V, Sashikala P, Chakraborty S. 2019. The impact of information technology and analytics on the performance of a hospital: Scale development in Indian context. *Int J Recent Technol Eng.* *8*(3), 2861–2869.
50. Kotlarsky J, Scarbrough H, Oshri I. 2014. Coordinating expertise across knowledge boundaries iin offshore-outsourcing projects. *MIS Quarterly.* *38*(2), 607–A5.
51. Deshkar S, Thanseeh RA, Menon VG. 2017. A review on IoT based m-Health systems for diabetes. *Int J Comput Sci Telecommun.* *8*(1), 13–18.
52. Bhatt V, Chakraborty S. 2021, March. Real-time healthcare monitoring using smart systems: A step towards healthcare service orchestration Smart systems for futuristic healthcare. In *2021 International Conference on Artificial Intelligence and Smart Systems (ICAIS)* (pp. 772–777). IEEE.
53. Apple I. 2019. *ECG App and Irregular Heart Rhythm Notification Available Today on Apple Watch.* Apple Newsroom.
54. Kukkar D, Zhang D, Jeon BH, Kim KH. 2022. Recent advances in wearable biosensors for non-invasive monitoring of specific metabolites and electrolytes associated with chronic kidney disease: Performance evaluation and future challenges. *TrAC Trends Anal Chem.* *150*, 116570.
55. Mohanta B, Das P, Patnaik S. 2019, May. Healthcare 5.0: A paradigm shift in digital healthcare system using Artificial Intelligence, IOT and 5G Communication. In *2019 International Conference on Applied Machine Learning (ICAML)* (pp. 191–196). IEEE.
56. Fatima M, Pasha M. 2017. Survey of machine learning algorithms for disease diagnostic. *J Intell Learn Syst Appl.* *9*(01), 1.
57. Knickerbocker JU, Budd R, Dang B, Chen Q, Colgan E, Hung LW, Kumar S, Lee KW, Lu M, Nah JW, Narayanan R. 2018, May. Heterogeneous integration technology demonstrations for future healthcare, IoT, and AI computing solutions. In *2018 IEEE 68th Electronic Components and Technology Conference (ECTC)* (pp. 1519–1528). IEEE.
58. Syed UA, Shamim HM, Ghulam M, Musaed A, Md. Abdur R. (2019). *Cognitive Smart Healthcare for Pathology Detection and Monitoring, 7.*
59. Alam MGR, Abedin SF, Moon SI, Talukder A, Hong CS. 2019. Healthcare IoT-based affective state mining using a deep convolutional neural network. *IEEE Access 7*, 75189–75202.
60. Tian S, Yang W, Le Grange JM, Wang P, Huang W, Ye Z. 2019. Smart healthcare: Making medical care more intelligent. *Glob Health J.* *3*(3), 62–65.
61. Yeong YC, Kalid KS, Sugathan SK. 2019. Cryptocurrency acceptance: A case of Malaysia. *Int J Engineer Adv Technol.* *8*(5), 28–38.
62. Bhatt V, Chakraborty S. 2020, October. Importance of trust in IoT based wearable device adoption by patient: An empirical investigation. In *2020 Fourth International Conference on I-SMAC (IoT in Social, Mobile, Analytics and Cloud)(I-SMAC)* (pp. 1226–1231). IEEE.
63. Wehbe Y, Al Zaabi M, Svetinovic D. 2018, November. Blockchain AI framework for healthcare records management: Constrained goal model. In *2018 26th Telecommunications Forum (TELFOR)* (pp. 420–425). IEEE.
64. Friesdorf M, Deetjen U, Sawant A, Gilbert G, Niedermann F. 2019. *Digital Health Ecosystems: A Payer Perspective* (p. 2). McKinsey & Company.

65. Sezen B. 2008. Relative effects of design, integration and information sharing on supply chain performance. *Supply Chain Manag Int J. 13*(3), 233–240.
66. Prajogo D. 2012. Olhager J, Supply chain integration and performance: The effect of long-term relationships, IT and sharing, and logistics integration. *Int J Prod Econ. 135*(1), 514–522.
67. Bagchi PK, Chun Ha B, Skjoett-Larsen T, BoegeSoerensen L. 2005. Supply chain integration: A European survey. *Int J Logist Manag. 16*(2), 275–294.

CHAPTER 4

Telemonitoring: Artificial Intelligence to Monitor Patients Remotely

ABSTRACT

The medical business has started using the statistical processing and interpretation capabilities of artificial intelligence in telemedicine, which mirrors the extensive use of artificial intelligence in several other areas. There is a need to strengthen the capabilities of telemedicine and customize its processes to handle specific challenges that have emerged throughout its introduction. The material reviewed in this study illustrates the boundless expansion possibilities presented by artificial intelligence and telemedicine. Constant patient checks, electronic health records, collaborative information analysis, diagnosis, and intelligence support are four areas where this technology is seeing increasing use. Each movement will be explained, with references to relevant modern literature and the issues they seek to solve provided as examples. The potential and growth of this present trend in telemedicine will be analyzed through the tabulation and classification of relevant references.

4.1 INTRODUCTION

The advancement of technology, namely in internet connectivity as well as information processing capabilities, has created avenues for the worldwide healthcare industry to thrive, notably in the field of telemedicine. Key domains for possible advancement in the intervening years include the interchange and assessment of information, as well as the World Wide Web of Things, connected devices, cloud computing, and robots. The use of artificial intelligence (AI) is essential in the management and application of medical technologies because of the extensive utilization of data in

DOI: 10.1201/9781779640819-4

healthcare, the requirement for consistent precision in complex operations, and the growing demand for medical services. Automating hospital logistics is essential to improving healthcare delivery and resource allocation [1]. The advent of telemedicine has made it possible to carry out consultations, diagnostic procedures, surgical procedures, and professional collaborations [2]. The "open and constantly growing science" [3] of telemedicine is often cited as the reason for its rapid development of technological innovations to address and adjust to the changing health conditions, demands, and environments of communities. The goals of telemedicine are primarily increased communication, reduced logistical costs, and accessibility. Over the previous 10 years, cost-benefit analyses, market penetration forecasts, and sensor/case study integration with EHRs and home monitoring are just some of the topics that have been studied about this technology, which has progressed greatly [4]. Teleradiology involves the remote transmission of digital radiological images (like X-rays), while telepathology involves the electronic transmission of pathological results, teledermatology deals with the remote transmission of medical information about skin conditions, and telepsychiatry involves the remote transmission of video and phone consultations and/or assessments with psychiatrists. However, advancements in AI and data analytics will allow for a broader application of the technology. The goal of telemedicine is to enhance effectiveness, personnel is allocated based on the specific demands and level of urgency of each patient. In this chapter, researchers look at the significance of AI and how some of its core ideas are already being applied to telemedicine's goals. Patient monitoring, healthcare IT, computer-assisted diagnostics, training simulations, and collaborative information analysis are just some of the topics that will be covered.

4.2 TELEMEDICINE

"Tele" comes from the term for distance in Greek. Telemedicine then offers online Medicare service, usually including several telecommunication resources, including laptops, cellular computers, and distant video links [5, 6]. The traditional method of providing medical care consisted of house calls from the doctor; however, hospitals and outpatient medical offices gradually took their place. Smartphones and rising interest have transformed a variety of industries, from accounting to transportation.

For instance, the increased use of ATMs in the bank lobby partially replaced bank tellers, who have since been entirely supplanted by the use of smartphone check deposits and Internet banking [6]. In a similar vein, recent advancements in telemedicine are set to return patient care to their homes from the doctor's office. The underlying growth opportunities available to healthcare organizations are depicted in Figure 4.1.

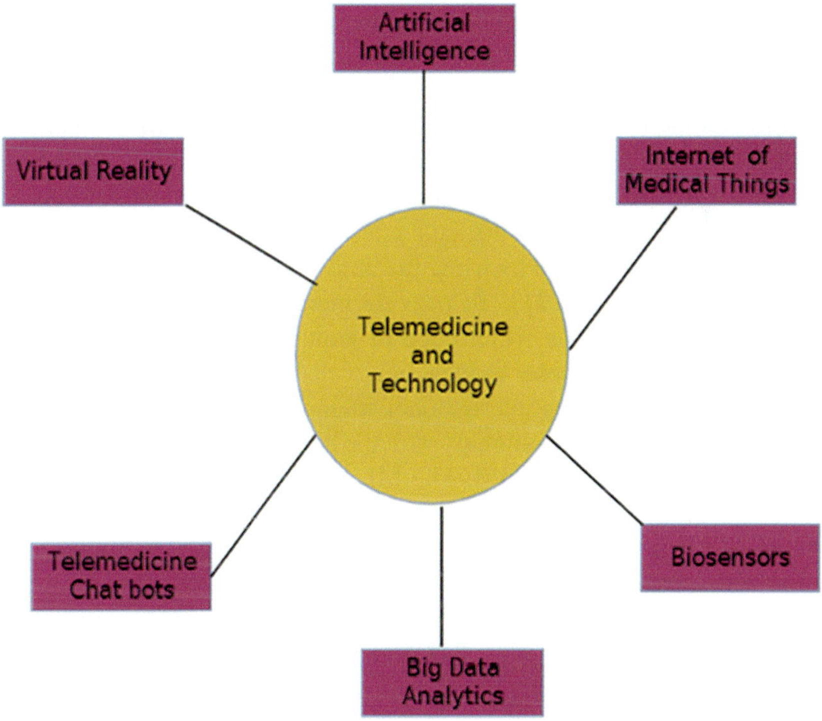

FIGURE 4.1 Telemedicine's expanding role in healthcare.

4.3 ARTIFICIAL INTELLIGENCE

Telemedicine's bright future lies in artificial intelligence, a branch of computer science that will soon allow machines to perform tasks as thoughtfully and purposefully as humans to better track patients [7] Growing in popularity, with the help of AI in several sectors, medical Scientists have been enhancing their ability to manage and interrupt telemedicine information gathered. Improving their knowledge and skills, and creating telemedicine-integration methods, are necessities for tackling certain issues. The adaptability of the two technologies discussed in this article, artificial intelligence and telemedicine, provided countless prospects for growth [8].

4.4 ARTIFICIAL INTELLIGENCE-ASSISTED TELEMEDICINE

Clinical, imaging, blood, and genetic signs may all play a role in a diagnosis's final verdict, but experts from different fields need to work together. Furthermore, discipline-specific testing may be required, for instance, neuropsychological tests, to obtain thorough mental health evaluations [9]. The cost of a few of these procedures would be prohibitive, and telemedicine might not be an option for individuals. Modern data-driven AI algorithms could solve this difficult multivariate challenge of choosing the best diagnostic method by using machine learning on massive disease population datasets [10, 11]. To provide more accurate predictions and better diagnoses across a wide range of populations, Without any prior statistical modeling, these models are capable of doing data-driven learning. There have been international attempts to forecast, prevent, and treat COVID-19 since its outbreak, with the help of combined datasets and data-driven methodologies [12]. The ML algorithm also incorporates an essential assessment that enables the pursuit of less costly remedies [13]. Synergistic variable combinations and redundant feature reduction can be tested with data-driven computational methodologies, allowing for more accurate diagnosis within the limitations of telemedicine [14]. According to projections by Collier et al. (2026) is the year when the widespread deployment of AI applications will enable the United States to save $150 billion annually on healthcare costs [15]. According to Wahl et al., applications of AI have a great potential to enhance effects on increasing spending on technological supports (such as mHealth, EMR, and online computing) and the widespread implementation of cellphones has a positive impact on the general health in nations with limited resources [16]. With the proliferation of mobile devices, digital healthcare transformations are gaining momentum and may soon be indispensable for the efficient and effective dissemination of information among healthcare providers and their patients [17]. When it comes to problem-solving and analytical reasoning, AI outperforms humans (especially when dealing with enormous volumes of data), and it can successfully solve the constraints of human function [18]. While artificial intelligence has the potential to save lives, its overuse could lead to the loss of critical physician abilities [13]. Even when using deep machine learning, AI still has difficulty fully assimilating and interpreting contextual data or differentiating between inputs of relevant and irrelevant data, which can harm rigid algorithm protocols and decision-making trees [19]. When deciding whether or not to use AI in the medical sector, it is important to measure the benefits against the human expertise needed to deal with the frequent occurrence of unexpected events [19–24]. A major roadblock to artificial intelligence's broad deployment is voice detection and comprehension making it imperative that the user experience and data input mechanisms be top-notch [25]. Many treatments and treatment decisions depend on subconscious human brain processes. Limitations in AI's ability to analyze qualitative or ambiguous data, as well as its lack of intuition and understanding, are major roadblocks in the healthcare industry, especially in urgent and time-sensitive situations [26]. Jarrahi demonstrates the value of combining AI with a human in the loop by comparing the accuracy of AI and human interpretation for using lymph node images to find cancer. The combined method is significantly more accurate (85%) than either method alone [26]. During COVID-19, telemedicine served as a vital patient continuity conduit despite disruptions in health service [27–29]. The defense of medical facilities and the reduction of risks to healthcare personnel during pandemics is another benefit [30–32]. When properly implemented, telemedicine can reduce healthcare and society's overall financial burden. This allows other doctors to provide prompt care to those who are more in need by providing these services remotely from medical facilities or via telecommunications to the customer. With the help of teleconsultations, doctors may examine patients, check for symptoms of infection, and simply keep track of those who are at a greater risk of becoming ill [33]. Using telemedicine technology saves doctors time by automatically completing insurance forms, allowing them to focus on patient care. Clinics are increasing their use of telehealth services to identify patients, it is necessary for COVID-19 testing to provide them with prompt medical care and limit public exposure [28, 31, 34]. Considering the significance of incorporating learning approaches for doctors and applicants early on in the telemedical structure along with how these innovations can tackle the difficulties of which link participants who are spread out Geographically divided (especially during a global epidemic) [35]; and the delivery of outstanding education, education and training, and timely care that is reliable and equivalent in standard to personal instruction [36, 37]. Virtual and augmented reality systems have the potential to improve teamwork among students and medical professionals [38]. Last but not least, consultation, therapy, diagnosis, and training can all benefit from the usage of immersive and telemedical technology, but these tools can only be useful if they can function reliably even when they aren't connected to the internet, as has been mentioned elsewhere in this paper [39]. This is particularly significant in places with spotty broadband internet service, which hinders the widespread adoption of such technology [40].

4.5 ROBOTICS-ASSISTED TELEMEDICINE

With the potential to revolutionize robotics may be a cutting-edge telemedicine tool for remote patient monitoring, clinical care, and physical examination [41, 42]. The Ebola and COVID-19 pandemics have shown the many potential applications of robotics and telemedicine [42,43]. Disinfection, drug and food distribution, monitoring vital signs, border control assistance, and automatic disinfection are all areas where robotics can be employed to reduce the spread of infectious diseases during epidemics [44, 45]. When used to connect patients in solitude with their loved ones and medical professionals, telepresence robots' two-way communication and remote control capabilities can be a lifeline [34]. Research into robots to combat the spread of infectious diseases could be sparked by exposure to COVID-19 [41]. With government support, it is possible to significantly impact the prevention of future pandemics by enabling the collaboration of experts in the fields of study including the field of engineering, audiovisual technological advances, and infectious disease. During a study conducted in a "Smart Field Hospital" in Wuhan, China, robots and Internet of Things (IoT) devices were used gadgets provide all of the necessary medical care to patients and healthcare staff while reducing the spread of the COVID-19 virus [46]. Health systems' capability and preparedness may be enhanced by investigating the use of robots in emergencies, such as those involving infectious diseases and other types of crises [46]. As part of its guidelines for robot-assisted surgery (RAS), the Society of European Robotic Gynecological Surgery also recommends using RAS rather than laparoscopic or open surgery for infection control [47]. Traditional laparoscopic surgery is advised over open surgery when RAS is not a possibility because of the smaller surgical team, lower risk of infection via aerosols and bodily fluids, and shorter recovery time [47, 48]. A similar set of guidelines, called COVID-19, was published by the European Association of Urology, which stressed the need to control smoke during The lowest possible intra-abdominal pressure should be maintained during robotic or laparoscopic surgery, and monitoring and controlling the flow of blood [49]. Disturbances in precision and interactivity as a result of the gap between the patient and the person operating the disruptions in the network and breakdowns in communication are all possibilities in the field of robotics-assisted telemedicine [48]. Surgeons' risk of contracting the COVID-19 virus may be reduced by the use of robots [50].

4.6 ARTIFICIAL INTELLIGENCE APPLICATIONS

Artificial intelligence has been the subject of extensive research and finds widespread use in many fields. The use of connecting computers with healthcare tools and data using current outcomes and procedure modifications can be utilized to generate solutions in many areas of healthcare, such as helping to evaluate patient data, pinpointing the source of problems, and arriving at effective treatments. Having the ability to quickly and accurately identify trends is a game-changer for identifying best practices and making informed medical decisions. In healthcare, identifying patterns in results is useful for both optimizing processes and anticipating potential issues. "Hospitals are currently implementing cutting-edge technologies to enhance the capabilities and achievements of professionals," states Dr Yulun Wang, CEO of In Touch Health in Santa Barbara [51]. In studies conducted in fields such as artificial neural networks, machine learning, dynamic logical reasoning, and similar areas, a range of different methods were used, such as the implementation of artificial intelligence.

4.7 TELEMEDICINE'S USE OF ARTIFICIAL INTELLIGENCE

Telemedicine refers to the provision of medical facilities via the use of electronic communication technology, allowing for distant delivery. The technology can the capacity to enhance access to healthcare, particularly in distant or underprivileged places. It has many applications, such as managing long-term health issues, providing assistance with mental health, and delivering basic healthcare. Telemedicine can enhance the availability of medical services, enhance operational effectiveness, and lower costs associated with healthcare. Telemedicine can provide a broad spectrum of offerings, including assessment, evaluation, and disease management. Additionally, it might be used for monitoring and providing subsequent care. Telemedicine may be administered by telephone, video conferencing, or web-based tools. Figure 4.2 illustrates the use of artificial intelligence in telemedicine.

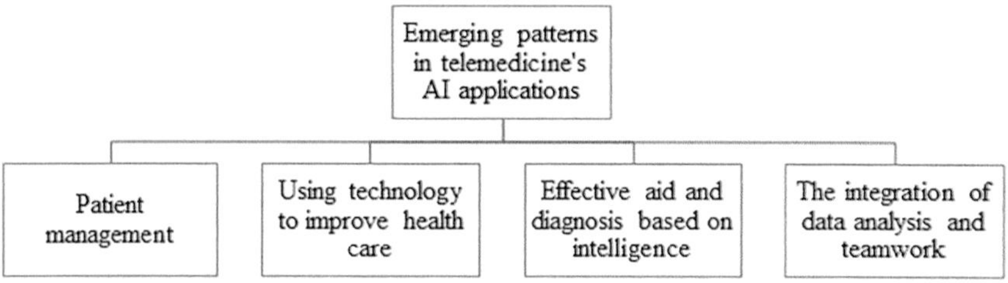

FIGURE 4.2 Utilization of AI in telemedicine.

4.7.1 PATIENT MANAGEMENT

One of the first and most common uses of telemedicine was for monitoring patients remotely. This facilitates remote doctor–patient consultations that can evaluate a patient's current condition and clinical outcomes more quickly and cheaply. By utilizing video conferencing technology and connecting digital medical equipment, investigators have created a system that can collect and record clinical data from a patient in a manner that is very similar to a face-to-face session. This development is being driven by a desire to give more convenient alternatives to traditional methods of patient monitoring that also save money. Modern telepresence robots are programmed to navigate their surroundings autonomously via a Wi-Fi connection and a user interface that allows for remote control [52]. The most recent development of this concept is the use of vision and AI systems together for autonomous navigation and obstacle avoidance. The Dr Rho Medical Telepresence Robot is a gadget designed to enable communication between doctors and patients. It is equipped with a screen and a moving body. During joint examinations and treatments, the device uses a microprojector and an artificial vision system to control cameras that track the doctor's every move [53]. More than one hospital has already put this robot, or a variant of it called a telepresence robot, to use. Using the help of AI, machine learning, sensors, and simultaneous mapping, the software can program the robot's route with only the destination as input from the user. In a similar vein, the robot's physical configuration, like the position of the screen or camera lens, can be modified with the same technology for the benefit of the patient. The study on using Machine Learning Classification and Feedback mounted on a Wireless Gyroscope demonstrates how AI and telemedicine can be used to monitor a patient's progress without the need for real-time video or face-to-face counseling. In this study, the investigator presents a system that combines a 3D-printed frame with a system that utilizes gyroscopes that communicate wirelessly. By linking the ankle rehabilitating system, which consists of a footplate, mobile device, and Bluetooth gyroscope device, with a mobile device, we can evaluate the effectiveness of the ankle rehabilitation system [54] and determine whether or not the rehabilitation approach is effective. The use of wireless vital sensors is demonstrated here to be useful in telemedicine since they can easily communicate data to devices that are critical to continuous monitoring [55, 56]. A web-based management system that utilizes machine learning methods enables the achievement of this possibility to collect data from sickle cell disease patients more quickly and in real time [57]. While the system's primary functions include using AI, healthcare facilities may enhance their management, patient accommodation, and surveillance capabilities. One specific benefit is the ability to predict medicine doses by analyzing historical data [58]. Recent advances in patient monitoring lend credence to self-diagnosis strategies and the use of telemedicine outside of traditional healthcare settings [59]. Each device ought to be created using a common data architecture [60] as capacity increases with the application of telemedicine on devices outside of hospitals. Most nonhospital technology and patient monitoring tools are used to keep tabs on the health and activities of the elderly and those with long-term conditions [61, 62].

4.7.2 HEALTHCARE INFORMATION TECHNOLOGY

Obtaining and preserving medical records will be challenging given the enormous amount of data being collected at medical facilities using both traditional approaches and the growing use of self-diagnostic technologies.

In addition, a unified database for all collaborating organizations is required [63] because telemedicine's ultimate purpose is to facilitate communication between healthcare providers located all over the world and their patients. Big data analytics and neural networks, cutting-edge innovation, are being used to organize and locate digital medical records. Utilizing artificial intelligence to streamline the process of organizing and examining data is one way that these challenges in healthcare settings are being tackled. Based on data from their study, the American College of Physicians developed Remedy to help doctors reclaim their time spent on electronic health records (EHR) and administrative tasks. Effective patient record management [64] is achieved by substituting the time-consuming procedure of manually checking a patient's vitals with a chat interface questionnaire, saving the information, and then delivering the results to the doctor. Due to the patient's ability to bring in photographs or videos for assessment, medicines and other information can be sent directly to them much more quickly. The use of cloud computing to address bandwidth limitations in some regions and the complexity of implementing patient monitoring systems is another emerging trend. By deploying the services in data centers and making use of distant servers for storage and management, this advancement hopes to enhance the effectiveness of gathering and disseminating patient data. In the study, a telemedicine service using cloud-based technology was used to accelerate clinical evaluation by delivering electrocardiogram wave data to multiple devices hosted on the cloud [65]. Connecting "emerging eHealth consumer electronics technology and traditional healthcare information system architecture" is another use case for cloud computing. The Microsoft Band 2 is a good illustration of this, which has a blood pressure monitor built in and an API specification for doing so [66]. When cloud computing is applied here, both data retrieval speed and transaction processing capacity will increase. Regional standardization of medical data and records is essential for the widespread adoption of an automated system in the region's healthcare facilities, in addition to facilitating data processing and communication [67]. As a result, telemedicine processes will be streamlined, and new initiatives will be rolled out more reliably and promptly. Wireless connections and the ongoing transmission of patient data provide a security risk in telemedicine [68]. One of the most problematic areas that arise frequently while attempting to deploy telemedicine in a facility. Wavelet-based security has been the subject of some research, particularly in the areas of artificial intelligence and image-processing watermarking. A technique for digital watermarking of medical photographs is proposed in this Indian study to protect patient privacy [69]. Device-to-device communication development with authentication and analysis of device demonstration for secure transmission procedure [70].

4.7.3 INTELLIGENT ASSISTANCE AND DIAGNOSIS

Two prominent contemporary themes in automation are the integration of mechanical assistance and the strategic use of healthcare data and discoveries. Each component is designed to improve the standard of care provided by hospitals, whether directly by helping patients or by evaluating data from the first stage of patient evaluation. These tools can be made more automated with the use of artificial neural networks and machine learning alone. The system can then use the new data and findings to refine and improve the technology over time. Self-diagnostic software and mobile phone apps are already being developed and released for use in telehealth, where intelligent diagnosis is being utilized. In line with the accepted standard in medical technology, self-diagnosing software, and devices have become more widely available, enabling quick assessments of heart rate, respiration rate, and other such vital indicators. Startups like Lemonaid Health evaluate and assess patients using an AI model once they've answered some questions and met some conditions, are one such example [71]. Screening results will be used to assign the patient to one of many categories, depending on their case's complexity [72]. Doctors will evaluate the circumstance and phone patients as necessary for consultations or send medications to patients' homes. A chatbot-based diagnostic assessment system has also been developed by Carbon Health. The patient's information will be summed up and the consultation, if necessary, will be scheduled automatically. Patients' medication use and any indicators of recurrence will be tracked and followed up on as part of the program as well [72]. Emergencies may also take advantage of wireless telemedicine technologies, including when hospitals located nearby require records about patients to be shared with ambulances so that they can all work together to provide rapid, high-quality care to the approaching patient. A study was done to examine the practicability and in other applications, such as disasters, it will be very helpful to assess the implementation's performance [73].

4.7.4 COLLABORATION IN INFORMATION ANALYSIS

Research and academic training/consultations in the medical field are examples of telemedicine's academic applications. Medical care around the world can benefit from the sharing of information and expertise made possible by technological advances in translation and communication. Applying genetic neural networks to pattern recognition and data analysis, and integrating the outcomes of clinical tests through big data analytics will have a profound impact on the pharmaceutical industry. Researchers are beginning to apply AI to clinical data to answer questions about the efficacy of pharmacy items and the outcomes of various therapies; this chapter discusses this recent development. As the need arises to not only store and be readily accessible but also evaluate healthcare data, this development will make extensive use of artificial intelligence's pattern-detecting capability. Since the computer analysis will be based solely on the results, it will be free of bias and views. Example of a Predictive Model for the Adoption of Assistive Technology among Individuals with Dementia model that employs neural networks to predict whether or not a given patient will adopt a particular technology by taking into account and analyzing a wide range of characteristics, behaviors, and other factors. The project aims to improve home-based care by developing prediction tools for improved understanding and interpretation [74]. Neural networks have many important uses, but one of the most important is in electronic health records, where they may be used to construct relationships between patients and their diagnoses (EHR). To utilize larger datasets for the study, may come from a network of medical centers spread across a region or a nation. If this plan is put into action successfully, new information on how to link patients' records as individuals and as a district about existing practices and environmental shifts may become available. The most up-to-date references on applying AI to these telemedicine application fields are listed in Table 4.1.

4.8 DIFFICULTIES IN IMPLEMENTATION

One of the main roadblocks to the widespread use of telemedicine is the high price tag associated with doing so. Even with the development of cost-effective models, hospitals and other facilities will still need to invest

TABLE 4.1 Trends in Artificial Intelligence

Journal Article	Year	Summary
Collaboration and Information Analysis		
A model to predict assistive technology adoption by dementia patients	2014	To develop an appropriate predictive tool that healthcare providers may utilize, this study analyzes the actions of people with dementia as they adapt to technology using data mining and k-nearest-neighbor algorithms.
Information Technology in Healthcare		
An application for telerehabilitation with preset consultation classes	2014	To address the issue of telemedicine in low-bandwidth network settings, this solution emphasizes the use of individualized consultation classes to demonstrate rehabilitation strategies with fixed parameters and an algorithm for dynamically adapting to network conditions.
Wavelet-Based Watermarking for Effective Telemedicine Security	2016	To ensure confidentiality, in this research, the researcher proposes an approach for adding and reading digital wavelet watermarks on medical photographs.
A cutting-edge biometrics technique to protect the use of wireless body area sensor networks in telemedicine and mobile health.	2006	This paper examines the integration of this channel into the BASN's security system, specifically how a biometrics method utilizes an inherent human bodily feature as the authentication identifier or protection mechanism for cipher key distribution to safeguard inter-BASN communications.
Patient Management		
Wi-Mon is a Dengue-specific wireless continuous patient monitoring system.	2017	This describes "a wireless system for keeping an eye on things based on the idea of wireless body area networks for patients who need continuous monitoring."
Wireless gyroscope ankle rehabilitation system with machine learning ankle classification and smartphone feedback	2015	The use of machine learning, wireless gyroscope technology, a smartphone app, and 3D printing are all used in this study to track therapy usage and results on an ankle and assess the effectiveness of the approach.
Intelligent Diagnosis Support		
Using intelligent decision-making in Medicine: a brief overview of patient care and medical diagnostics	2015	The study found that machine learning algorithms such as genetic algorithms, neural networks, supported vector machines, Bayesian decision, k-nearest neighbor, etc., can consequently recognize a wide range of serious ailments, including insulin resistance, breast, pancreas, and pulmonary cancers, cardiac arrest, and genetic predisposition.

TABLE 4.1 *(Continued)*

Journal Article	Year	Summary
Data-Driven Predictive Monitoring for Mobile Patients from Wearable Sensors and Clinical Observations	2014	The objective of this chapter is to investigate systematic machine-learning methods for analyzing extensive volumes of frequently collected, diverse physiological information from portable patient monitors. The aim is to detect early indications of critical physiological circumstances, enabling the provision of proactive care to a certain extent.

in installation and training to complete implementation [3]. As it may be essential to make improvements to the infrastructure, which can be highly tough, especially in rural or underdeveloped facilities, slow and inconsistent delivery of high-quality telemedicine information is an issue [75]. Considering the present problems with keeping healthcare information private and secure during telemedicine consultation and operations, the field of artificial intelligence has made healthcare information a major focus for future developments. There is still a chance that sensitive information could be compromised while using connections like satellites or the internet as discussed in the section on healthcare information technology. Studies that attempt to solve this issue are still being developed, thus it may take some time before they can be used to the telemedicine technology itself. Similar to other medical procedures and tools, malpractice is a concern that has resulted in the need for education and certification before telemedicine can be practiced equipment safely. Because it increases the cost and length of the project, this could prevent facilities from implementing. The consistency and preferences of patients may be impacted by negligence and illiteracy, which could lead to a disregard for the application of or advancement of technology.

4.9 CONCLUSION

While AI is still in its infancy at the moment, it already shows promise of vastly surpassing the performance of existing technologies and even human-run operations. This study highlights the importance of using technology like this in healthcare and showcases its seamless applicability. Due to the flexibility and capacity for the expansion of telemedicine, the field will likely continue to expand in ways that will have far-reaching effects on people's lives. Although some problems must yet be worked out, it appears that Telemedicine has embraced the usage of artificial intelligence to keep up with current trends. Since the greatest impact will come from putting these findings into practice, it is crucial to start looking for ways to reduce the price of this technology so it can be used in places like remote villages and inadequately financed clinics.

KEYWORDS

- **technology**
- **healthcare**
- **robotics**
- **telemedicine**
- **artificial intelligence**

REFERENCES

1. Fernandez-Marcelo P. 2013. *Telehealth and eMedicine*. Presentation, National Telehealth Center.
2. Dinya E, Tóth T. 2013. *Health Informatics: eHEALTH and TELEMEDICINE*. Presentation, Semmelweis University Institute of Health Informatics.
3. World Health Organization. 2010. *2010 Opportunities and Developments Report on the Second Global Survey on eHealth Global Observatory for eHealth Series—Volume 2 TELEMEDICINE in Member States WHO Library Cataloging-in-publication Data*. Report, WHO Press.
4. Pattichis CS, Kyriacou E, Voskarides S, Pattichis MS, Istepanian R, Schizas CN. 2002. *IEEE Antennas Propag. Mag. 44*(2), 143–153.
5. Labiris G, Panagiotopoulou EK, Kozobolis VP. 2018. A systematic review of teleophthalmological studies in Europe. *Int J Ophthalmol. 11*(2), 314–325. https://doi. org/10.18240/ijo.2018.02.22.
6. Dorsey ER, Topol EJ. 2016. State of telehealth. *N Engl J Med. 375*(2), 154–161. https://doi. org/10.1056/NEJMra1601705
7. Armstrong GW, Lorch AC. 2020. A(eye): A review of current applications of artificial intelligence and machine learning in ophthalmology. *Int Ophthalmol Clin. 60*(1), 57–71. https://doi. org/10.1097/ IIO.0000000000000298.
8. Pacis DMM, SubidoJr ED, Bugtai NT. 2018, February. Trends in telemedicine utilizing artificial intelligence. In *AIP Conference Proceedings* (Vol. 1933, No. 1, p. 040009). AIP Publishing LLC.

9. Huys QJM, Maia TV, Frank MJ. 2016. Computational psychiatry as a bridge from neuroscience to clinical applications. *Nat Neurosci. 19*, 404–413. https://doi. org/10.1038/nn.4238
10. Kuziemsky C, Maeder AJ, John O, Gogia SB, Basu A, Meher S, et al. 2019. Role of artificial intelligence within the telehealth domain. *Yearb Med Inform. 28*, 35–40. https://doi. org/10.1055/s-0039-1677897.
11. Aractingi S, Pellacani G. 2019. Computational neural network in melanocytic lesions diagnosis: Artificial intelligence to improve diagnosis in dermatology? *Eur J Dermatol. 29*, 4–7. https://doi. org/10.1684/ejd.2019.3538
12. Luo EM, Newman S, Amat M, Charpignon ML, Duralde ER, Jain S, et al. 2020. MIT COVID-19 datathon: Data without boundaries. *BMJ Innov. 7*(1), 231–234. https:// doi. org/10.1136/bmjinnov-2020-000492.
13. Ahuja AS. 2019. The impact of artificial intelligence in medicine on the future role of the physician. *PeerJ. 7*, e7702. https://doi. org/10.7717/peerj.7702
14. Pacis DMM, Subido EDC, Bugtai NT. 2018. Trends in telemedicine utilizing artificial intelligence. *AIP Conf Proc. 1933*, 040009. https://doi. org/10.1063/1.5023979
15. Accenture. 2020. Why Artificial intelligence is the future of growth. Available online at: https://www.accenture.com/us-en/insight-artificialintelligence-future-growth (Accessed September 19, 2020).
16. Wahl B, Cossy-Gantner A, Germann S, Schwalbe NR. 2018. Artificial intelligence (AI) and global health: How can AI contribute to health in resource-poor settings? *BMJ Glob Health 3*, e000798. https://doi. org/10.1136/bmjgh-2018-000798
17. Thierry JP. 2020. The human resource: Cornerstone of the digital transformation of the healthcare plan. *Soins 65*, 46–47. https://doi. org/10.1016/j.soin.2020.01.009
18. Huang M-H, Rust RT. 2018. Artificial intelligence in service. *J Serv Res. 21*, 155–172. https://doi. org/10.1177/1094670517752459
19. Heinrichs B, Eickhoff SB. 2020. Your evidence? Machine learning algorithms for medical diagnosis and prediction. *Hum Brain Mapp. 41*, 1435–1444. https://doi. org/10.1002/hbm.24886
20. Grote T, Berens P. 2020. On the ethics of algorithmic decision-making in healthcare. *J Med Ethics. 46*, 205–211. https://doi. org/10.1136/med ethics-2019-105586
21. London AJ. 2019. Artificial intelligence and black-box medical decisions: Accuracy versus explainability. *Hastings Cent Rep. 49*, 15–21. https://doi. org/10.1002/hast.973
22. McDougall RJ. 2019. The computer knows best? The need for value flexibility in medical AI. *J Med Ethics. 45*, 156–160. https://doi. org/10.1136/med ethics-2018-105118
23. Sun W, Nasraoui O, Shafto P. 2020. Evolution and impact of bias in human and machine learning algorithm interaction. *PLoS One 15*, e0235502. https://doi. org/10.1371/journal.pone.0235502
24. Ash JS, Berg M, Coiera E. 2004. Some unintended consequences of information technology in health care: The nature of patient care information system-related errors. *J Am Med Inform Assoc. 11*, 104–112. https://doi. org/10.1197/jamia.M1471
25. Davenport T, Kalakota R. 2019. The potential for artificial intelligence in healthcare. *Future Healthc J. 6*, 94–98. https://doi. org/10.7861/futurehosp.6-2-94

26. Jarrahi MH. 2018. Artificial intelligence and the future of work: Human-AI symbiosis in organizational decision making. *Bus Horiz. 61*, 577–586. https://doi. org/10.1016/j. bushor.2018.03.007
27. Hollander JE, Carr BG. 2020. Virtually perfect? telemedicine for Covid-19. *N Engl J Med. 382*, 1679–1681. https://doi. org/10.1056/NEJMp2003539
28. Bhaskar S, Bradley S, Chattu VK, Adisesh A, Nurtazina A, Kyrykbayeva S, et al. 2020. Telemedicine as the new outpatient clinic gone digital: Position paper from the pandemic health system REsilience PROGRAM (REPROGRAM) international consortium (Part 2). *Front Public Health 8*, 410. https://doi. org/10.3389/ fpubh.2020.00410
29. Bhaskar S, Bradley S, Chattu VK, Adisesh A, Nurtazina A, Kyrykbayeva S, et al. 2020. Telemedicine across the globe—position paper from the COVID-19 pandemic Health System Resilience Program (REPROGRAM) international consortium (Part 1). *Front Public Health 8*, 556720. https://doi. org/10.3389/fpubh.2020.556720.
30. Bhaskar S, Bradley S, Israeli-Korn S, Menon B, Chattu VK, Thomas P, et al. 2020. Chronic neurology in COVID-19 era: Clinical considerations and recommendations from the REPROGRAM consortium. *Front Neurol. 11*, 664. https://doi. org/10.3389/ fneur.2020.00664
31. Bhaskar S, Rastogi A, Chattu VK, Adisesh A, Thomas P, Alvarado N, et al. 2020. Key strategies for clinical management and improvement of healthcare services for cardiovascular disease and diabetes patients in the coronavirus (COVID-19) settings: Recommendations from the REPROGRAM consortium. *Front Cardiovasc Med. 7*, 112. https://doi. org/10.3389/fcvm.2020.00112
32. Bhaskar S, Sharma D, Walker AH, McDonald M, Huasen B, Haridas A, et al. 2020. Acute neurological care in the COVID-19 era: The pandemic health system REsilience PROGRAM (REPROGRAM) consortium pathway. *Front Neurol. 11*, 579. https://doi. org/10.3389/fneur.2020.00579
33. Sinha S, Kern LM, Gingras LF, Reshetnyak E, Tung J, Pelzman F, et al. 2020. Implementation of video visits during COVID-19, Lessons learned from a primary care practice in New York City. *Front Public Health 8*, 514. https://doi. org/10.3389/ fpubh.2020.00514
34. Bakas T, Sampsel D, Israel J, Chamnikar A, Ellard A, Clark JG, et al. 2018. Satisfaction and technology evaluation of a telehealth robotic program to optimize healthy independent living for older adults. *J NursScholarsh 50*, 666–675. https:// doi. org/10.1111/jnu.12436
35. Lucey CR, Johnston SC. 2020. The transformational effects of COVID-19 on medical education. *JAMA 324*, 1033–1034. https://doi. org/10.1001/jama.2020.14136
36. Jumreornvong O, Yang E, Race J, Appel J. 2020. Telemedicine and medical education in the age of COVID-19. *Acad Med. 95*(12), 1838–1843. https://doi. org/10.1097/ ACM.0000000000003711.
37. Aron JA, Bulteel AJB, Clayman KA, Cornett JA, Filtz K, Heneghan L, et al. 2020. A role for telemedicine in medical education during the COVID-19 pandemic. *Acad Med. 95*(11), e4–e5. https://doi. org/10.1097/ACM.0000000000003572.
38. Bremner R, Gibbs A, Mitchell ARJ. 2020. The era of immersive health technology. *EMJ Innov. 4*, 40–47.

39. Institute of Medicine (US) Committee on Assuring the Health of the Public in the 21st Century. 2002. *The Future of the Public's Health in the 21st Century*. National Academies Press The Health Care Delivery System: Washington, DC. Available online at: https://www.ncbi.nlm.nih.gov/books/ NBK221227/ (Accessed September 19, 2020).
40. Drake C, Zhang Y, Chaiyachati KH, Polsky D. 2019. The limitations of poor broadband internet access for telemedicine use in Rural America: An observational study. *Ann Intern Med. 171*, 382–384. https://doi. org/10.7326/M19-0283.
41. Tavakoli M, Carriere J, Torabi A. 2020. Robotics, smart wearable technologies, and autonomous intelligent systems for healthcare during the COVID-19 pandemic: An analysis of the state of the art and future vision. *AdvIntell Syst. 2*, 2000071. https:// doi. org/10.1002/aisy.202000071
42. Yang G-Z, Nelson JB, Murphy RR, Choset H, Christensen H, Collins HS, et al. 2020. Combating COVID-19—The role of robotics in managing public health and infectious diseases. *Sci Robot. 5*, eabb5589. https://doi. org/10.1126/scirobotics.abb5589
43. Deng B. 2015. Robo-rescuers battle it out in disaster challenge. *Nature 519*, 14–15. https://doi. org/10.1038/519014a
44. Kovach CR, Taneli Y, Neiman T, Dyer EM, Arzaga AJA, Kelber ST. 2017. Evaluation of an ultraviolet room disinfection protocol to decrease nursing home microbial burden, infection, and hospitalization rates. *BMC Infect Dis. 17*, 186. https://doi. org/10.1186/s12879-017-2275-2
45. Yang G, Lv H, Zhang Z, Yang L, Deng J, You S, et al. 2020. Keep healthcare workers safe: Application of teleoperated robot in isolation ward for COVID-19 prevention and control. *Chin J Mech Eng. 33*, 47. https://doi. org/10.1186/s10033-020-00464-0
46. Hornyak T. 2020. CNBC. What America can learn from China's use of robots and telemedicine to combat the coronavirus. Available online at https:// www. cnbc.com/2020/03/18/how-china-is-using-robots-and-telemedicineto-combat-the-coronavirus.html (Accessed September 14, 2020).
47. Kimmig R, Verheijen RHM, Rudnicki M. 2020. Robot-assisted surgery during the COVID-19 pandemic, especially for gynecological cancer: A statement of the Society of European Robotic Gynaecological Surgery (SERGS). *J Gynecol Oncol. 31*, e59. https://doi. org/10.3802/jgo.2020.31.e59
48. Avgousti S, Christoforou EG, Panayides AS, Voskarides S, Novales C, Nouaille L, et al. 2016. Medical telerobotic systems: Current status and future trends. *BioMedEng Online 15*, 96. https://doi. org/10.1186/s12938-016-0217-7
49. Mottrie A. 2020. ERUS 2020. ERUS (EAU Robotic Urology Section) guidelines during COVID-19 emergency. Available online at: https://uroweb. org/wp-content/ uploads/ERUS-guidelines-for-COVID-def.pdf (Accessed April 27, 2020).
50. Samalavicius NE, Siaulys R, Janusonis V, Klimasauskiene V, Dulskas A. 2020. Use of 4 robotic arms performing Senhance R robotic surgery may reduce the risk of coronavirus infection to medical professionals during COVID-19. *Eur J ObstetGynecolReprod Biol. 251*, 274–275. https://doi. org/10.1016/j.ejogrb.2020.06.014.
51. Chea T. 2013. Telepresence robots let medical specialists 'beam' into remote hospitals | Lubbock Online | Lubbock Avalanche-Journal. 2013-11-17. [Online]. Available: http://lubbockonline.com/filed-online/2013-11-17/telepresence-robots-let-medical-specialists-beam-remote-hospitals. (Accessed Jun 24, 2017)

52. iRobot Corp., FDA clears first autonomous telemedicine robot for hospitals | business wire. [Online]. Available: http://www.businesswire.com/news/home/20130124005134/en/FDA-Clears-Autonomous-Telemedicine Robot-Hospitals. Accessed Jun 24, 2017).
53. Choudary S. 2014. Dr Rho—edical telepresence robot: Create the future design contest. 2014-07-2. [Online]. Available: https://contest.techbriefs.com/2014/entries/medical/5078. (Accessed Jun 24, 2017).
54. LeMoyne R, Mastroianni T, Hessel A, Nishikawa K. 2015. Ankle rehabilitation system with feedback from a smartphone wireless gyroscope platform and machine learning classification. In *2015 IEEE 14th International Conference on Machine Learning and Applications (ICMLA)* (pp. 406–409), (IEEE, Miami, FL).
55. Islam SK, Fathy A, Wang Y, Kuhn M, Mahfouz M. 2014. *IEEE Microw Mag. 15*(7), S25–S33.
56. Sohbati M, Toumazou C. 2015. *IEEE Potentials 34*(2), 33–37.
57. Khalaf M, Hussain AJ, Al-Jumeily D, Keenan R, Fergus P, Idowu IO. 2015. Robust approach for medical data classification and deploying self-care management system for sickle cell disease. In *2015 IEEE International Conference on Computer and Information Technology; Ubiquitous Computing and Communications; Dependable, Autonomic and Secure Computing; Pervasive Intelligence and Computing* (pp. 575–580), (IEEE, Liverpool, UK).
58. Khalaf M, Hussain AJ, Al-Jumeily D, Keenan R, Keight R, Fergus P, Idowu IO. 2015. Applied difference techniques of machine learning algorithm and web-based management system for sickle cell disease. In *2015 International Conference on Developments of E-Systems Engineering (DeSE)* (pp. 231–235), (IEEE, Dubai, UAE).
59. Kazantsev A, Ponomareva J, Kazantsev P, Digilov R, Huang P. 2012. Development of e-health network for in-home pregnancy surveillance based on artificial intelligence. In *Proceedings of 2012 IEEE-EMBS International Conference on Biomedical and Health Informatics* (pp. 82–84), (IEEE, Hong Kong).
60. Lasierra N, Alesanco A, Garcia J. 2014. *IEEE J Biomed Heal Informatics 18*(3), 896–906.
61. Juarez JM, Ochotorena JM, Campos M, Combi C. 2013. Multiple temporal axes for visualising the behaviour of elders living alone. In *2013 IEEE International Conference on Healthcare Informatics* (pp. 387–395), (IEEE, Philadelphia, PA).
62. Kurnianingsih, Nugroho LE, Widyawan, Lazuardi L, Non-alinsavath K. 2015. Ontology-based context-aware for ubiquitous home care for elderly people. In *2015 2nd International Conference on Information Technology, Computer, and Electrical Engineering (ICITACEE)* (pp. 454–459), (IEEE, Semarang).
63. Demiris G. 2003. *J Am Med Inform Assoc. 10*(4), 310–314.
64. Bankson AM. 2017, January. Can artificial intelligence expand health care access? - MIT Sloan School of Management. [Online]. Available: http://mitsloan.mit.edu/newsroom/articles/can-artificial-intelligence-expand-healthcare-access/. (Accessed Jun 23, 2017).
65. Matlani P, Londhe ND. 2013. A cloud computing based telemedicine service. In *2013 IEEE Point-of-Care Healthcare Technologies (PHT)* (pp. 326–330), (IEEE, Bangalore).

66. Garai A, Adamko A. 2017. Comprehensive healthcare interoperability framework integrating telemedicine consumer electronics with cloud architecture. In *2017 IEEE 15th International Symposium on Applied Machine Intelligence and Informatics (SAMI)* (pp. 000411–000416), (IEEE, Herl'any).
67. Al-Tamimi A-K, Khalifeh A. 2014. Mobile mules: Modular e-health information synchronization framework. In *2014 8th International Symposium on Medical Information and Communication Technology (ISMICT)* (pp. 1–5), (IEEE, Firenze).
68. Larburu N, Widya I, Bults RGA, Hermens HJ. 2014. Making medical treatments resilient to technological disruptions in telemedicine systems. In *IEEE-EMBS International Conference on Biomedical and Health Informatics (BHI)* (pp. 285–288), (IEEE, Valencia).
69. Singh J, Patel AK. 2016. An effective telemedicine security using wavelet-based watermarking. In *2016 IEEE International Conference on Computational Intelligence and Computing Research (ICCIC)* (pp. 1–6), (IEEE, Chennai).
70. Zhang A, Wang L, Ye X, Lin X. 2017. *IEEE Trans Inf Forensics Secur*. *12*(3), 662–675.
71. "Lemonaid Health—Healthcare. Refreshingly Simple. AZ, CA, CT, FL, GA, Il, MI, NY, OH, OR, PA, RI, VA and WA Only." [Online]. Available: https://www.lemonaidhealth.com/#how-it-works. (Accessed Jun 24, 2017).
72. Wang C. 2016, December. How telemedicine and health AI are transforming healthcare experience | Chuhan Wang | Pulse | LinkedIn," [Online]. Available: https://www.linkedin.com/pulse/how-telemedicine-health-ai-transforming-healthcare-experience-wang. (Accessed Jun 23, 2017).
73. Mukhopadhyay A, Raghunath S, Kruti M. 2016. Feasibility and performance evaluation of VANET techniques to enhance real-time emergency healthcare services. In *2016 International Conference on Advances in Computing, Communications and Informatics (ICACCI)* (pp. 2597–2603), (IEEE, Jaipur).
74. Shuai Zhang, McClean SI, Nugent CD, Donnelly MP, Galway L, Scotney BW, Cleland I. 2014. *IEEE J Biomed Heal Informatics* *18*(1), 375–383.
75. Bhatia JS, Singh C. 2014. Impact of usage of discrete networks on Telemedicine capabilities especially in India. In *2014 International Conference on Medical Imaging, m-Health and Emerging Communication Systems (MedCom)* (pp. 311–318), (IEEE, Greater Noida).

CHAPTER 5

Disease Management and Patient Care with Artificial Intelligence

*Corresponding author

ABSTRACT

A major concern in today's fast-developing and evolving world is the creation and spread of new illnesses. Using technology for disease prevention, control, and prevention has become an enormous problem for the medical community. With today's hectic schedules, it is almost hard to stick to a healthy routine. The difficulties mentioned above may be overcome by using a smart health monitoring (SHM) system. Industry 5.0 and 5G have just ushered in a new era of affordable, high-tech sensors that can be used for real-time health monitoring of persons. Faster, cheaper, and more trustworthy health monitoring services from far-flung locales are now feasible thanks to the SHM, which was previously impossible with conventional medical infrastructure. The inclusion of blockchain architecture has increased the security and privacy of patients' sensitive data and reduced the risk of data abuse. Using Deep Learning and Machine Learning to examine health data for numerous goals has aided in the achievement of preventative healthcare and fatality control. As a result, chronic illnesses may now be identified earlier than ever before. Cloud computing and cloud storage have been integrated to make the services more real-time and cost-effective. This chapter provides a comprehensive overview of SHM, discussing both past and contemporary achievements in the field with the problems that still need to be solved.

Computational Intelligence for Patient Care: Blockchain, AI, and ML in Healthcare.
Rishabha Malviya, Rishav Sharma, Sathvik Belagodu Sridhar, and Suraj Kumar (Authors)

DOI: 10.1201/9781779640819-5

5.1 INTRODUCTION

In the age of breakthroughs, artificial intelligence (AI) plays a vital role in the medical sector. The field of AI has had tremendous development over the last ten years and is now expanding quickly. One of the most modern technologies enhances many established healthcare practices. While keeping scientific cultures, the workforce, and society at large in mind, AI synergies for responsible innovation and tangible potential for healthcare development from preventive to diagnostic therapies might carry unintended repercussions of automation caused by AI and algorithms. Most healthcare institutions now employ machines for a variety of tasks, including diagnosis and referrals [1, 2]. These tasks range from electronic data collection and storage to next-generation sequencing and electronic data collection. Due to sensors and cutting-edge algorithms that enable patient health metrics to be continually computed and saved, big data processing and processing has reached exponential heights, surpassing human natural data analysis and interpretation skills. AI enhances experts' abilities to identify, anticipate danger, choose the best drug, and expedite procedures in the healthcare system. To function, AI algorithms need extensive data, which can typically be found in the form of pictures, notes, profiles, information from genetic tests, and recordings from medical devices, but is not restricted to these things. Electronic health records (EHR), computers, cellphones, watches, servers used by clinics and hospitals, and wearable devices all save this specific information. The introduction of cloud-based storage, which offers the assurance of limitless storage and access to data, has helped significantly address the data infrastructure problem thus far. AI may be used to detect and diagnose prevalent diseases early on. AI technologies are currently being employed in clinics all around the globe due to their ability to interpret and deliver a diagnosis based on vision identification. AI is used in radiology as a scanning instrument. AI will also help assess life-threatening symptoms that need medical care to be referred for urgent treatment by a specialist. AI would decrease the workload of increasingly overburdened clinicians by screening patients so they can concentrate on more important cases. AI can decide where services can be guided and put to effective use through the assessment of patients. Figure 5.1 illustrates the multiple uses of AI in the healthcare industry [3].

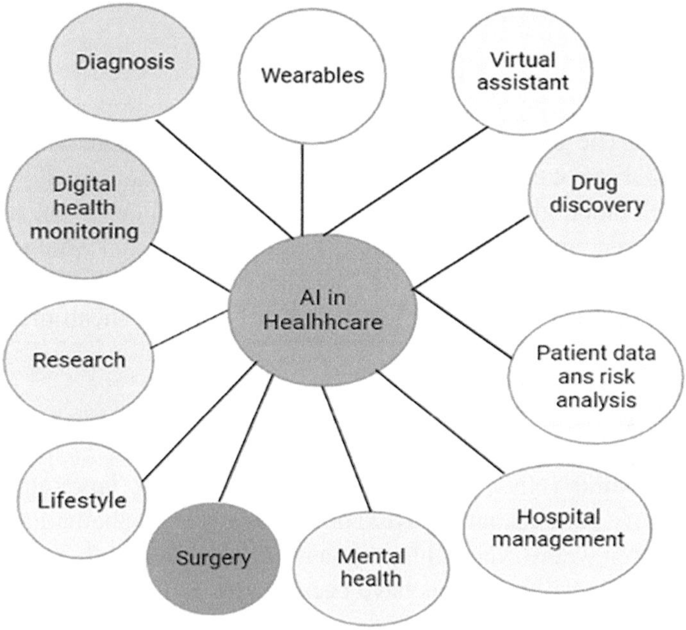

FIGURE 5.1 Applications of AI in healthcare.

5.2 AI IN DIABETES MANAGEMENT

AI is being used increasingly in four primary areas of diabetes care: autonomous retinal screening, clinical decision support, predictive population risk stratification, and patient self-management [2]. The purpose of this study is to summarize the potential and current applications of AI in the field of diabetes research, diagnosis, and therapy. The use of AI to treat diabetes is both possible and desired, as it would allow for more efficient data processing and the creation of software and equipment to aid in its control. It is recommended to provide stable designs, safety reserves, and procedural protections to provide a safer infrastructure through AI, with all uncertainties defined with all future technological systems. Three key areas of diabetes treatment can be affected and improved by AI: diabetes patients, healthcare providers, and healthcare networks. For patients with diabetes, AI also added additional levels of self-management, implemented fast and efficient decision-making, and convenient follow-up for health care providers, and improved usage of services in health care networks [3].

5.3 CASE-BASED REASONING (CBR)

CBR is widely utilized in diabetes control [4,5] because it is an AI approach for solving new issues by learning from comparable previous encounters. The Diabetes Support System is one example of the use of CBR in diabetes care. The goal of the system is to automatically identify issues with blood glucose management, provide solutions to the observed issues, and remember which solutions were successful and which were not for specific patients [4]. With CBR, patients with diabetes may tailor their insulin treatment to their specific needs over a range of mealtimes [5].

5.4 ARTIFICIAL NEURAL NETWORKS (ANNS)

Neural networks (NNs) have been created to evaluate large amounts of data, identify patterns, and provide unique answers. Diabetic diagnosis is only one area where NN technology has been put to novel and extensive use [6]. Intelligent algorithms have been created to investigate the impact of various factors on glycemic indices [7].

5.5 CELL BIOLOGY AND BIOMARKER DISCOVERY

The investigation of molecular interactions and the exposure of fundamental cell biology at varying concentrations are both made possible by tracking individual molecules [8]. Researchers from Osaka University and RIKEN have developed an AI system that can see and monitor single molecules within live cells [9]. The AI system was built using NNs that had been trained to pinpoint the exact location of a sample. In addition, designers need to separate individual fluorescent molecules inside thriving cells. Using the AI approach, imaging and investigating epidermal growth factor receptors (EGFRs) in numerous cells in plaques over a day was successfully performed. Using methods that rely on AI, researchers have been able to successfully differentiate between the natural and modified variants of EGFR [9]. The field of drug development is one area where AI is useful. New molecule design, toxicity and off-target impact prediction, and optimal medication dose selection for studies are just a few examples of how AI is put to work in the pharmaceutical industry [10, 11]. One advantage of adopting AI-inspired prediction is that it may help reduce medication toxicity. Organizations have sprung up all across the globe to apply AI to find novel chemical structures and identify unknown molecules. Several medications have been demonstrated to stimulate the immune system, which may then be used to effectively treat many different types of cancer. The revolutionary impact of checkpoint inhibitors in cancer therapy may be directly attributed to a robust immune response in malignant diseases [12]. Patients need individualized attention since their immunological responses are distinct. The precise dose of inhibitors may be administered based on AI predictions of how patients would respond during treatment. AI is extremely descriptive and may illustrate even modest variances in the therapeutic impact and the reactions of patients [13], thus the "one size fits all" approach to drug research and therapy would not work in tandem with AI. More data is required for computer modeling to develop procedures and models that account for all the many features of tumors/immune interactions and clinical trials, therefore bioinformaticians, biomedical scientists, and clinicians will need to collaborate on this [8].

5.6 MEDICAL TISSUE ENGINEERING AND REGENERATIVE MEDICINE

In addition, AI has been used in the fields of regenerative medicine, stem cell treatment, and tissue engineering. In a significant development, algorithms have been created to anticipate how individual patients would react to therapy with stem cells and manufactured products. There is great potential for people to improve their health and live a more fulfilling life thanks to advances in regenerative medicine and tissue engineering. The area of regenerative medicine is still in its youth, and as a result, there is a dearth of data on best practices. Most research relies on trial-and-error approaches, making it susceptible to human error. As a result, a lot of effort is expended before a satisfactory answer can be found. Algorithms based on AI might be used to reduce wasteful resource use [8].

5.7 OPHTHALMOLOGY

Several studies have compared the accuracy of different algorithms to that of ophthalmologists when determining the cause of eye issues. It is essential to have a team of specialists mark up the photographs or pictures.

Following accurate labeling, NNs may be trained using hundreds of thousands, if not millions, of images [14, 15]. It might be difficult to detect diabetic retinopathy in its early stages. Diabetic retinopathy might one day be diagnosed using NNs and clinical image analysis. Reproducing anything by the tens of thousands, NNs are more accurate in diagnosing diabetic retinopathy than human ophthalmologists [16, 17]. Significantly, the use of computational algorithms for the diagnosis of conditions other than diabetic retinopathy and age-related macular degeneration will be made possible by the development of new and better referral algorithms [18, 19]. An algorithm has been demonstrated to outperform retinal experts and optometrists when it comes to making recommendations using optical coherence tomography (OCT) pictures [20, 21]. Apart from circumstances where it performed as well as or better than professionals when presented with OCT pictures and patient notes. For this research, researchers used a pair of NNs, one for deciphering OCT images and another for assigning those categories.

5.8 CARDIOLOGY

Electrocardiograms (ECGs) and echocardiograms are cardiologists' primary tools for gathering information. Research on the use of deep neural networks (DNNs) for ECG and echocardiography has been conducted on several occasions [22, 23]. Until now, DNNs have been able to diagnose heart failure and other cardiac problems as accurately as human specialists [24, 25]. The accuracy of DNNs when applied to echocardiogram pictures (92%) was higher than that of DNN cardiologists (79%), according to the Precision for the Expert's metric [26]. DNNs have been shown in retrospective studies to be more accurate than cardiologists in classifying hypertrophic cardiomyopathy and cardiac amyloid [27].

5.9 BIOMETRICS

Smartphones have sparked growth in the field of biometric sensors. A variety of wireless health monitoring devices are now on the market, including blood pressure cuffs, thermometers, pulse oximeters, heart rate monitors, and blood glucose meters. These gadgets often transmit data to a smartphone app that keeps track of the measurements. These days, several smartwatches already can record vital signs like an ECG. First-to-market trials have shown high accuracy for screening for atrial fibrillation and other heart disorders compared to the gold standard of outpatient ECGs [28–30]. New capabilities such as smartphone-based spirometry, video plethysmography, and seizure detection, are now in the works [31]. Apart from blood glucose monitors, which undergo stricter regulation, the vast majority of items fall under the Food and Drug Administration (FDA's) purview as class II medical devices, which means they are safe to use but not checked for accuracy. Demand for health monitoring via electronic devices is on the rise, and this is driving improvements in biometric surveillance in terms of precision and utility [32].

5.10 NANOROBOTS

The development of micro- and nano-electromechanical frameworks has made it possible to produce implantable robots for a variety of uses, including the regulation of medicine or gene delivery [33, 34]. As a result of the spectacular advancements in nanoscience, there has been an increased amount of focus placed on the fabrication of nanorobots that include a combination of an active or passive power source, sensors, and AI [35, 36]. Traditional medicines may benefit from enhanced effectiveness and reduced adverse effects when encoded, signaled, sensed, acted upon, sent data on, executed biological activities at cellular levels, and distributed locally by these intelligent entities [37, 38]. Tracking hazardous substances and theranostics applications are two areas where nanorobots show a lot of promise [39, 40]. The direction guidelines, collision avoidance, target recognition rule, tracking, and connection rule, drug distribution rule, task complete rule, and drain mode triggering contributing to the excretion of bio-nano robots are included in the Bionanorobot rule framework. The use of AI in molecular production automation offers the possibility of regulating the action or movement of nanorobots [41, 42]. The experimental verification of participatory and adaptive behaviors of nanorobots or nanorobot-based drug carrier mechanisms has been achieved via the use of simulation and modeling tools [43, 44]. After being administered intravenously, nanorobots can move freely throughout the body and participate in activities such as crawling and swimming by using bio-actuation mechanisms [45, 46]. Microrobots that swim for controlled drug delivery, transient microrobots systems for targeted drug delivery using touch or nano communication mechanisms, or remotely controlled and intensely penetrable microrobots are some of the new types of controlled drug release that have been proposed for targeted therapy for a variety of disorders, especially chronic ones that would benefit greatly from personalized medicine [47]. Swimming microrobots for controlled drug delivery have also been proposed as a new type of controlled drug release for targeted therapy [47].

5.11 REMOTE-CONTROLLED CAPSULE FOR SPECIFIC DELIVERY

The microthrusters were used for the first time as the actuation mechanism in a novel RCC built on MEMS technologies. The electrical energy for lighting the microthrusters was just 120 mW, and the drug release duration was restricted to less than 1 second. The thrusters were activated upon receipt of an activation signal, and the shifting force against the drug reservoir was created by the ignition of propellants. In regular beagle puppies, the novel RCC was found to be both well enough and secure to use. The circuits and the installation of the microthrusters were performed efficiently, but certain procedures needed to be developed in the development of the capsule. The findings of the *in vitro* experiment and the initial beagle research have shown that the innovative activation mechanism in the RCC for site-specific delivery systems in the GI tract has been successfully implemented [48].

5.12 SERVICES UTILIZING AI IN THE HEALTHCARE DOMAIN

Currently, available healthcare AI services are discussed in Figure 5.1 depicts some of these services, which include healthcare and related assistance. The services under examination are compiled from many sources, such as academic publications and private market researchers [49]. The research focuses on services that either provide immediate care or direct assistance for care. One example is the use of a robot to aid in surgery; another is the ability to participate in a clinical trial; a third is the availability of virtual nursing and consulting services; a fourth is the ability to diagnose an image; a fifth is the elimination of unnecessary side effects; a sixth is the ease with which medications. Problems like fraud detection, administrative and workflow support, cybersecurity, linked machines, and medication advancements have been the focus of previous research and offer indirect services for healthcare procedures without compromising direct patient care; these issues are not addressed in the current study. Investigators also classified healthcare services and apps according to the extent to which they use AI and include human input in clinical decision-making [50]. Some of the most common AI methods now being used in healthcare applications and services are briefly outlined below. As seen in Figure 5.2, several applications and methods of AI.

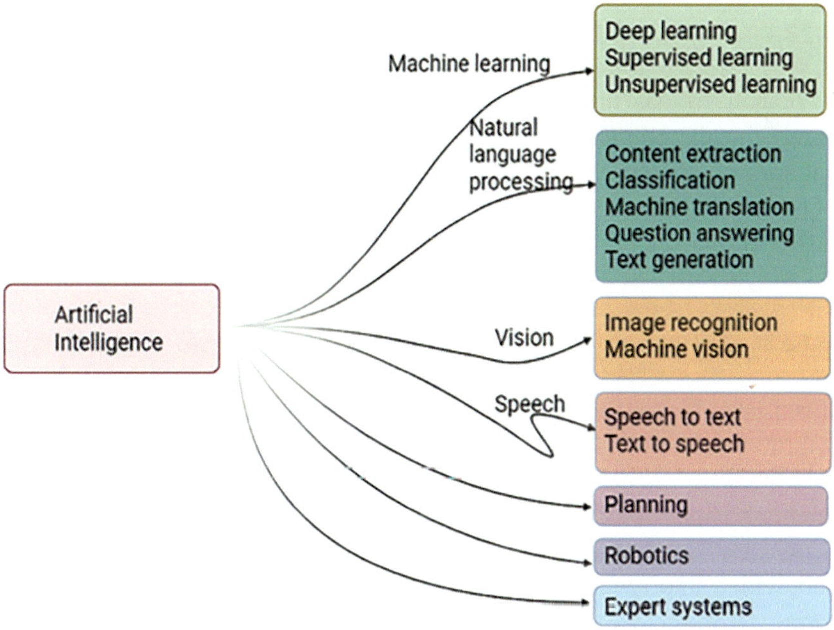

FIGURE 5.2 AI methods and applications.

5.12.1 MACHINE LEARNING (ML)

The discipline of AI delivers AI solutions that may be modified to fit individual requirements. The ML may be divided into three distinct parts. The goal of supervised learning algorithms is to create a mathematical model that, given a known set of inputs and intended outputs, can reliably forecast the future occurrence of the result [51]. Algorithms in unsupervised learning use an input-only data set and discover hidden patterns and relationships within it, such as clustering and grouping. Without any predetermined labels or categories, test data is used to teach algorithms in unsupervised learning [52]. Validation learning methods may be used for any problem, regardless of whether or not the user has a thorough understanding of the underlying mathematical model for a stochastic control process operating in discrete time. Reinforcement learning is used as an alternative to real-time feedback in situations when the self-driving car does not have access to information about whether its judgments are good or bad.

5.12.2 NATURAL LANGUAGE PROCESSING (NLP)

A branch of AI, linguistic computing is teaching machines to read, comprehend, and infer meaning from human languages to facilitate more natural interactions with people. One medical use of NLP is the prediction of health issues using the analysis of a patient's voice and electronic health information [53].

5.12.3 NN

It consists of taking a digital input, such as an image or voice, and running it through a series of hidden layers of interconnected artificial neurons that each react to distinct elements and provide different outputs. Particular attention should be paid to DNNs due to their widespread application in healthcare AI solutions. DNNs are a portion of NNs, which can be further subdivided into recurrent, convolutional, transfer, and generative adversarial, reinforcement, representation, and transfer networks. DNNs are also known as ANNs. The analysis of clinical pictures (such as those seen in pathology, skin lesions, the retina, and endoscopy) and data are two of the most common uses of DNN in the medical profession (such as those found in medical scans, ECGs, and vital signs).

5.13 COMPUTER-ASSISTED SURGERY (CAS) AND ROBOTIC-ASSISTED SURGICAL SYSTEMS (RASS)

Since its conception in 1985, the RASS has been used by several surgical subspecialties including cardiothoracic, gastrointestinal, gynecological, orthopedic, spinal, transplant, urological, and general surgery [54–57]. There are three basic categories under RASS, each of which reflects a different degree of autonomy: supervisory controlled surgery, telesurgical surgery, and shared control surgery. In conventional surgery, doctors can only fix what they can see, and open operations are the only method to have a good look at the patient's internals. With RASS, surgeries may be carried out with pinpoint accuracy using cameras and instruments that can be introduced via a tiny incision. Patient recovery durations and surgical problems are hoped to be decreased by using a less invasive technique. Additionally, RASS might minimize the surgical team's physical workload. Additionally, RASS allows for the recording of the whole surgical procedure, including all hand motions, incisions, and suturing, to be used afterward for analysis and improvement of the surgical procedure. Manufacturers of RASS ship their products all over the globe [58, 59]. This chapter describes the DaVinci RASS, created by Intuitive Surgical Inc. and now one of the most popular RASS. As of September 2019 [60–62], there were 5406 DaVinci installations. CAS provides an alternative method for assisting surgeons. CAS uses computers for surgical planning and improves surgeon supervision, whereas RASS focuses on the physical surgery robot, its control, and its applications. CAS methods may either take an active role in the operation or help surgeons with tasks like instrument placement and navigation [63]. When it comes to enhancing surgical efficiency and effectiveness before, during, and after surgery, CAS includes a suite of apps utilized in the operating room. To perform its core responsibilities, a CAS must be able to generate a virtual image of the patient, do diagnostic analysis and processing on that image, plan for the surgery, simulate it, and guide the surgeon throughout the procedure. CAS has been essential in the development of RASS. Shorter hospital stays, less blood loss, and fewer complications were just some of the positive clinical outcomes associated with RASS in prostatectomy, hysterectomies, and nephrectomies, as well as cardiac surgery, according to a 2011 systematic evaluation of studies conducted in Canada [64]. In certain RASS procedures, like a laparoscopic prostatectomy, the time it takes to do the procedure is greatly decreased, but in others, like an open prostatectomy or an open hysterectomy, it is significantly lengthened. Prostatectomy, heart surgery, nephrectomy, and hysterectomy all had their financial evidence weighed in the same review. Hospitalization expenses were shown to be lower for robotic radical prostatectomy patients compared to those who had laparoscopic or open surgery because of the shorter duration of stay after the procedure. But the high purchase and maintenance expenses of surgical robots mean that robot-assisted procedures will increase the cost by around 75% of all operations. However, a greater rate of RASS use may cut expenses. In 2017, researchers analyzed the efficacy, safety, and cost of RASS for the treatment of gynecological cancers [65]. Materials were reviewed to determine the efficacy of RASS in the treatment of gynecologic cancers. According to the findings, the safety of RASS is comparable to that of traditional surgical techniques for cancer patients, but the high application, acquisition, and maintenance costs of RASS equipment will drive up total prices. Studying the cost and effectiveness of robotic hepatectomy revealed that the RASS group had a longer operational time (20%), shorter length of stay (35% shorter), higher preoperative expenditures (10%), and lower postoperative costs (36% lower) than the regular open surgery group. According to the results, RASS is more cost-effective than open surgery by a margin of 22%. Similar rates of complications were seen in patients undergoing RASS and those undergoing open surgery [66].

5.14 VIRTUAL NURSE ASSISTANTS (VNAS) FOR HEALTHCARE

As the healthcare industry has become more digitized, it has begun using virtual assistants similar to those already used in other industries. Hospitals may lessen the number of unscheduled patient visits and ease the strain on medical staff by employing virtual nursing aides. These virtual assistants can hear, speak, and make suggestions. The usage of chatbots and other embodied conversational agents (ECAs) has been the subject of several types of research over the last two decades, all of which have shown that healthcare outcomes increase significantly when ECAs are used. Multi-choice and utterance surveys take advantage of user input that has been made possible by the vast majority of these ECAs. The most recent breakthroughs in AI have enabled the creation of conversational systems that can replicate human communication, allowing for the creation of virtual assistants or virtual agents [67, 68]. AI- and ML-based virtual health assistants use NHS data in the United Kingdom to tailor preventative treatment to each individual. The preprimary care service will take action before the patient decides to go to the main care service. MD is a smartphone app and website that allows users to self-diagnose medical conditions from the comfort of their homes. Twenty of the most prevalent medical disorders were correctly diagnosed 85% of the time. MD benchmark tests using validated test cases from Harvard University and the Royal College of General Practitioners [69]. In some other studies, multiple symptom assessment applications were compared to five general practitioners in terms of 200 vignettes designed to mimic real-world scenarios and assess the best results in terms of condition coverage, the accuracy of recommended conditions, and performance in providing urgent advice (GPs). The service ADA had the greatest results, with a condition recommendation coverage of 99%, a suggestion for the top three conditions of 70.50% (GPs average: 82.10%), and a proposal for safe urgent advice of 97.0% (GPs average: 97.0%) [70]. The AI used to power the virtual nurse is sophisticated. The system can keep tabs on a patient's health by using information from his or her medical record. In addition to scheduling and attending to patients' appointments, the VNA may also provide care in between scheduled doctor visits and anticipate patients' subsequent needs. In 2019, individuals with persistent heart failure participated in a clinical study of the platform. Readmission rates were shown to be 75% lower using the platform, while patient monitoring costs were reduced by 66% when compared to the traditional care technique [71, 72].

5.15 MEDICATION MANAGEMENT AND MEDICATION ERROR REDUCTION (MMMER)

Remarkable savings in healthcare spending and reduced incidences of avoidable injuries and fatalities are both possible thanks to the efficacy of MMMER services. Nonoptimized pharmaceutical treatment was expected to cause $528 billion in yearly expenses in the United States due to drug-related death and morbidity. This amounts to $1600 billion, or 16% of 2016 healthcare spending in the United States [72]. Mistakes with medications prescribed to patients result in serious adverse events, unnecessary hospitalizations, and high healthcare costs. According to the National Audit Commission [73], there are around 7000 fatalities that occur annually in the United States as a direct result of adverse prescription reactions and other pharmaceutical blunders. Despite this, the need of taking measures and the sense of urgency associated with doing so is highlighted. AI has many potential applications in the field of medication management and dosage error reduction, including but not limited to the following: improving medication safety, preventing drug overdoses, predicting health risks and outcomes across large populations, saving time and money, and monitoring patient adherence.

5.15.1 IMPROVING MEDICAL SAFETY

MedAware developed a program to identify drug mistakes. Researchers found that the ML-based approach was clinically effective in identifying 75% of probable prescription mistakes or difficulties, with 18.80% categorized as having medium clinical value and 56.20% of the valid warnings classed as having high clinical [74].

5.15.2 MONITORING MEDICATION ADHERENCE

It is well established that poor medication adherence is a major contributor to both rising healthcare expenses and poor patient outcomes. The cost of medication failure to work as intended is from $100 billion to $300 billion annually in the US [73]. An AI platform on mobile devices was shown to be useful in assessing and enhancing medication adherence among stroke patients undergoing prolonged anticoagulant therapy. In the research, participants were found to adhere to their prescribed medical regimen at a rate of 100% in the intervention group compared to 50% in the control group. The AI program could tell who the patient was, what they were taking, and whether or not they had taken it. Subsequently, plasma samples and pill counts were used to determine adherence [75]. Clinical research also looked at another AI platform for adherence monitoring; this one used a NN technique for machine vision. Visual patient and medication identification and ingestion confirmation were achieved via the use of machine vision and a NN. According to the research, the AI group had a greater rate of adherence than the standard-of-care group, which used a modified direct observation treatment protocol [76].

5.15.3 CLINICAL TRIAL PARTICIPATION

Clinical trial interventions are those described in the study design or protocol, as specified by the FDA and the National Library of Medicine. Drugs, medical technologies, and surgical procedures are all examples of possible treatments. So are dietary adjustments and other lifestyle modifications. There are three common frameworks for clinical studies.

1. One method of evaluating a potential new medical treatment is to evaluate it through established methods.
2. Contrast the new method with an inert placebo.
3. Contrast with the new method, in which any changes are avoided [77].

It is also important to note that developing and commercializing a new treatment typically takes between 10 and 15 years and $1.5 and $2.0 billion. About half of the effort and cost in developing a new medicine goes into clinical trials [78]. While up to 20% of potentially eligible participants were included in a Mayo Clinic research on cancer, only 3–5% of patients were included in clinical studies [79]. This finding highlights the need for more thorough clinical trials. The usage of AI has expanded to include the design of clinical trials and the automated discovery of patterns of meaning in massive, unstructured datasets, including voice, text, and pictures. Human–machine interfaces that make use of NLP enable more fluid communication between people and machines by comprehending and making sense of text written or spoken in a variety of languages. These features aid in enhancing patient-trial match and recruitment before real trials by matching various and vast datasets including medical literature, EHRs, and databases. In a real clinical study, AI may be utilized automatically and constantly to monitor patients. Furthermore, using AI improves adherence, endpoint assessment efficiency, control, and yield dependability. IBM did research based on this history to increase the number of people who sign up for clinical trials. Using IBM's Watson AI platform, this study found that cancer clinical trial enrollment may be increased by 80%. The Mayo Clinic saw a rise in this area. Thanks to this innovative setup, mass screening could now be carried out quickly and effectively [79].

5.15.4 PRELIMINARY DIAGNOSIS AND PREDICTION

Health records and patient diagnoses have been used by diagnostic services for decades to improve patient care and prognoses. The following investigation demonstrates that because of recent developments in AI research, computers can now surpass human doctors in several medical specialties when it comes to the speed and accuracy of making diagnoses.

5.15.5 DIABETES PREDICTION

Diabetes prediction may make use of four types of technology applications: retinal screening, clinical decision assistance, predicting population risk, and patient self-management. Diabetic retinopathy, macular edema, and exudates are just a few of the problems that may be picked up on a retinal scan using a screening program. Diabetic nephropathy, neuropathy, and wounds are just some of the complications that may be identified and monitored with the use of a clinical decision support application or service. Predictive or population risk stratification aims to classify those with diabetes that are more likely to have complications, hospitalizations, and subsequent readmissions. The artificial pancreas, AI enhanced glucose monitors, and food and activity monitoring devices are all examples of self-management aids now in use by patients. The Guardian Connect from Medtronic is one of the systems available for monitoring diabetes. It was the first continuous glucose monitoring (CGM) system to be powered by AI to get FDA approval. Guardian Connects advanced ML algorithm enables it to foresee substantial deviations in glucose levels. Up to 60 minutes in advance, changes may be foreseen. The system also has a sensor that may be worn on the belly. Glucose levels in the blood are tracked every 5 minutes using this sensor. Nearly 98.5% of hypoglycemia incidents were detected by the system and a warning was sent. As a result of these notifications, patients might take preventative measures to restore healthy blood sugar levels [80].

5.15.6 CANCER PREDICTION

In the United States, researchers at Houston Methodist used keywords and free-text radiology and pathology information from 543 patients to build a NLP-based algorithm that can evaluate mammography data. The app's accuracy reaches 99% when measured against that of human doctors. The amount of time saved by just manually validating the application's correctness for 10% of these 543 patients is remarkable. It took between 50 and 70 hours to manually validate 54 cases [81].

5.15.7 TUBERCULOSIS DIAGNOSIS

Both AlexNet and GoogLeNet, deep convolutional NNs trained using positive and negative X-rays for TB, were used in diagnostic testing. One hundred fifty examples were used to evaluate the models' performance. Combining AlexNet with GoogLeNet resulted in a 96% accurate AI model with the maximum functionality. Thirteen out of 150 instances showed discrepancies between the two deep convolutional neural network models. In these instances, the radiologist's diagnosis was spot-on. Deep learning (DL) has improved the accuracy of ML, which was previously only at an 80% success rate. AI-assisted TB diagnosis may become a crucial weapon in the war against the disease shortly [82].

5.15.8 MEDICAL IMAGING AND IMAGE DIAGNOSTICS (MID)

One of the most valuable and difficult to understand a type of patient information is data generated by medical imaging. Conventionally, reading medical imaging images has been a labor-intensive, manual process that has required a great deal of education and experience. Significant improvements in patient care have resulted from the use of AI technologies like DNNs and DLs, which have been found to accelerate, improve, and reduce the overall cost of medical image interpretation. MID may be used to diagnose a variety of medical conditions, from heart abnormalities to musculoskeletal ailments to neurological diseases to thoracic issues and even common cancers. By 2026 [83], the MID AI industry is expected to be worth $265 billion, up from $21 billion in 2018.

5.15.9 PATIENT HEALTH MONITORING (PHM)

Patients' duration of stay in the hospital, as well as their time to recovery and mortality rate, may all benefit from continuous PHM. Preventive health management (PHM) may be used at home to give guidance and prompts for routine checkups and other preventative measures. In this work, investigators define PHM as a set of services and solutions (used by patients and doctors alike regularly) that use AI techniques to keep tabs on their health in real-time, evaluate their condition, and look for any signs of illness. In both institutional and noninstitutional settings, patients benefit from HM's assistance. Studies on the general adoption of HM services have shown that AI-based health condition monitoring solutions rank first among the most significant technologies in healthcare and second among the services that healthcare professionals are keen to utilize [83].

5.15.10 HEART FAILURE MONITORING

A prototype of a computer-assisted diagnostic system for the detection of cardiac disease has been created by Italian researchers utilizing AI. The program was developed to assist primary care doctors and nurses who do not have specialized training in cardiology. The diagnostic and prognostic information for a patient is derived from both anamnestic (preinformation) and instrumental (instrument-related) data. When establishing a diagnosis, the system takes into account the patient's medical history. Furthermore, the device collects data from heart failure patients, creating a resourceful data warehouse for later use. When comparing the three severity levels, the AI method known as NNs fared the best, correctly classifying 98 out of 100 patients in the training population and 31 out of 36 patients in the test group. In terms of accuracy across the board for the test population, the best of the assessed systems achieved 86.10% [84]. Including the findings presented in this chapter has led us to the conclusion that there are several applications where AI techniques might be utilized to improve healthcare delivery.

1. By using AI, healthcare workers may save valuable time.
2. Provide a reliable diagnosis.
3. Produce Predictions Based on Medical Pictures and Documentation.
4. Monitor health conditions and predict the occurrence or progress of diseases.
5. Boost the quality of care being offered.
6. Improve surgical procedures by minimizing problems.
7. Regulate patient compliance and prevent drug abuse.
8. Contribute to the process of clinical decision-making.

Identified benefits are shown in Figure 5.3. Researchers propose the following minimum requirements for the effective deployment of AI technologies into healthcare services:

1. A large, clinically verified dataset for training and testing AI systems.

2. Academic studies in which healthcare practitioners and creators of AI techniques collaborate to verify the efficacy of new and current AI approaches.
3. Improvement has been shown in a clinical setting or by scientific means for a particular healthcare use.
4. Certification of the gadget for use in the intended market.
5. Make it very clear to patients that AI does not independently decide on their medical treatment. It merely offers advice, aids in therapeutic tasks, and supports physicians in decision-making.

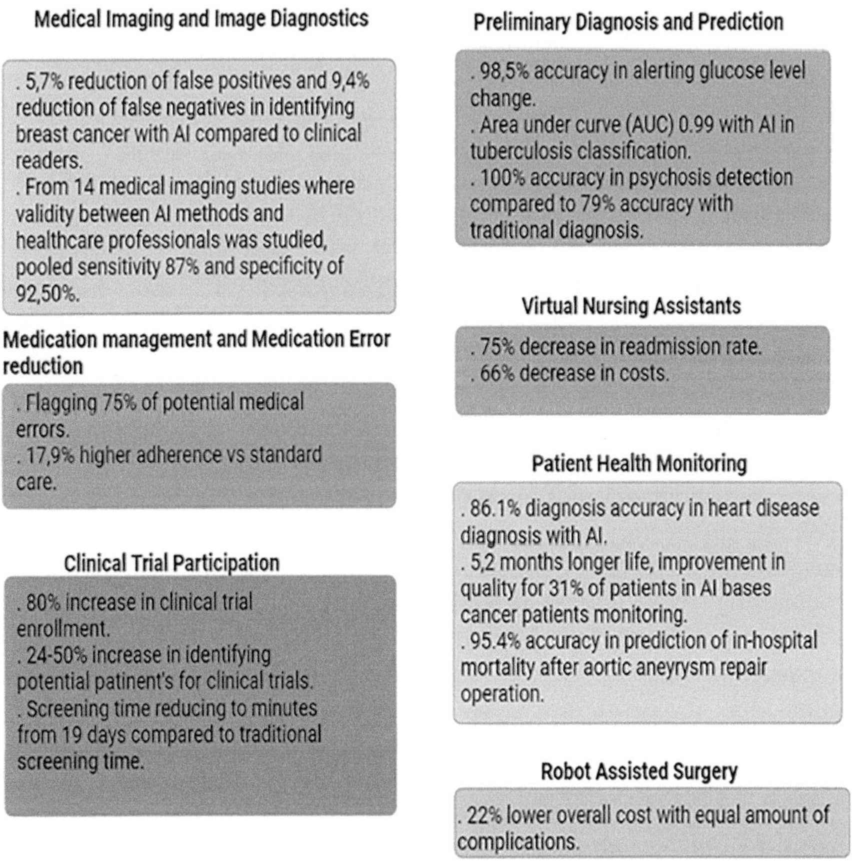

FIGURE 5.3 Benefits of AI in healthcare.

5.16 REMOTE PATIENT MONITORING

It is currently noninfectious disorders, including asthma, cancer, heart disease, diabetes, and mental health concerns, that cause the most death and disability globally [85, 86]. Due to both the aging population and the prevalence of bad lifestyles, the percentage of persons dealing with various chronic illnesses is expected to rise. The lack of a quick fix is the biggest problem presented by chronic diseases. Those with chronic diseases must constantly take care of their health to avoid experiencing acute symptoms. This means keeping close tabs on their eating habits, exercise routines, and prescription use consistently. As a result, there is a growing interest and demand for patient monitoring solutions as a crucial entry point to lessening the burden of chronic illness management and, in particular, bettering self-management [87, 88]. Remote patient monitoring is a developing area of medicine that aims to manage patients' health and disease via the use of information technology and telecommunications capabilities to treat or identify an illness. Using these devices, data about a user's health may be gathered in the comfort of their own homes or while going about their daily routines, and then either stored or sent to medical experts for analysis and advice [89]. Patient monitoring outside of a hospital environment is referred to variously as telemedicine, telehealthcare, and mobile health, all of which use some of the same terminology as remote patient monitoring. Remote patient monitoring satisfies the research interest in the signals and actions of people at risk of acute symptoms due to chronic conditions. This enhances therapy, gives the patient peace of mind for the monitoring of unexpected health assaults, and decreases the need for hospitalizations. Remote monitoring has several advantages, including real-time and continuous symptom monitoring, early disease detection or prevention, reduced healthcare costs, more knowledge about health concerns, and the potential for expanded service and emergency medical aid in the future [90]. An aging population, increasing demands, limited resources, and the prospect of healthy aging are some of the key drivers behind the use of remote health monitoring [91]. The typical components of a remote monitoring system include a data acquisition integrated user-facing data processing, storage, and display along with some kind of network for exchanging messages. The information gathering apparatus includes a variety of sensors and gadgets, such as smartphones internal sensors transmission without wires, etc.

The terminal, which may be a computer at the hospital or a database on the device or smartphone, receives and sends data via the data processing system. In most cases [92, 93], a healthcare practitioner would be able to communicate with the user and the data processing system. Information may be continually gathered and used by the patient and delivered to a healthcare practitioner on an as-needed basis, or information may be continuously supplied to the healthcare professional for evaluation. The patient's health, the details of the data, and the degree of intricacy are all factors. The patient may need to be encouraged to seek medical attention, provide first aid, take medicine, or make contact with a healthcare provider. There is a wide range of technological sophistication, channels of communication, and sensor integration among today's remote monitoring systems. Figure 5.4 shows an example of the architecture used for remote patient monitoring.

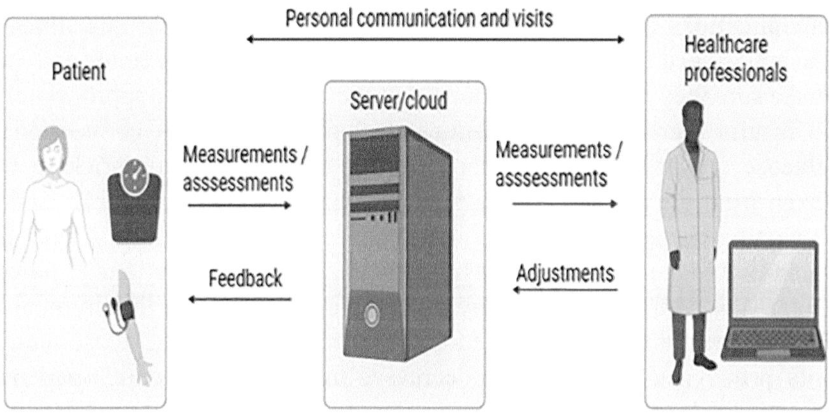

FIGURE 5.4 Remote patient monitoring architecture.

5.17 IMPLEMENTING PATIENT MONITORING SYSTEMS

Patient's vital signs are captured via remote monitoring systems using sensors and other data entry mechanisms. Heart rate, blood pressure, respiratory rate and airflow, blood oxygen volume, ECG, electroencephalogram, electromyogram, body temperature, skin temperature, and blood glucose levels are some of the most often recorded metrics by current systems. They may also be supplemented by information on the patient's physical environment, routine, waking hours, calorie intake, and weight. Conventional monitoring devices typically employ electrodes attached to the skin or other external body components to acquire data [93]. Technological developments in electronics and wireless networking have led to the miniaturization and proliferation of wireless sensors and monitoring devices. In addition, cell phones and tablets are being used to operate a growing variety of modern machines.

5.18 PATIENT MONITORING IN HEALTHCARE TODAY

Medical illnesses as diverse as diabetes, cardiovascular disease, and neurological disorders all benefit from remote patient monitoring ability to decrease the need for hospitalization, increase survival rates, and enhance care and service. Achieving and maintaining stable blood glucose levels and minimizing the development of diabetes-related complications calls for diligent care of this common, chronic illness. Diabetics need to monitor their blood glucose levels many times daily to make sure they are within the normal range and responding appropriately to insulin therapy. Electrochemical techniques, used by conventional glucose sensors, require a blood sample the size of a pinprick to be taken from the patient, which is cumbersome and intrusive [94]. CGM is a game-changer for patients with type 1 and type 2 diabetes, helping them live longer and healthier lives. CGMs record fluctuations in blood sugar levels throughout the day and displays the data so that hypo and hyperglycemia may be detected and treated. Continuous glucose monitors' primary advantage is the decreased frequency with which patients experience hypoglycemia. Improved levels of hemoglobin A1c (HbA1c), a critical indicator of diabetes, are also linked to these [95]. In conjunction with an insulin pump, CGMs allow for more regular monitoring and changes, greatly improving glucose management. Currently, only a small number of manufacturers, including Medtronic and Dexcom (with Tandem), provide closed-loop systems, and none of them is suitable for continuous monitoring [96]. Additionally, despite the obvious advantages, CGM devices have met with very limited clinical acceptability and adoption. Figure 5.5 is a representation of a closed-loop system for the management of glucose levels that makes use of a glucose sensor and an insulin pump for the delivery of insulin.

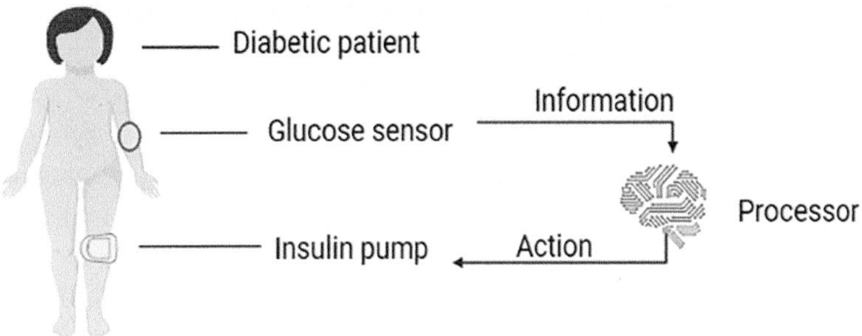

FIGURE 5.5 Illustration of closed-loop glycemic management system using glucose sensor and insulin pump for insulin delivery.

The World Health Organization estimates that 26 million individuals are living with heart failure globally [97]. The risk of hospitalization and death due to this condition is high. Without post-treatment monitoring, patients with heart failure have a greater chance of being readmitted and developing new health problems. When compared to in-person visits by medical personnel, the cost of remote patient monitoring is far lower. ECG, blood pressure, heart rate, and weight are just some of the parameters that are taken with regular weigh-ins and phone check-ins as part of the monitoring process. Some of these depend on telemonitoring, while others employ videoconferencing or monitoring and intervention techniques that are based on mobile phones [98]. The positive impacts that such monitoring systems have on patients have been the focus of a significant number of clinical trials, with differing outcomes from each of those investigations. On the other hand, there is widespread consensus that monitoring at home for heart failure may minimize the risk of mortality and readmission to the hospital [99]. Remote patient monitoring has the potential to aid patients with a variety of neurological conditions, including Parkinson's disease, epilepsy, multiple sclerosis, and dementia. Assessing the impact of treatment on a patient's symptoms and functioning is one of the main problems for clinicians dealing with these conditions. Due to the correlation between inactivity and a host of health problems, tracking how much you move about is crucial for diagnosing and treating a wide range of neurological disorders. The study of predictors, outcomes, and decision support may all benefit from remote monitoring, which allows for the assessment of physical activity outside of the clinic. Patients with Parkinson's disease may benefit from the use of accelerometry devices in physical activity monitors to predict fall risk and evaluate mistakes [100]. Actigraph and Omron are two examples of such gadgets on the market; they track the user's arm and leg movements as they walk or reach for an item. They analyze variables including walking posture, swing duration, and pace. Users and doctors get feedback from these systems, which improves their ability to analyze the situation and give optimal rehabilitative and therapeutic management [101]. Figure 5.6 shows an example of data collection and sensor setup to monitor the physical activity of Parkinson's disease patients.

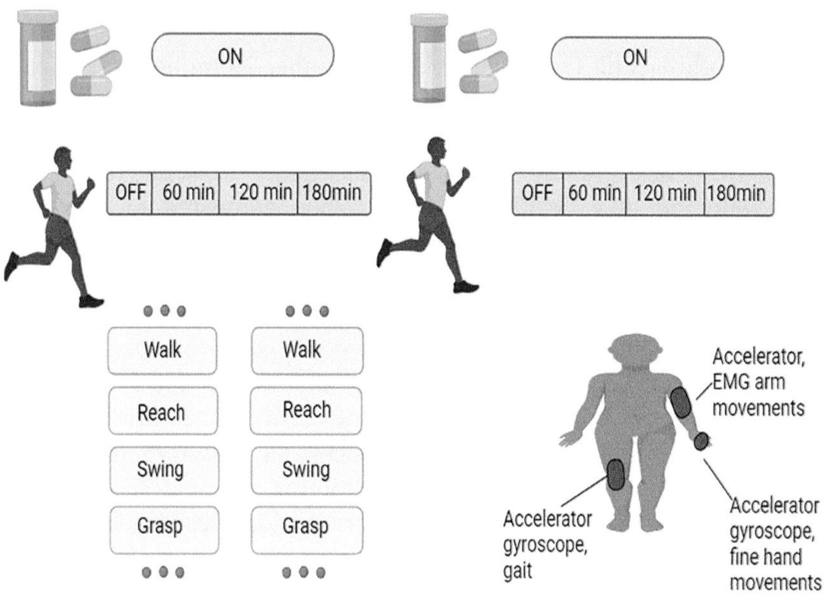

FIGURE 5.6 Data collection and sensor setup for physical activity monitoring of patients with Parkinson's.

5.19 ENHANCED HEALTHCARE OUTCOMES THROUGH REMOTE PATIENT MONITORING

Clinical research and pilot projects have shown several uses for remote patient monitoring that result in better clinical results. However, numerous studies, even for the same monitoring technology or condition, indicate no significant increase in clinical outcomes. Due to the diverse range of applications and medical conditions that may be monitored remotely, it is difficult to make generalized statements about the effectiveness of remote patient monitoring systems. The area of remote patient monitoring is very specialized, with most monitoring systems concentrating their attention just on a single form of illness or kind of technology. Reductions in morbidity, death, or biometric indicators like HbA1c in the case of diabetes have been the primary focus of most debates on clinical outcomes up until this point. However, several critical markers of therapeutic impact, such as adherence, are ignored. Adherence is the rate at which a patient follows their doctor's orders and other treatment recommendations. This includes taking medications as prescribed and making use of any other recommended treatments. Adherence needs to be recognized as a critical component in the deployment of patient monitoring to keep good management and generate superior health outcomes [101, 102]. Adherence monitoring using remote monitoring systems, such as mHealth apps, has been more popular over the last decade and is currently one of the primary uses for these technologies. To increase the possibility that patients will adhere to their treatment programs, several methods, ranging from simple text message reminders to sensor-based monitoring systems with integrated medical aid, may be used. In a review of clinical studies, Hamine et al. found that 56% of the studies had a significant effect on adherence, while only 40% of the studies had a significant effect on clinical outcomes [103]. This result is based on the fact that throughout the clinical investigations, researchers kept tabs on both patient adherence and more traditional measures of outcome. Increases in adherence rely heavily on the practitioner, with a focus on patient participation and open communication. Moreover, it was shown that the most popular and successful method of increasing adherence is the usage of text message reminders. Engaging patients actively is crucial to retaining a large user base, which in turn leads to better adherence and therapeutic results. Because it takes additional work and the outcomes may not be seen right away, patients frequently lack the motivation to increase their adherence. It is not simple to get people to start doing anything new, particularly if it does not provide any kind of entertainment value or quick reward. However, acceptance is crucial if these adherence tools are to make it beyond the stage of clinical trials and pilot projects and into actual use in the real world. There are several possible explanations [104] for the slow pace of device and system adoption. The majority of monitoring devices are worn, and due to their size and the need for precise positioning of the body, they may be cumbersome and limiting in their use.

Many monitoring systems are prone to connectivity difficulties including latency, data loss, and broken network connections, all of which may lead to a frustrating user experience. Clinicians utilizing the monitoring system may also have concerns about the accuracy and dependability of clinical decision assistance if it was primarily designed and tested in simulated environments. In the end, there is a common deficiency in user participation and interaction. A substantial obstacle to adoption [105, 106] exists because users typically have the impression that they are active data collectors yet have extremely restricted access to all of the data they have gathered. These monitoring systems may be enhanced for wider usage if greater attention is paid to the user's perspective and they are designed to meet their needs. Product success in healthcare depends not only on the approval of healthcare professionals but also on the understanding and cooperation of patients.

5.20 AI'S ROLE IN HEALTHCARE AND PATIENT MONITORING

5.20.1 HARNESSING THE POWER OF CONSUMER TECHNOLOGY

AI is increasingly being used in remote monitoring as society becomes more dependent on such innovations. According to a 2015 study conducted by the Pew Research Centre in the United States, 81% of adults in the nation own smartphones, with over 62% of those smartphone owners using their devices to do searches relating to their health and wellness. According to research that was carried out in 2018 and looked at the ownership of smartphones as well as the usage of health apps among sensitive groups [107], in the United States, 39% of participants report using a mobile app to monitor their current health state. To meet the demands of today's savvy consumers, the fields of AI, big data, and ML are growing quickly in this arena. Several factors, including population growth and aging, rising healthcare costs, healthcare disparities, and the rise in the incidence of chronic diseases like asthma, diabetes, dementia, and Parkinson's, have contributed to an increased demand for healthcare technologies at the community level [108]. This requires regular monitoring of dietary intake, physical activity, and medication administration. As a result, researchers are paying close attention to the prospect of using AI solutions for remote patient monitoring as a means of reducing the stress associated with chronic illness treatment and improving the standard of self-management.

Workforce shortages are another area of rising concern, particularly in the United States healthcare system [109]. According to the results of the 2010 AAMC Consumer Survey of Health Care Access [110], vulnerable persons living in rural and urban areas are anticipated to be the most negatively affected by these gaps. In addition, the current workforce in the healthcare industry in the United States is becoming older, which contributes to the rising number of people retiring [111]. Therefore, AI has been more thoroughly integrated into remote patient monitoring to develop more innovative health monitoring systems that may help individuals deal with the ever-increasing costs of healthcare. Most importantly, these technologies aim to stabilize patients, reduce the length of time patients spend in hospitals, save costs connected with medical care, allow patients to complete treatments and diagnoses under medical supervision, and keep tabs on their progress as they recover at home. In addition, there is evidence that indicates that people with lower earnings have worse health conditions, and access to health services, and is more likely to be careless about their health and predominantly well in hazardous environments [108]. This is because people with lower earnings are more likely to be careless about their health and to reside in environments that pose a risk to their health. There are many factors in society, economics, culture, behavior, environment, and healthcare system that all contribute to these discrepancies. As a result, there is a great deal of mistrust and complications between these folks and healthcare practitioners whenever the system is inattentive or insufficiently receptive to their worries.

5.20.2 AMBIENT ASSISTED LIVING

The term "ambient aided living (AAL)" is used to describe the practice of incorporating new technology into one's everyday life to better meet the growing need for medical care and other forms of help, hence enhancing the standard of living for the individual concerned. AI-based AAL systems are especially helpful for the elderly, the handicapped, and those living with chronic diseases. They provide vital healthcare solutions including remote patient monitoring, aid in times of crisis, training for independent living, and home care [112]. For example, new technologies may be very useful for remote monitoring because AI-based sensors can be utilized to keep tabs on patients throughout the day and to provide constant assistance to caretakers for the elderly. Smart homes also have the potential to assist in the management of energy consumption and reduce carbon emissions [113]. Automatic activity recognition of humans (HAR) is an essential component of AAL systems. The Internet of Things (IoT) and AI are its main building blocks. AAL systems can process large datasets, evaluate them with the right models, find the right pattern, and provide actionable predictions thanks to the use of AI techniques like big data and ML. To distinguish between the different types of motion, HAR makes use of computational methods such as random forests, naive Bayes, k-means, and IBK classifiers. For example, an AAL system can track the patient's position and motion in space in real-time as they do things like sit, lie down, stand up, walk on a horizontal surface, walk downstairs, or walk upstairs [114]. The IoT, together with a variety of sensors, and various AI algorithms, have collaborated to make this a reality. The accelerometer and gyroscope found in modern smartphones are often used by AAL systems. Davis-Owusu et al. [113] utilized data collected from seniors utilizing a smartphone and its built-in sensors. The researchers used three independent ML strategies to determine six unique behaviors: support vector machines (SVMs), ANNs, and a hybrid method combining HMMs and SVMs (SVM–HMM) (sitting, walking, lying, and standing, descending, and ascending the stairs). For AAL systems, HAR was implemented like DL-based methods [115]. And there has been related work using convolution NNs, where commonplace motions like running, climbing stairs, walking, sitting, and standing were identified [116]. It is possible to construct an AAL system using a wide range of sensors. The use of cell phones and wearable sensors, especially when they are not intrusive and are affordable, is key to the success of AAL systems like e-textile, smart homes, and assistance robots [117].

5.20.3 AI FOR DIABETES PREDICTION AND MONITORING

Diabetes is a major cost burden on the healthcare system, affecting more than 463 million persons worldwide. Despite the availability of many treatments, there is still a need for disease management services that may help improve the quality of life for individuals with diabetes and reduce the risk of complications. Managing diabetes requires more than just monitoring blood glucose and glycated hemoglobin (HbA1C) levels [118]. It also necessitates improving mood and gaining as much knowledge as possible. New digital and device technologies provide a chance to reimage diabetic care. Development into the potential of AI to enhance the lives of diabetics has exploded in the last decade. These sorts of systems may be used for a variety of purposes, including but not limited to the following: screening for diabetes; identifying the condition; treating it; and monitoring its effects.

5.20.4 DIABETES

Diabetes was developed by BCT and is available for iOS and Android. Diabetics may now monitor their glucose levels in real-time and plan for any fluctuations up to an hour in advance. It is only one of numerous diabetes management options that are now available on the commercial market for remote patient monitoring. Diabetes employs several ML methods on data collected from CGM, smartphone sensors, and user input to forecast glucose levels in the future. Patients may use this function to proactively take steps toward keeping their blood glucose levels within the healthy range. In addition, this is integrated with tools for analyzing past data to monitor and manage the condition and achieve better control of blood glucose [119]. Diabetes is an app that individuals with type 1 and type 2 diabetes may use to better control their illness on an individual level by building a model of their blood sugar levels. Additionally, it assists the user in grasping the influence of different stimuli, such as meals, on the pattern of blood sugar, which may help in the prevention of both hypoglycemia and hyperglycemia. When used in tandem with either the Dexcom CGMs or the third-party program The Night Scout app allows users to access their CGM data. Heart rate, calories burned, and steps taken can all be monitored with the help of a fitness tracker or wristwatch. The prediction efficacy benefits from these further data points. Diabetes's ML system learns a user's physiology over 37 days, and it improves its ability to forecast blood glucose as it does so. SVM and unsupervised DL techniques are utilized here, with the choice being made based on data volume and the presence or absence of individual or population-level data. However, autoregressions can only accurately anticipate blood sugar levels up to 30 minutes in advance [110].

5.20.5 SYSTEMATIC APPROACHES TO CLINICAL DECISION-MAKING

The application of ML, DL, and NLP in cardiovascular disease decision support systems is on the rise. These systems are designed to simulate the decision-making process of a human expert. IBM's Watson for Health, for example, draws on extensive information from electronic medical records, laboratory and imaging results, and other internet resources [120]. These cutting-edge AI systems, which rely heavily on ML and DL, are fashioned after how the human brain makes decisions. IBM is working on a smart assistant to aid cardiologists' and radiologists' decision-making in the field of cardiovascular care. Among the many imaging-related capabilities that IBM's Medical Sieve project provides for cardiac monitoring is the automatic detection of coronary stenoses in angiograms [110].

5.21 AI IN VIRTUAL REALITY, AUGMENTED REALITY, AND VOICE-POWERED VIRTUAL ASSISTANTS

AI techniques have found significant use in the field of cardiology mixed reality approach, combining elements of both VR and AR. The vast majority of the virtual reality designs that are now on the market are focused on periprocedural and preprocedural modalities, such as cardiac interventions and preintervention stress management for patients [121]. AR systems are also utilized to help the interventionist during cardiac surgeries by providing them with real-time data from many screens. However, virtual assistants that can be controlled by voice like Google Assistant, Siri, and Alexa from Amazon require sophisticated AI systems for voice detection. With the use of speech-based virtual assistants, medical professionals, such as physicians and operators, can get online information or search the electronic medical record system with the utmost speed, ease, and convenience using just their voice signature passwords [122].

5.22 CONCLUSION AND FUTURE SCOPE

Smart health monitoring (SHM) has been quite effective, especially when compared to the old health monitoring system, which only allowed for a delay in services, latency in medicine, and precautions. In terms of data security and data privacy, the integration of Cloud computing and blockchain technologies in SHM has earned the confidence of both medical care providers and their patients. It was discovered that SHM could meet the unique requirements of seriously sick patients, in addition to the more general health monitoring services necessary to realize individualized health objectives and promote healthy lifestyles. More research into SHM's potential applications in athletics and healthcare, in general, is possible as new technologies emerge. The SHM opens up several doors for the future of medicine that were previously unattainable. This study provides a comprehensive overview of the smart health monitoring frameworks that have effectively adopted and deployed DL and ML strategies and algorithms to improve their performance. There is a shortage of reporting on efforts that incorporate ML and DL into SHM in the comparable review works. Due to the widespread use of IoMT in SHM, medical services that rely on remote monitoring in real-time have become much more accessible and efficient.

KEYWORDS

- **smart health monitoring**
- **remote health monitoring**
- **machine learning**

REFERENCES

1. vanGemert-Pijnen JE, Nijland N, van Limburg M, et al. 2011. A holistic framework to improve the uptake and impact of eHealth technologies. *J Med Internet Res. 13*(4), e111.
2. Dankwa-Mullan I, Rivo M, Sepulveda M, Park Y, Snowdon J, Rhee K. 2019. Transforming diabetes care through artificial intelligence: The future is here. *Popul Health Manag. 22*(3), 229–42. https://doi. org/10.1089/pop.2018.0129.
3. Ellahham S. 2020. Artificial intelligence: The future for diabetes care. *Am J Med. 133*(8), 895–900. https://doi. org/10.1016/j.amjmed.2020.03.033.
4. Marling C, Wiley M, Bunescu R, Shubrook J, Schwartz F. 2012. Emerging applications for intelligent diabetes management. *AI Mag. 33*(2), 67.

5. Pesl P, Herrero P, Reddy M, et al. 2017. Case-based reasoning for insulin bolus advice: Evaluation of case parameters in a six-week pilot study. *J Diabetes Sci Technol. 11*, 37–42.
6. Shankaracharya, Odedra D, Samanta S, Vidyarthi AS. 2010. Computational intelligence in early diabetes diagnosis: A review. *Rev Diabet Stud.* 7(4), 252–62. https://doi.org/10.1900/RDS.2010.7.252.
7. Buch V, Varughese G, Maruthappu M. 2018. Artificial intelligence in diabetes care. *Diabet Med. 35*, 495–7.
8. Integrating Artificial and Human Intelligence: A Partnership for Responsible Innovation in Biomedical Engineering and Medicine
9. Yasui M, Hiroshima M, Kozuka J, Sako Y, Ueda M. 2018. Automated single-molecule imaging in living cells. *Nat Commun. 9*, 3061.
10. Schneider G. 2018. Automating drug discovery. *Nat Rev Drug Discov. 17*, 97–113
11. Thomford NE, Senthebane DA, Rowe A, et al. 2018. Natural Products for Drug Discovery in the 21st Century: Innovations for novel drug discovery. *Int J Mol Sci 19*, pii: E1578.
12. Poleszczuk J, Enderling H. 2018. The optimal radiation dose to induce robust systemic anti-tumor immunity. *Int J Mol Sci. 19*, pii: E3377.
13. Dzobo K. 2019. Epigenomics-guided drug development: Recent advances in solving the cancer treatment "jigsaw puzzle". *OMICS 23*, 70–85
14. Cheng PM, Malhi HS. 2017. Transfer learning with convolutional neural networks for classification of abdominal ultrasound images. *J Digit Imaging 30*, 234–243
15. Wang L, Yang Y, Min R, Chakradhar S. 2017. Accelerating deep neural network training with inconsistent stochastic gradient descent. *Neural Netw. 93*, 219–229.
16. Rahimy E. 2018. Deep learning applications in ophthalmology. *Curr Opin Ophthalmol. 29*, 254–260.
17. Wong TY, Bressler NM. 2016. Artificial intelligence with deep learning technology looks into diabetic retinopathy screening. *JAMA 316*, 2366–2367
18. Leibig C, Allken V, Ayhan MS, Berens P, Wahl S. 2017. Leveraging uncertainty information from deep neural networks for disease detection. *Sci Rep. 7*, 17816.
19. Ramachandran N, Hong SC, Sime MJ, Wilson GA. 2018. Diabetic retinopathy screening using deep neural network. *Clin Exp Ophthalmol. 46*, 412–416.
20. De Fauw J, Ledsam JR, Romera-Paredes B, et al. 2018. Clinically applicable deep learning for diagnosis and referral in retinal disease. *Nat Med. 24*, 1342–1350.
21. Li F, Chen H, Liu Z, Zhang X, Wu Z. 2019. Fully automated detection of retinal disorders by image-based deep learning. *Graefes Arch Clin Exp Ophthalmol. 257*, 495–505
22. Iqbal U, Wah TY, Habib Ur Rehman M, Mujtaba G, Imran M, Shoaib M. 2018. Deep deterministic learning for pattern recognition of different cardiac diseases through the internet of medical things. *J Med Syst. 42*, 252.
23. Yao Z, Chen Y. 2018. Arrhythmia classification from single lead ECG by multi-scale convolutional neural networks. *Conf Proc IEEE Eng Med Biol Soc. 2018*, 344–347.
24. Strodthoff N, Strodthoff C. 2019. Detecting and interpreting myocardial infarction using fully convolutional neural networks. *Physiol Meas. 40*, 015001.

25. Willems JL, Abreu-Lima C, Arnaud P, et al. 1991. The diagnostic performance of computer programs for the interpretation of electrocardiograms. *N Engl J Med. 325*, 1767– 1773.
26. Zhang Y, Chen Y, Ma L. 2018b. Depression and cardiovascular disease in elderly: Current understanding. *J Clin Neurosci. 47*, 1–5.
27. Madani A, Arnaout R, Mofrad M, Arnaout R. 2018. Fast and accurate view classification of echocardiograms using deep learning. *NPJ Digital Med. 1*, 6
28. Nelson BW, Allen NB. 2019. Accuracy of consumer wearable heart rate measurement during an ecologically valid 24-hour period: Intraindividual validation study. *JMIR Mhealth Uhealth. 7,* e10828.
29. Thomson EA, Nuss K, Comstock A, et al. 2019. Heart rate measures from the Apple Watch, Fitbit Charge HR 2, and electrocardiogram across different exercise intensities. *J Sports Sci. 37*, 1411–1419.
30. Haberman ZC, Jahn RT, Bose R, et al. 2015. Wireless smartphone ECG enables large-scale screening in diverse populations. *J Cardiovasc Electrophysiol. 26*, 520–526.
31. Ahmed A, Ahmad W, Khan MJ, Siddiqui SA, Cheema HM. 2017. A wearable sensor based multi-criteria-decision-system for real-time seizure detection. *Conf Proc IEEE Eng Med Biol Soc. 2017*, 2377–2380.
32. Jim HSL, Hoogland AI, Brownstein NC, Barata A, Dicker AP, Knoop H, Gonzalez BD, Perkins R, Rollison D, Gilbert SM, Nanda R, Berglund A, Mitchell R, Johnstone PAS. 2020. Innovations in research and clinical care using patient-generated health data. *CA Cancer J Clin. 70*(3), 182–199. https://doi. org/10.3322/caac.21608.
33. Lixin D, Li Z, Dominik JB, Bradley JN, Detlev G. 2006. Hybrid nanorobotic approaches for fabricating NEMS from 3D helical nanostructures. In *Proceedings—IEEE International Conference on Robotics and Automation* (pp. 1396–1401).
34. Hassanzadeh P, Atyabi F, Dinarvand R. 2016. Creation of nanorobots: Both state-of-the-science and state-of-the-art. *Biomed. Rev. 27*, 37–44.
35. Hamdi M, Ferreira A. 2009. Multiscale design and modeling of protein-based nanomechanisms for nanorobotics. *Int. J. Robot. Res. 28*(4), 436–449.
36. Robert A. 2005. Current status of nanomedicine and medical nanorobotics. *J. Computl. Theor. Nanosci. 2*, 1–25.
37. Banharnsakun A, Achalakul T, Batra RC. 2016. Drug delivery based on swarm microrobots. *Int. J. Comput. Intel Appl. 15*, 1–25.
38. Patel GM, Patel GC, Patel RB, Patel JK, Patel M. 2006. Nanorobot: A versatile tool in nanomedicine. *J. Drug Target 14*, 63–67.
39. Couvreur P, Vauthier C. 2006. Nanotechnology: Intelligent design to treat complex disease. *Pharm. Res. 23*, 1417–1450.
40. Cavalcanti A, Shirinzadeh B, Kretly LC. 2008. Medical nanorobotics for diabetes control. *Nanomedicine 4*, 127–138.
41. Saadeh Y, Vyas D. 2014. Nanorobotic applications in medicine: Current proposals and designs, *Am. J. Robot Surg. 1*, 4–11.
42. Toth-Fejel T. 2000. Agents, assemblers, and ANTS: Scheduling assembly with market and biological software mechanisms. *Nanotechnology 11*, 133–137.
43. Cavalcanti A, Freitas RA. 2005. Nanorobotics control design: A collective behavior approach for medicine. *IEEE Transact. Nanobiosci. 4*, 133–140.

44. Ntika M, Kefalas P, Stamatopoulou I. 2014. Formal modelling and simulation of a multiagentnano-robotics drug delivery system. *Scal Comput. 15*, 217–230.
45. Zhou W, Wang LZ. 2011. *Three-Dimensional Nanoarchitectures Designing Next Generation Devices*. Springer: New York.
46. Cavalcanti A, Shirinzadeh D, Freitas A, Hogg T. 2008. Nanorobot architecture for medical target identification. *Nanotechnology 19*, 1–15.
47. Hassanzadeh P, Atyabi F, Dinarvand R. 2019. The significance of artificial intelligence in drug delivery system design. *Adv Drug Deliv Rev. 151–152*, 169–190. https://doi.org/10.1016/j.addr.2019.05.001.
48. Xitian P, Hongying L, Kang W, Yulin L, Xiaolin Z, Zhiyu W. 2009. A novel remote controlled capsule for site-specific drug delivery in human GI tract. *Int J Pharm. 382*(1–2), 160–164. https://doi. org/10.1016/j.ijpharm.2009.08.026.
49. Collier M, Fu R, Yin L, Christiansen P. 2017. *Artificial Intelligence: Healthcare's New Nervous System*. Accenture plc.
50. Rao AS, Verweij G. 2017. Sizing the prize: What's the real value of AI for your business and how can you capitalise. PwC Publication, PwC, pp. 1–30.
51. Russell SJ. 2010. *Artificial Intelligence a Modern Approach*. Pearson Education, Inc.
52. Tucker AB. 2004. *Computer Science Handbook*. Chapman and Hall/CRC.
53. Chowdhury GG. 2003. Natural language processing. *Ann Rev Inform Sci Technol. 37*(1), 51–89.
54. Kypson AP, Chitwood WR Jr. 2004. Robotic applications in cardiac surgery. *Int J Adv Robot Syst. 1*(2), 87–92.
55. Melfi FM, Menconi GF, Mariani AM, Angeletti CA. 2002. Early experience with robotic technology for thoracoscopic surgery. *Eur J Cardio-thoracic Surg. 21*(5), 864–868.
56. Hyun MH, Lee CH, Kim HJ, Tong Y, Park SS. 2013. Systematic review and meta-analysis of robotic surgery compared with conventional laparoscopic and open resections for gastric carcinoma. *J Br Surg. 100*(12), 1566–1578.
57. Herron DM, Marohn MJSE. 2008. A consensus document on robotic surgery. *Surg Endosc 22*(2), 313–325.
58. DiGioia A, Jaramaz B, Picard F, Nolte LP. (Eds.), 2004. *Computer and Robotic Assisted Hip and Knee Surgery*. Oxford University Press.
59. Shweikeh F, Amadio JP, Arnell M, Barnard ZR, Kim TT, Johnson JP, Drazin D. 2014. Robotics and the spine: A review of current and ongoing applications. *Neurosurg Focus 36*(3), E10.
60. Hameed AM, Yao J, Allen RD, Hawthorne WJ, Pleass HC, Lau H. 2018. The evolution of kidney transplantation surgery into the robotic era and its prospects for obese recipients. *Transplantation 102*(10), 1650–1665.
61. Lee DI. 2009. Robotic prostatectomy: What we have learned and where we are going. *Yonsei Med J. 50*(2), 177–181.
62. Väänänen A, Haataja K, Vehviläinen-Julkunen K, Toivanen P. 2021. AI in healthcare: A narrative review. *F1000Research 10*(6), 6.
63. Jenny JY. 2006. The history and development of computer assisted orthopaedic surgery. *Der Orthopade 35*(10), 1038–1042.

64. Ho C, Tsakonas E, Tran K, Cimon K, Severn M, Mierzwinski-Urban M, Corcos J, Pautler S. 2013. Robot-assisted surgery compared with open surgery and laparoscopic surgery: Clinical effectiveness and economic analyses.
65. Kristensen SE, Mosgaard BJ, Rosendahl M, Dalsgaard T, Bjørn SF, Frøding LP, Kehlet H, Høgdall CK, Lajer H. 2017. Robot-assisted surgery in gynecological oncology: Current status and controversies on patient benefits, cost and surgeon conditions—a systematic review. *Acta Obstetriciaet Gynecol Scand 96*(3), 274–285.
66. Sham JG, Richards MK, Seo YD, Pillarisetty VG, Yeung RS, Park JO. 2016. Efficacy and cost of robotic hepatectomy: Is the robot cost-prohibitive. *J Robot Surg. 10*(4), 307–313.
67. Laranjo L, Dunn AG, Tong HL, Kocaballi AB, Chen J, Bashir R, Surian D, Gallego B, Magrabi F, Lau AY, Coiera E. 2018. Conversational agents in healthcare: A systematic review. *J Am Med Inform Assoc. 25*(9), 1248–1258.
68. Radziwill NM, Benton MC. 2017. Evaluating quality of chatbots and intelligent conversational agents. *arXiv preprint arXiv:1704.04579.*
69. Carr-Brown J, Berlucchi M. 2016. *Pre-Primary Care: An Untapped Global Health Opportunity*. Your.MD.
70. Chambers D, Cantrell AJ, Johnson M, Preston L, Baxter SK, Booth A, Turner J. 2019. Digital and online symptom checkers and health assessment/triage services for urgent health problems: Systematic review. *BMJ Open 9*(8), e027743.
71. Sensely. 2019. An integrated payer/provider wanted to intervene in a timelier manner with its chronic heart failure (CHF) patients.
72. Watanabe JH, McInnis T, Hirsch JD. 2018. Cost of prescription drug–related morbidity and mortality. *Annal Pharmacother. 52*(9), 829–837.
73. Williams DJ. 2007. Medication errors. *J-R Coll Physicians Edinb. 37*(4), 343.
74. Schiff GD, Volk LA, Volodarskaya M, Williams DH, Walsh L, Myers SG, Bates DW, Rozenblum R. 2017. Screening for medication errors using an outlier detection system. *J Am Med Inform Assoc. 24*(2), 281–287.
75. Labovitz DL, Shafner L, Reyes Gil M, Virmani D, Hanina A. 2017. Using artificial intelligence to reduce the risk of nonadherence in patients on anticoagulation therapy. *Stroke 48*(5), 1416–1419.
76. Bain EE, Shafner L, Walling DP, Othman AA, Chuang-Stein C, Hinkle J, Hanina A. 2017. Use of a novel artificial intelligence platform on mobile devices to assess dosing compliance in a phase 2 clinical trial in subjects with schizophrenia. *JMIR Mhealth Uhealth 5*(2), e7030.
77. Hanania NA, King MJ, Braman SS, Saltoun C, Wise RA, Enright P, Falsey AR, Mathur SK, Ramsdell JW, Rogers L, Stempel DA. 2011. Asthma in the elderly: Current understanding and future research needs—a report of a National Institute on Aging (NIA) workshop. *Journal Allergy Clin Immunol. 128*(3), S4–S24.
78. Harrer S, Shah P, Antony B, Hu J. 2019. Artificial intelligence for clinical trial design. *Trends Pharmacol Sci. 40*(8), 577–591.
79. Haddad TC, Helgeson J, Pomerleau K, Makey M, Lombardo P, Coverdill S, Urman A, Rammage M, Goetz MP, LaRusso N. 2018. Impact of a cognitive computing clinical trial matching system in an ambulatory oncology practice. *J Clin Oncol. 36.* http//:doi:10.1200/JCO.2018.36.15_suppl.6550

80. Christiansen MP, Garg SK, Brazg R, Bode BW, Bailey TS, Slover RH, Sullivan A, Huang S, Shin J, Lee SW, Kaufman FR. 2017. Accuracy of a fourth-generation subcutaneous continuous glucose sensor. *Diabetes Technol Ther. 19*(8), 446–456.
81. Patel TA, Puppala M, Ogunti RO, Ensor JE, He T, Shewale JB, Ankerst DP, Kaklamani VG, Rodriguez AA, Wong ST, Chang JC. 2017. Correlating mammographic and pathologic findings in clinical decision support using natural language processing and data mining methods. *Cancer 123*(1), 114–121.
82. Lakhani P, Sundaram B. 2017. Deep learning at chest radiography: Automated classification of pulmonary tuberculosis by using convolutional neural networks. *Radiology 284*(2), 574–582.
83. Researcher DBM. Global artificial intelligence in medical imaging market-industry trends-forecast to 2026. *Reference Source*.
84. Guidi G, Iadanza E, Pettenati MC, Milli M, Pavone F, BiffiGentili G. 2012, June. Heart failure artificial intelligence-based computer aided diagnosis telecare system. In *International Conference on Smart Homes and Health Telematics* (pp. 278–281). Springer: Berlin, Heidelberg.
85. Wickramasinghe N, John B, George J, Vogel D. 2019. Achieving value-based care in chronic disease management: Intervention study. *JMIR Diabetes 4*(2), e10368.
86. Blackwelder A, Hoskins M, Huber L. 2021. Peer reviewed: Effect of inadequate sleep on frequent mental distress. *Prev Chronic Dis. 18*, E61.
87. Wickramasinghe N, Troshani I, Tan J. (Eds.) 2016. *Contemporary Consumer Health Informatics*. Springer.
88. Wickramasinghe N. 2019. Essential considerations for successful consumer health informatics solutions. *Yearb Med Inform. 28*(01), 158–164.
89. Vegesna A, Tran M, Angelaccio M, Arcona S. 2017. Remote patient monitoring via non-invasive digital technologies: A systematic review. *Telemed e-Health 23*(1), 3–17.
90. Malasinghe LP, Ramzan N, Dahal K. 2019. Remote patient monitoring: A comprehensive study. *J Ambient Intell Humaniz Comput. 10*(1), 57–76.
91. Albahri OS, Zaidan AA, Zaidan BB, Hashim M, Albahri AS, Alsalem MA. 2018. Real-time remote health-monitoring Systems in a Medical Centre: A review of the provision of healthcare services-based body sensor information, open challenges and methodological aspects. *J Med Syst. 42*(9), 1–47.
92. Klersy C, De Silvestri A, Gabutti G, Regoli F, Auricchio A. 2009. A meta-analysis of remote monitoring of heart failure patients. *J Am Coll Cardiol. 54*(18), 1683–1694.
93. Gopalsami N, Osorio I, Kulikov S, Buyko S, Martynov A, Raptis AC. 2007. SAW microsensor brain implant for prediction and monitoring of seizures. *IEEE Sens J. 7*(7), 977–982.
94. Yoo EH, Lee SY. 2010. Glucose biosensors: An overview of use in clinical practice. *Sensors 10*(5), 4558–4576.
95. Rodbard D. 2016. Continuous glucose monitoring: A review of successes, challenges, and opportunities. *Diabetes Technol Ther. 18*(S2), S2–S3.
96. Chen C, Zhao XL, Li ZH, Zhu ZG, Qian SH, Flewitt AJ. 2017. Current and emerging technology for continuous glucose monitoring. *Sensors 17*(1), 182.
97. Savarese G, Lund LH. 2017. Global public health burden of heart failure. *Card Fail Rev. 3*(1), 7.

98. Bashi N, Karunanithi M, Fatehi F, Ding H, Walters D. 2017. Remote monitoring of patients with heart failure: An overview of systematic reviews. *J Med Internet Res. 19*(1), e6571.
99. Ong MK, Romano PS, Edgington S, Aronow HU, Auerbach AD, Black JT, De Marco T, Escarce JJ, Evangelista LS, Hanna B, Ganiats TG. 2016. Effectiveness of remote patient monitoring after discharge of hospitalized patients with heart failure: The better effectiveness after transition–heart failure (BEAT-HF) randomized clinical trial. *JAMA Int Med. 176*(3), 310–318.
100. Block VA, Pitsch E, Tahir P, Cree BA, Allen DD, Gelfand JM. 2016. Remote physical activity monitoring in neurological disease: A systematic review. *PLoS One 11*(4), e0154335.
101. Lonini L, Dai A, Shawen N, Simuni T, Poon C, Shimanovich L, Daeschler M, Ghaffari R, Rogers JA, Jayaraman A. 2018. Wearable sensors for Parkinson's disease: Which data are worth collecting for training symptom detection models. *NPJ Digit Med. 1*(1), 1–8.
102. DiMatteo MR. 2004. Variations in patients' adherence to medical recommendations: A quantitative review of 50 years of research. *Med Care 42*(3), 200–209.
103. Hamine S, Gerth-Guyette E, Faulx D, Green BB, Ginsburg AS. 2015. Impact of mHealth chronic disease management on treatment adherence and patient outcomes: A systematic review. *J Med Internet Res. 17*(2), e3951.
104. Baig MM, GholamHosseini H, Moqeem AA, Mirza F, Lindén M. 2017. A systematic review of wearable patient monitoring systems—current challenges and opportunities for clinical adoption. *J Med Syst. 41*(7), 1–9.
105. Milenković A, Otto C, Jovanov E. 2006. Wireless sensor networks for personal health monitoring: Issues and an implementation. *Comput Commun. 29*(13–14), 2521–2533.
106. Deshmukh SD, Shilaskar SN. 2015, January. Wearable sensors and patient monitoring system: A review. In *2015 International Conference on Pervasive Computing (ICPC)* (pp. 1–3). IEEE.
107. Vangeepuram N, Mayer V, Fei K, Hanlen-Rosado E, Andrade C, Wright S, Horowitz C. 2018. Smartphone ownership and perspectives on health apps among a vulnerable population in East Harlem, New York. *Mhealth 4*, 31.
108. Gibbons MC, Shaikh Y. 2019. Introduction to consumer health informatics and digital inclusion. In *Consumer Informatics and Digital Health* (pp. 25–41). Springer: Cham.
109. Dall T, West T, Chakrabarti R, Iacobucci W. 2015. *The Complexities of Physician Supply and Demand: Projections from 2013 to 2025.* Association of American Medical Colleges: Washington, DC.
110. Jeddi Z, Bohr A. 2020. Remote patient monitoring using artificial intelligence. In *Artificial Intelligence in Healthcare* (pp. 203–234). Academic Press.
111. Buerhaus PI. 2008. Current and future state of the US nursing workforce. *JAMA 300*(20), 2422–2424.
112. Darwish M, Senn E, Lohr C, Kermarrec Y. 2014, June. A comparison between ambient assisted living systems. In *International Conference on Smart Homes and Health Telematics* (pp. 231–237). Springer, Cham.
113. Davis K, Owusu E, Bastani V, Marcenaro L, Hu J, Regazzoni C, Feijs L. 2016, July. Activity recognition based on inertial sensors for ambient assisted living. In *2016 19th International Conference on Information Fusion (fusion)* (pp. 371–378). Ieee.

114. Chetty G, White M, Akther F. 2015. Smart phone based data mining for human activity recognition. *Procedia Comput Sci. 46*, 1181–1187.
115. Ronao CA, Cho SB. 2016. Human activity recognition with smartphone sensors using deep learning neural networks. *Expert Syst Appl. 59*, 235–244.
116. De-La-Hoz-Franco E, Ariza-Colpas P, Quero JM, Espinilla M. 2018. Sensor-based datasets for human activity recognition—a systematic review of literature. *IEEE Access 6*, 59192–59210.
117. Majumder S, Mondal T, Deen MJ. 2017. Wearable sensors for remote health monitoring. *Sensors 17*(1), 130.
118. Fagherazzi G, Ravaud P. 2019. Digital diabetes: Perspectives for diabetes prevention, management and research. *Diabetes Metab. 45*(4), 322–329.
119. Hayeri A. 2019. 922-P: Diabits—An AI-powered smartphone application for blood glucose monitoring and predictions. *Diabetes 68*(Supplement_1).
120. Syeda-Mahmood T. 2018. Role of big data and machine learning in diagnostic decision support in radiology. *J Am College Radiol. 15*(3), 569–576.
121. Silva JN, Southworth MK, Dalal A, Van Hare GF, Silva JR. 2017. Improving visualization and interaction during transcatheter ablation using an augmented reality system: First-in-human experience. *Circulation 136*(suppl_1), A15358–A15358.
122. Steinhubl SR, Topol EJ. 2018. Now we're talking: Bringing a voice to digital medicine. *Lancet 392*(10148), 627.

CHAPTER 6

Intelligent Blockchain-Based Healthcare Data Management Systems for Patient Care

*Corresponding author

ABSTRACT

Health information is stored in electronic health records (EHRs). EHRs are shared across healthcare stakeholders, making them vulnerable to power outages, data abuse, a lack of privacy, security, and an audit trail. Blockchain, on the other hand, is a revolutionary technology that allows nodes in a list of networks to join without a central authority. It might overcome EHR management's limitations and establish a more secure, decentralized, and safer EHR data exchange environment. Also, blockchain is a distributed ledger that stores and shares data in a cryptographically secure, verified, and unanimously agreed-upon way across all mining nodes. The blockchain saves data securely and cannot be manipulated. Smart contracts and machine-learning algorithms may be trusted to make judgments and analyze data. Yet, blockchain has scalability and complexity difficulties that may make it inefficient. Mixing AI with blockchain technology can mitigate some of these two technical ecosystems' limitations. Data helps AI computers learn, evaluate, and draw conclusions. The highlighted taxonomy integrates blockchain and AI, allowing us to examine the potential uses of both technologies in healthcare data management. Future study topics and unanswered questions are discussed to round out the chapter.

Computational Intelligence for Patient Care: Blockchain, AI, and ML in Healthcare.
Rishabha Malviya, Rishav Sharma, Sathvik Belagodu Sridhar, and Suraj Kumar (Authors)

DOI: 10.1201/9781779640819-6

6.1 INTRODUCTION

Researchers in the medical and healthcare areas emphasize the need of being able to collect and evaluate data from diverse sources to improve the quality of patient care. This paves the way for the detection of public health threats, the development of individualized treatments, and the administration of targeted medicine [1]. Patient health records and patient portals are only two examples of how this data can be used to better individual health information systems. Despite being the principal owners of personal data, practitioners often restrict patient access to their medical records. The key to success is embedding easily available technology like blockchain and AI into the very fabric of a company [2, 3]. Using technology to provide user- and customer-centric interfaces and data-driven decisions for novel approaches to data processing and enhanced results is essential for advancing medical research and achieving patient centricity [3, 4]. For example, AI could help determine which patients need to be monitored and developed first for a treatment, which is crucial for both regular drug manufacturing and shorter development times [3]. Clinical trial data were analyzed for reusing existing drugs, testing new drug formulations, and determining appropriate dosing [5] using numerical drug design techniques and AI. Blockchain makes it possible to build a system for generating and managing ledgers, or blocks of content, that include cryptographically secure and automatically analyzed data. Doctors, hospitals, and insurance companies will have quick access to the latest health data because it will be collected and evaluated safely. Nevertheless, due to the vast processing resources required, it would be prohibitively expensive to store massive documents on the blockchain, such as comprehensive electronic medical records or genetic data records. This is a significant problem with blockchain technology since it complicates the process of doing data queries within a blockchain. However, artificial intelligence algorithms incorporated into the blockchain can assist address this limitation [3, 5–8]. To better comprehend health trends and patterns, AI has begun to learn and reason like a doctor. Unstructured data is collected from the patient, the radiologist, and the images. The computing abilities of AI extend to the execution of sophisticated algorithms and the evaluation of massive data sets. Blockchain makes it possible to build a system for generating and managing ledgers, or blocks of content, that include cryptographically secure and automatically analyzed data. Doctors, hospitals, and insurance companies will have quick access to the latest health data because it will be collected and evaluated safely. Nevertheless, due to the vast processing resources required, it would be prohibitively expensive to store massive documents on the blockchain, such as comprehensive electronic medical records or genetic data records. This is a significant problem with blockchain technology since it complicates the process of doing data queries inside of a blockchain [9]. Artificial intelligence started to learn and reason like a doctor to comprehend health trends and patterns. It gathers unstructured information from the patient, the radiologist, and the images themselves. Artificial intelligence can also quickly and accurately evaluate vast amounts of patient data and perform sophisticated computing procedures. Some doctors are still reluctant to utilize AI in healthcare, especially in positions where it could have an impact on a patient's health, although AI has demonstrated that it can execute multiple dynamic and cognitive operations faster than a human [10–13]. The automotive industry has already proven it can successfully employ AI to create fully autonomous vehicles. To prove the extent of AI's maturity, however, several companies have already developed machine learning-based approaches for detecting fraud and identifying financial hazards [14]. The fundamental concepts and terminology of intelligent technology in healthcare are discussed below. Researchers examine the development of intelligent technologies and the security requirements for their application in the medical field. In addition, modular information technology systems have emerged since the 1970s, when healthcare provisioning was first put into practice. Healthcare in this era is sometimes referred to as "version 1.0." Due to financial constraints, digital system coordination and expansion of healthcare services were not possible at the time. But, biomedical machines did not exist and did not communicate with other connected electronics. Healthcare institutions often employed paper-based medication and report at this time, which raised both expenses and time [15]. The era of Healthcare 2.0 lasted from 1991 until 2005. During this period, the healthcare and IT infrastructures upon which modern healthcare is built were established. As part of this procedure, automated monitoring was introduced, giving medical professionals access to imaging equipment with which to evaluate patients' conditions. Along with the rise of social media, new user-enabled innovations emerged in the healthcare industry. Providers and patients alike can now have constant access to their medical records and paperwork thanks to the proliferation of online forums dedicated to the exchange of information and experience in the healthcare industry [16]. At the time, naysayers complained that patients' privacy had been violated and that they had been given false information. Doctors were able to have better, faster access to patient information because of the usage of networked electronic health management techniques and clinical imaging technologies. Healthcare 3.0 was released at the same time as the World Wide Web, empowering users to alter the flow of information on a patient's medical history. The interfaces that users interact with are now easier to use and more specifically designed to meet their needs. The advent of electronic health records (EHRs) as well as wearable and implantable technologies has made continuous, near-constant healthcare monitoring possible. Similarly, EHR systems [17] emerging with support for storing patient data on non-networked, standalone systems like social media platforms. Industry 4.0's emphasis on integrating high-tech and human elements into all aspects of production led to a proliferation of care periods, which in turn led to the development of blockchain that provide near-instantaneous access to patients' clinical records. The primary focus throughout this time frame is on enhancing virtualization to facilitate real-time individualized healthcare [18]. Teamwork, consistency, and integration are increasingly prioritized as researcher utilizes artificial intelligence to deliver patient-specific, prognostic treatment. This chapter intends to explore the potential of AI-blockchain to manage EHRs by addressing the following scenario, demonstrating the obstacles and future horizons involved. In this meta-analysis, the investigator looks at the literature on managing EHRs using blockchain technology, including studies that present conceptual solutions, experimental results, prototypes, and blockchain implementations [19].

6.2 IMPLEMENTATION OF EHR SYSTEM

EHRs often include data including a patient's medical history, personal statistics (such as age and weight), laboratory test results, and more. Therefore, these records must be protected from public view. Nevertheless, countries like the United States subject hospitals to rigorous governmental monitoring [20–23]. There are several challenges associated with healthcare system deployment and implementation. Centralized server architectures, already discussed, are vulnerable to single-point attacks and malicious insider attacks. When users (including patients) have their data outsourced or housed in these EHR systems, they no longer have control over their information. They are completely in the dark about who is accessing it and for what reasons (i.e., privacy breaches). Another risk is that malicious insiders will leak this information to a third party, such as an insurance company that will then refuse to cover the patient because of the information in the released medical data [24]. A schematic representation of the proposed system's EHR architecture is presented in Figure 6.1. The blockchain's major stakeholders are the hospital, the patient, and the doctor. As a result of the distributed ledger's private keys, every participant in the blockchain ecosystem will have their special authority. There could be restrictions on what features medical professionals, patients, and hospitals can use. The doctor will be able to log onto the website (Frontend) using his or her private key. The individual exchanges data with the physician using his key. The two parties will exchange health data employing a front-end web application. After obtaining care, patients are required to conduct business via smart contract.

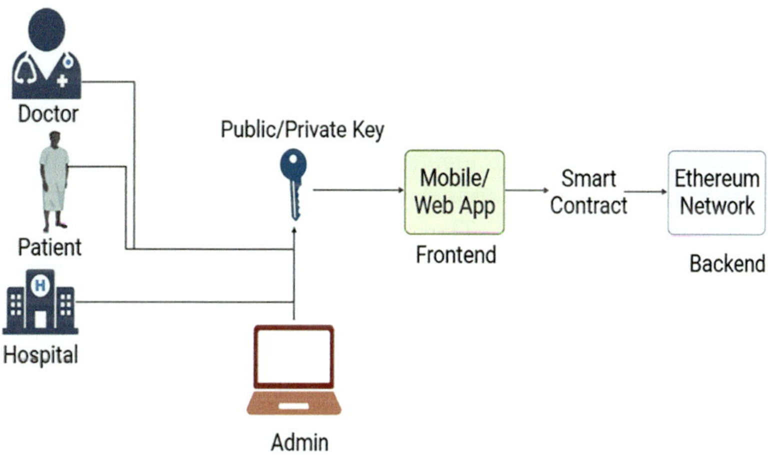

FIGURE 6.1 EHR technology.

6.3 THE BENEFIT OF USING BLOCKCHAIN IN AI

Blockchain and AI provide several potential solutions to the coronavirus outbreak. The blockchain has numerous practical applications that can be put to use in the fight against the coronavirus outbreak. By having people install client software for a blockchain network on their mobile devices, blockchain might be used to track the global spread of coronavirus infections. The capacity of blockchain to prevent the release of user information is crucial, as is its role in facilitating the early detection of outbreaks [25]. It makes vaccination trials more efficient and transparent and keeps track of all fundraising activities and donations, both of which aid in managing epidemics and coordinating treatments. Artificial intelligence can aid in several ways in the fight against the coronavirus. Viruses can be detected and their spread predicted with the help of AI by examining data on environmental factors [26], access to healthcare, and the transmission process. Artificial intelligence can assist establish if coronaviruses are present in small-scale disease outbreaks by classifying samples. Heart virus infections can cause a variety of serious side effects, including pneumonia, acute respiratory distress syndrome, and kidney failure. While the impact of a virus is dependent on individual immunity and genome structure and no single treatment can effectively treat all symptoms at present, a genome-based neural network that has already been developed for personalized care could prove for a great help in managing adverse events or symptoms caused by the coronavirus. Accelerating the development of new immunizations against developing coronaviruses [27] could be assisted by AI. Finally, AI might be used to create an automated model or correlation between medical records and outcomes. The rapid identification of diagnostic and treatment options provided by these models should improve clinical protocols for coronavirus-like epidemics. These potential benefits have led to a recent request from the White House to use AI to aid the US government in reacting to the coronavirus outbreak [28]. Disintermediation is considered to occur when there is no single entity responsible for amassing, processing, and validating all of the designed and shared data and models. Time, effort, and money spent on processes to develop and maintain a predictive model for use in clinical practice and risk management can be minimized. Blockchain-verified transactions and the data they contain are immutable; they cannot be altered or deleted, which both guarantees their veracity and increases the safety of the underlying system [29, 30].

6.4 HEALTHCARE SYSTEM

Current healthcare systems have been scrutinized after the COVID-19 epidemic. The current COVID-19 outbreak could put a strain on already overcrowded healthcare services. There is currently no reliable data monitoring mechanism [31] to provide essential healthcare organizations with the information they need about potential epidemics in real time. Unfortunately, most of what researchers know about coronaviruses now comes from disparate, unmonitored sources like the general population, hospitals, and clinical labs. Potential outbreak identification and quarantine are hampered by the use of incorrect information. The current method of coronavirus identification is time-consuming and inaccurate, frequently taking several hours to complete virus tests. In light of the speed with which the coronavirus is spreading, this cannot stand. Learning to quickly and reliably identify coronaviruses is crucial. When dealing with complicated patterns and large amounts of data, analyzing coronavirus data with human-dependent medical software is extremely challenging. When it comes to fighting pandemics, blockchain technology offers some intriguing security solutions. The blockchain can produce unalterable transaction ledgers for healthcare information exchange networks. Also, central servers are no longer required to guarantee fairness among transaction parties thanks to the integration of blockchain and smart contract technologies [32–34]. Blockchain's core features, traceability, and decentralization, are not present in more conventional security methods. In addition, blockchain technology allows for trustworthy data analyses. The first step of disease analytics is to gather the necessary data. To have high-quality disease data analytics, it is crucial to know how to guarantee the accuracy of data during data collection [35–38]. Analytical errors caused by inaccurate data or unreliable database sources can have devastating effects, such as failing to detect a life-threatening illness. Furthermore, in an emergency epidemic situation, data on contagious diseases are gathered from numerous unprotected sources, including hospitals, the general public, and the media. The quality of the data collected and analyzed would suffer as a result of these problems. Blockchain is in great demand in this setting because of the need to guarantee the integrity of the data being collected. Blockchain's consensus methods also guarantee the right sequencing of records as they go from data sources to final destinations (like hospitals or clinical labs), so ensuring data quality. These blockchain characteristics would for trustworthy illness analysis by guaranteeing precise data acquisition [39–41]. The mass surveillance of the population to monitor the coronavirus raises privacy concerns, which brings us to our final argument. To prevent the transmission of the COVID-19 coronavirus, for instance [42], healthcare groups can monitor users' cell phones without a court order. But, privacy and human rights advocates have voiced their opposition to the initiative because it could lead to the disclosure of sensitive personal information on residents, which would in turn violate their fundamental rights. Users' privacy must be ensured inside real-time monitoring systems to prevent the spread of the coronavirus. A growing number of people are interested in private blockchain networks, which employ Privacy by Blockchain Design technology to permit granular adjustment of privacy settings [43].

6.5 BLOCKCHAIN

A blockchain is a publicly distributed ledger that includes records of all legitimate and finalized transactions. These blocks are shared between all peers in the network. The length of the chain increases as more blocks are added. Blockchain technology uses asymmetric encryption and P2P distributed consensus to keep the ledger secure and private. Thus, a cryptographic hash [44] connects these blocks with timestamps. Each block typically comprises peer-verified transaction records, also called "miner" verifications. It's a never-ending process of adding blocks to the end of the chain, stretching it out. However, the header of each subsequent block is effectively a cryptographic hash and is referenced in the new block (e.g., SHA-256). Pseudonymity, transparency, and immutability [45, 46] were all prioritized during the development of each block. A Merkle tree consists of a set of nodes, each of which can be either a leaf node representing a single transaction or a non-leaf node representing the two child nodes that make up the leaf node and store their hash value. Each node can independently verify the existence and integrity of a transaction without taxing the network by comparing only the hash value of the two concatenated child nodes that make up the leaf node, as opposed to the complete Merkle tree. There will be one and only one root hash, even though each transaction will produce a new hash value whenever the top-level data is updated. The maximum number of transactions allowed in a block depends on both the block size and the size of individual transactions [47]. When the hashing algorithm is used, all blocks will be connected. Since confirmed data in the blockchain cannot be altered or removed, any new information will simply be appended to the chain of blocks. The block's digital signature and the associated link relationship are both modified whenever there is a change to the block, creating a new block. Blockchain technology is fundamentally immutable and secure [48].

6.6 DIGITAL SIGNATURE

In an untrusted scenario, asymmetric cryptography is widely employed for transaction authentication [49]. Transactions on the Blockchain are sent and verified using asymmetric cryptography. Transactions in a peer-to-peer network are signed using the sender's private key before being sent to the recipient. The elliptic curve digital signature algorithm [50] is used by the vast majority of an existing blockchain. When a transaction is requested or initiated, a block is created to represent it and sent out to the P2P network, where all peers have equal Privileges, for verification. The other nodes will receive this block shortly. Using the sender's public key and a set of predetermined block validation rules, we may verify that the block we've received is legitimate. Until all nodes agree that the block is legitimate, it will be broadcast to them. Otherwise, it will be thrown away during the process. The blockchain network only accepts and stores blocks that are legitimate [51]. With her private key, she starts a transaction that is later validated by the network. If Alice's public key is available, then anyone can check the transaction. Second, the P2P network broadcasts the trade to other nodes in the network. Third, the transaction is checked by each node against a set of rules. At step 4, once the miner has found a solution, all of the confirmed transactions will be sorted by time and included in a new block. Then, the new block will be replicated and updated on all nodes [52].

6.7 ALGORITHMS FOR BUILDING CONSENSUS

The blockchain operates with no central authority. Hence, the Byzantine Generals Problem [53], a form that was first developed in the context of distributed networks in 1982, is a crucial problem [54]. If the Byzantine generals who have surrounded the city don't all strike at once, they have very little chance of winning. In a geographically distributed setting, the presence of traitors is an open question. Hence, they will either have to attack or retreat. A similar problem faces the blockchain infrastructure. The addition of a new block to the blockchain necessitates a consensus process across all the distributed nodes, and many such methods have been devised [55].

- **PoW (Proof of Work):** PoW is the name of the consensus algorithm used by Bitcoin (PoW). A miner node with a specified amount of computing (hashing) power must prove he is not malevolent by performing the time-consuming work of mining before earning any rewards [56–58]. The node must repeatedly execute hash computations until it discovers a nonce value that is less than (or equal to) the target hash value. Nonces are difficult to produce, but other nodes can verify their authenticity with little effort. Due to the extensive computations needed, the project is prohibitively expensive (computational resources). An extreme scenario would be a 51% attack [59] on the blockchain network. By controlling more than 51% of the network's hashing power, a single miner or group of miners can prevent fresh blocks from being generated and forge transaction records to their advantage.
- **Proof of Stake (PoS):** PoS is more energy efficient than PoW. The highest-stakes nodes (those with the most money invested) are thought to be less inclined to launch an attack on the network. Since the wealthiest node is more likely to seize control of the network, making it centralized, it is unjust to make decisions based on account balances [60].
- **Delegated Proof of Stake (DPoS):** DPoS can serve the same purpose as PoS. In contrast to PoS, which selects based on any nodes, DPoS is based on a democratically representative sample of voters [61]. Delegates can be chosen by stakeholders to determine who creates and verifies blocks. Faster transaction confirmation occurs when fewer nodes are required to validate a block. The removal of untrustworthy representatives would also simplify network upkeep.
- **Proof of Capacity (PoC):** PoC is a consensus technique that, instead of relying on computational resources, uses free space on the hard disk to reach an agreement. More space means you can keep more solutions on hand, which in turn raises the probability that a new block will be created. A growing tendency is to mix many consensus algorithms to increase performance in a wide range of applications, rather than relying on a single consensus algorithm alone [62].

- **Smart Contract:** Smart contracts are a type of blockchain-based software that can run independently of human intervention. They've worked in banking, healthcare, and government, among other places. When a transaction invoking a contract is sent to the correct contract address, the system can carry out complicated programmed functionality. In a safe container, the predefined terms of the smart contract will be automatically carried out. Decentralized applications (Dapps) 544 can be built on Ethereum since it is the first open-source blockchain platform to offer Turing-complete smart contract languages. Dapps, built on the blockchain, eliminate the need for a middleman between patients and doctors by facilitating direct communication through the Ethereum network. Patients will have more say in their medical histories [48] because of this.

6.8 HEALTHCARE BLOCKCHAIN APPLICATIONS

Data management in electronic medical records: The potential of blockchain technology in healthcare settings has been an area of some initial investigation. After developing and launching a blockchain-based pilot platform in the United States, Booz Allen Hamilton Consulting was retained by the Food and Drug Administration's Office of Translational Sciences to advise them on the potential applications of the technology known as blockchain in healthcare data management. The Ethereum Foundation is in charge of the pilot project, which currently operates at four major hospitals to regulate data access via VPNs using Ethereum. Using off-chain cloud components and cryptographic strategies, IPFS may encrypt user data and reduce data replication, making it easier for users to work together on a project [63].

Blockchain and health services data Protection: There is compatibility between blockchain technology and the EU's General Data Protection Regulation (GDPR). Even though data portability, data traceability, and legal access auditing are all possible, blockchain technology is highly valued by GDPR. Information presented thus far suggests several problems may arise (real control may be decreased when the technical implementation of the smart contract over data). A possible approach that satisfies the permission requirement of the GDPR is dynamic consent management [51].

According to the GDPR [64], enterprise blockchain are thought to be especially well-suited for compliance because transactions that involve digital copies of stored data can be altered and eliminated by the private parties or authorities who own and manage the network, using a specific kind of consensus algorithm. These individual blockchains are controlled by a single entity and are restricted to users who meet strict criteria [65]. A medical chain is a blockchain application [66] that facilitates the application and approval of many healthcare agents for access to a patient's medical records and subsequent communication. Doctors, clinics, labs, pharmacies, and medical health plans are all examples of such intermediaries. Every action in the healthcare supply chain is documented in a transaction on the distributed ledger, which is permanently auditable and transparent.

6.9 AN OVERVIEW OF AI IN HEALTHCARE INFORMATION SYSTEMS

Artificial intelligence systems in healthcare typically employ either supervised or unsupervised learning. Supervised learning teaches computers to make predictions based on labeled data, where the predictors are the inputs. In contrast, the 645 unsupervised techniques do not rely on labeled data and do not try to predict an outcome. To categorize variables or observations into similar groups, it looks for patterns and correlations in the data [67, 68]. Most present machine learning architectures in the healthcare sector use supervised learning approaches [69], including ones that construct electronic phenotyping systems. This study provides a brief introduction to a variety of machine-learning techniques, including random forests, support vector machines, supervised and unsupervised models for deep learning, and neural networks [70], which are frequently used to classify clinical data from EHRs.

6.10 MANAGING EHR USING AI AND BLOCKCHAIN

Healthcare system optimization and the delivery of intelligent services are two areas where machine learning can be of assistance. One of the biggest challenges for real-world ML systems is figuring out how to keep sensitive data safe during storage, transfer, and training. The privacy and integrity of data sets are being strengthened through the integration of machine learning and blockchain [71]. To ensure the privacy and security of sensitive information while it is being shared amongst multiple computing nodes, federated learning is a machine learning approach. Sharing encrypted datasets enables medical institutions to work together to develop reliable prediction models. Blockchain as a regulator can record related training transactions in an immutable and transparent fashion, thereby establishing responsibility and fostering dependable cooperation. To improve patient care and population health, medical institutions and researchers will be more likely to share encrypted datasets under these conditions. The blockchain serves as a trustworthy foundation for ML algorithms, guaranteeing the safety of all input data. Huge datasets being shared between apps and domains is the first issue brought up by Abdellatif et al. [72]. Yet, homomorphic encryption has a very high computational cost. Hopefully, one day soon researchers will be able to encrypt private information without compromising the efficacy of machine learning in providing personalized services. Blockchain can also be used to store rollback models in the event of a high rate of erroneous predictions. The blockchain provides a secure and immutable location for storing the references to the primary data of retrained models. Retraining models referenced by blockchain pointers may enhance continuous distant system accuracies, as was argued by Gai et al. [73] in the case of irregular arrhythmia alarm rates. Smart contract manufacturing can be automated with the help of AI, leading to more reliable and versatile procedures. There has been a rise in interest in using blockchain technology in the healthcare industry from both the academic community and the entrepreneurial community [74]. In contrast to their publication [75], in which they claim to have pioneered the use of blockchain for EHR management, this report presents a system for exchanging EHRs with an emphasis on security and portability. However, implementation and verification of the system's claimed improvements remain to be done. MedRec, a distributed system for managing EHRs, was developed using blockchain technology [76]. Their in-house data storage system was paired with their modular design for ease of use and scalability. To verify the network's PoW [77], they encouraged members of the medical community and EHR stakeholders to act as miners. In return, access to the aggregated and de-identified data will be allowed. The prototype was created and tested in conjunction with the Harvard Medical

School Teaching Hospital. They proposed that to facilitate precision medicine and targeted research, future studies should concentrate on regions where miners can rank their preferences for data traits (demographic, gender, age group, etc.).

6.11 AI IN HEALTH RECORDS: CHALLENGES

The application of AI to the responsibility of keeping medical records includes considerations such as the portability and openness of the aforementioned algorithms and the need for adequate training sizes to obtain desirable levels of productivity.

- **Transparency:** A major hurdle in employing complex machine learning algorithms for phenotyping tasks, especially when the stakes are high and end-user confidence is vital, is the lack of transparency surrounding the implementation of such algorithms. When the possibilities are great, this is extremely important to remember. Some professionals, like doctors, would rather have their decision-making guided by algorithms than merely dictated [78]. On the other hand, regulatory bodies have a requirement that algorithms must be decipherable for purposes of transparency. This is because their classification system may have significant repercussions in terms of the law or finances [79]. As a consequence of this, it is of the utmost importance to enhance the interpretability of models of this "black box" variety. Extensive prior research [80] that interpreted the results of deep learning model predictions by using a method that had only recently been developed yielded impressive results. To determine the most relevant terms from clinical content, researchers [81] adopted a modified version of saliency, dubbed saliency [63], which was then used for prediction using convolutional neural networks. According to the authors, these vocabularies would be more useful to clinicians in describing and understanding the target feature than the most important traits identified by an extraction-based NLP approach. This is because these labels better describe and fit the ideal quality [82]. The use of mappings for class activation by radiologists' assessments, developed heatmaps capturing the most significant components of chest X-ray images used by their deep neural network for the prediction of chest illnesses [33]. Techniques like these to make complex machine learning models more transparent and interpretable improve the probability that doctors and other end users will adopt and employ these technologies.

- **Transportability:** A significant amount of research on electronic phenotyping was carried out in a single-site context [83]. This was done for a variety of reasons, including privacy concerns and administrative constraints. An increasing number of researchers and healthcare organizations are showing an interest in sharing their algorithms to increase their flexibility, but only if they are given sufficient time and money to do so [84]. There may be progression in this direction, as evidenced by the existence of resources like the Phenotype Knowledgebase, a website designed to aid researchers in the creation, exchange, and evaluation of electronic phenotyping algorithms [85]. However, not many phenotyping approaches have been modified for usage in a wide range of settings, especially those that make use of machine learning. Scalable phenotyping algorithms are built by first having the algorithms independently verified for portability, and then, if necessary, updating the algorithms to account for testing environment specifics. Phenotyping algorithms that make use of natural language processing systems might benefit greatly from this "validation-adaptation" approach, even though it can be extremely time-consuming and labor-intensive [86].

There are significant challenges in the way of data transparency, traceability, immutability, audit, data provenance, adaptable access, trust, privacy, and security in today's healthcare data management systems. Blockchain is a new and potentially disruptive decentralized technology that might drastically alter the current healthcare data management system (Figure 6.2).

6.12 ARTIFICIAL NEURAL NETWORKS (ANN)

It was in the 1980s that [87] popularized the use of ANNs, originally proposed by McCulloch and Pitts [86]. Many classification problems are within their capabilities. The term "neutral" refers to a class of algorithms

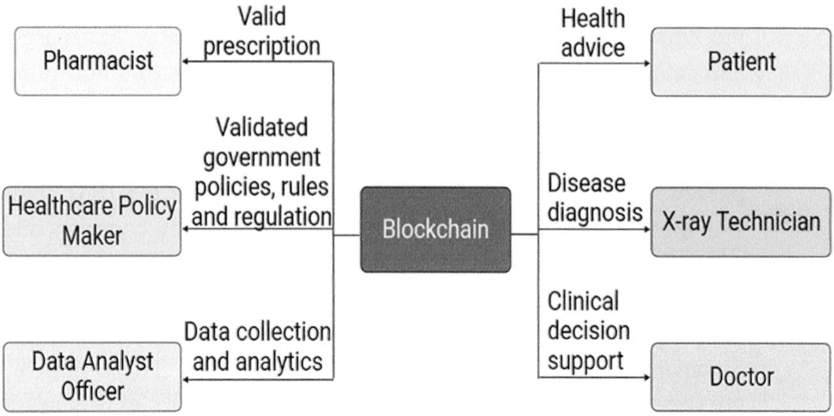

FIGURE 6.2 Blockchain's potential for managing medical records.

that draws inspiration from the way humans' brains learn to classify information. ANNs were developed as a means of simulating the human brain, which consists of a very large number of neurons connected via numerous axons. Reinforcing labeled training data can strengthen or decrease neuron connections, just as it might in biological learning [88]. This network of nerve fibers can be represented by a weighted matrix. This matrix is a "layer," like the cortical layers of the brain. A sort of 'biological learning,' the training data employed in ANNs can be thought of as a tool for human education. While input and output layers are always present in an Ann model, additional hidden layers are possible. To find answers to issues, ANNs are taught to generate a solution from a collection of inputs [89].

6.13 POTENTIAL BENEFITS OF BLOCKCHAIN IN THE HEALTHCARE INDUSTRY

The use of blockchain technology confers a variety of advantages on individuals, as well as on medical researchers and suppliers of health care [90]. The creation of a single storage site for all health data, the tracking of personalized data in real-time, and the setting of data access rights at a granular level would be beneficial to research as well as personalized care [91]. Researchers in the field of medicine require complete data sets to make significant strides in their understanding of the disease, speed up the process of biomedical discovery, keep a close eye on the rapid development of new drugs, and devise personalized treatment strategies based on the patient's genetic makeup, lifecycle, and surrounding environment [92]. If patients from a variety of racial, socioeconomic, and geographical backgrounds were included in the shared data system of Blockchain, it would produce a data set that encompassed a wide range of information. Because it captures health data throughout a person's lifetime, blockchain is an excellent source of information for longitudinal studies [93]. A healthcare blockchain will enable the incorporation of data from underserved or underrepresented groups who do not often take part in medical or scientific research [94]. Blockchain's distributed database technological setting makes it easier for traditionally "hard-to-reach" audiences to get interested, and it also allows the general public to produce results that are more reflective of the population as a whole [95]. A blockchain for the healthcare industry will almost certainly stimulate the development of a new breed of "smart" healthcare provider apps. These programs would sidestep the most recent medical research and create individualized treatment routes. Both the patient and the health care provider would have access to the same information, allowing for the possibility of engaging in a collaborative and informed discussion of treatment options that are supported by research as opposed to those that are based on the patient's best-case intuition [96].

6.14 CONCLUSION

There is a lot of curiosity about blockchain technology among individuals and businesses of all sizes. It has the potential to revolutionize established industries thanks to properties like decentralization, anonymity, durability, and audibility. It is anticipated that blockchain applications will utilize AI techniques to revolutionize the healthcare industry. The process would not only be transparent and secure, but it would also boost healthcare quality while reducing costs. In the suggested framework, the authors discuss the use of blockchain technology in healthcare, naming both the key research programs and future research opportunities. This chapter discussed several studies that propose tamper-resistant systems employing blockchain technology and AI technologies to guarantee the accuracy of health data.

KEYWORDS

- **healthcare system**
- **blockchain**
- **digital signature**
- **artificial neural networks**

REFERENCES

1. Kumari A, Tanwar S, Tyagi S, Kumar N. 2018. Fog computing for healthcare 4.0 environment: Opportunities and challenges. *Comput Electr Eng. 72*, 1–3.
2. Campanella P, Lovato E, Marone C, Fallacara L, Mancuso A, Ricciardi W, Specchia ML. 2016. The impact of electronic health records on healthcare quality: A systematic review and meta-analysis. *Eur J Public Health 26*(1), 60–64.
3. Tanwar S, Parekh K, Evans R. 2020. Blockchain-based electronic healthcare record system for healthcare 4.0 applications. *J Inf Secur Appl. 50*, 102407.
4. Mistry I, Tanwar S, Tyagi S, Kumar N. 2020. Blockchain for 5G-enabled IoT for industrial automation: A systematic review, solutions, and challenges. *Mech Syst Sig Proc. 135*, 106382.
5. Tagde P, Tagde S, Bhattacharya T, Tagde P, Chopra H, Akter R, Kaushik D, Rahman MH. 2021. Blockchain and artificial intelligence technology in e-Health. *Environ Sci Pollut Res. 28*, 52810–52831.
6. Vora J, Italiya P, Tanwar S, Tyagi S, Kumar N, Obaidat MS, Hsiao KF. 2018, Jul. Ensuring privacy and security in e-health records. In *2018 International Conference on Computer, Information and Telecommunication Systems (CITS)* (pp. 1–5). IEEE.
7. Kubo T, Yanasan A, Herbosa T, Buddh N, Fernando F, Kayano R. 2019. Health data collection before, during and after emergencies and disasters—the result of the Kobe expert meeting. *Int J Environ Res Public Health 16*(5), 893.
8. Puaschunder JM. 2019. Artificial intelligence in the healthcare sector. *SCIENTIA MORALITAS—Int J Multidisc Res 4*(2), 1–4.
9. Feng Q, He D, Zeadally S, Khan MK, Kumar N. 2019. A survey on privacy protection in blockchain system. *J Netw Comput Appl. 126*, 45–58.
10. Lin C, He D, Huang X, Khan MK, Choo KK. 2020. DCAP: A secure and efficient decentralized conditional anonymous payment system based on blockchain. *IEEE Trans Inf Forensics Secur. 15*, 2440–2452.
11. Zhang J, Cheng Y, Deng X, Wang B, Xie J, Yang Y, Zhang M. 2021. A reputation-based mechanism for transaction processing in blockchain systems. *IEEE Trans Comput. 71*(10), 2423–2434.
12. Lamport L, Shostak R, Pease M. 2019, Oct. The Byzantine generals problem. In *Concurrency: The Works of Leslie Lamport* (pp. 203–226).

13. Wang W, Hoang DT, Hu P, Xiong Z, Niyato D, Wang P, Wen Y, Kim DI. 2019. A survey on consensus mechanisms and mining strategy management in blockchain networks. *IEEE Access 7*, 22328–22370.
14. Siyal AA, Junejo AZ, Zawish M, Ahmed K, Khalil A, Soursou G. 2019. Applications of blockchain technology in medicine and healthcare: Challenges and future perspectives. *Cryptography 3*(1), 3.
15. Shahnaz A, Qamar U, Khalid A. 2019. Using blockchain for electronic health records. *IEEE Access 7*, 147782–147795.
16. Nguyen DC, Ding M, Pathirana PN, Seneviratne A. 2021. Blockchain and AI-based solutions to combat coronavirus (COVID-19)-like epidemics: A survey. *IEEE Access 9*, 95730–95753.
17. Cyran MA. 2018. Blockchain as a foundation for sharing healthcare data. *Blockchain in Healthcare Today*. 1. https://doi.org/10.30953/bhty.v1.1
18. Kaye J, Whitley EA, Lund D, Morrison M, Teare H, Melham K. 2015. Dynamic consent: A patient interface for twenty-first century research networks. *Eur J Hum Genet. 23*(2), 141–146.
19. Lima C. 2018. *Blockchain-GDPR Privacy by Design How Decentralized Blockchain Internet will Comply with GDPR Data Privacy*. IEEE Blockchain Group.
20. Villani C, Bonnet Y, Rondepierre B. 2018. For a meaningful artificial intelligence: Towards a French and European strategy. *Conseil National Numérique*.
21. Zhang P, White J, Schmidt DC, Lenz G, Rosenbloom ST. 2018. FHIRChain: Applying blockchain to securely and scalably share clinical data. *Comput Struct Biotechnol J. 16*, 267–278.
22. Salah K, Rehman MH, Nizamuddin N, Al-Fuqaha A. 2019. Blockchain for AI: Review and open research challenges. *IEEE Access 7*, 10127–10149.
23. Resta M, Sonnessa M, Tànfani E, Testi A. 2018. Unsupervised neural networks for clustering emergent patient flows. *Oper Res Health Care 18*, 41–51.
24. Omar IA, Jayaraman R, Salah K, Yaqoob I, Ellahham S. 2021. Applications of blockchain technology in clinical trials: Review and open challenges. *Arab J Sci Engineer. 46*, 3001–3015.
25. Ford E, Carroll JA, Smith HE, Scott D, Cassell JA. 2016. Extracting information from the text of electronic medical records to improve case detection: A systematic review. *J Am Med Inform Assoc. 23*(5), 1007–1015.
26. Shivade C, Raghavan P, Fosler-Lussier E, Embi PJ, Elhadad N, Johnson SB, Lai AM. 2014. A review of approaches to identifying patient phenotype cohorts using electronic health records. *J Am Med Inform Assoc. 21*(2), 221–230.
27. Foster KR, Koprowski R, Skufca JD. 2014. Machine learning, medical diagnosis, and biomedical engineering research-commentary. *Biomed Engineer Online 13*, 1–9.
28. Kemp R, Prasad V. 2017. Surrogate endpoints in oncology: When are they acceptable for regulatory and clinical decisions, and are they currently overused. *BMC Med. 15*(1), 1–7.
29. Kavakiotis I, Tsave O, Salifoglou A, Maglaveras N, Vlahavas I, Chouvarda I. 2017. Machine learning and data mining methods in diabetes research. *Comput Struct Biotechnol J. 15*, 104–116.
30. McCelloch WS, Pitts W. 1943. A logical calculus of the idea immanent in neural nets. *Bull Math Biophys. 5*, 115–133.

31. Schmidhuber J. 2015. Deep learning in neural networks: An overview. *Neural Netw. 61*, 85–117.
32. Uddin S, Khan A, Piraveenan M. 2015, Jan. Administrative claim data to learn about effective healthcare collaboration and coordination through social network. In *2015 48th Hawaii International Conference on System Sciences* (pp. 3105–3114). IEEE.
33. Dubovitskaya A, Novotny P, Thiebes S, Sunyaev A, Schumacher M, Xu Z, Wang F. 2019, August. Intelligent health care data management using blockchain: Current limitation and future research agenda. In *Heterogeneous Data Management, Polystores, and Analytics for Healthcare: VLDB 2019 Workshops, Poly and DMAH, Los Angeles, CA, USA*, Revised Selected Papers 5 2019 (pp. 277–288). Springer International Publishing.
34. Khatoon A. 2020. A blockchain-based smart contract system for healthcare management. *Electronics 9*(1), 94.
35. Yaqoob I, Salah K, Jayaraman R, Al-Hammadi Y. 2021. Blockchain for healthcare data management: Opportunities, challenges, and future recommendations. *Neural Comput Appl*. 1–6.
36. Rajawat AS, Bedi P, Goyal SB, Shaw RN, Ghosh A, Aggarwal S. 2022. Ai and blockchain for healthcare data security in smart cities. In *AI and IoT for Smart City Applications* (pp. 185–198).
37. Quasim MT, Algarni F, Radwan AA, Alshmrani GM. 2020, Jul. A blockchain based secured healthcare framework. In *2020 International Conference on Computational Performance Evaluation (ComPE)* (pp. 386–391). IEEE.
38. Theodouli A, Arakliotis S, Moschou K, Votis K, Tzovaras D. 2018, Aug. On the design of a blockchain-based system to facilitate healthcare data sharing. In *2018 17th IEEE International Conference on Trust, Security and Privacy in Computing and Communications/12th IEEE International Conference on Big Data Science and Engineering (TrustCom/BigDataSE)* (pp. 1374–1379). IEEE.
39. Pham QV, Nguyen DC, Huynh-The T, Hwang WJ, Pathirana PN. 2020. Artificial intelligence (AI) and big data for coronavirus (COVID-19) pandemic: A survey on the state-of-the-arts. *IEEE Access 8*, 130820–130839.
40. Xu W, Zhang J, Zhang Q, Wei X. 2017, Feb. Risk prediction of type II diabetes based on random forest model. In *2017 Third International Conference on Advances in Electrical, Electronics, Information, Communication and Bio-Informatics (AEEICB)* (pp. 382–386). IEEE.
41. Forssen H, Patel R, Fitzpatrick N, Hingorani A, Timmis A, Hemingway H, Denaxas S. 2017. Evaluation of machine learning methods to predict coronary artery disease using metabolomic data. In *Stud Health Technol Inform* (Vol. 235, pp. 111–115). IOS Press.
42. Liang X, Zhao J, Shetty S, Liu J, Li, D. 2017. Oct. Integrating blockchain for data sharing and collaboration in mobile healthcare applications. In *2017 IEEE 28th Annual International Symposium on Personal, Indoor, and Mobile Radio Communications (PIMRC)* (pp. 1–5). IEEE.
43. Zheng X, Mukkamala RR, Vatrapu R, Ordieres-Mere J. 2018, Sep. Blockchain-based personal health data sharing system using cloud storage. In *2018 IEEE 20th International Conference on e-health Networking, Applications and Services (Healthcom)* (pp. 1–6). IEEE.

44. Yaji S, Bangera K, Neelima B. 2018, Dec. Privacy preserving in blockchain based on partial homomorphic encryption system for AI applications. In *2018 IEEE 25th International Conference on High Performance Computing Workshops (HiPCW)* (pp. 81–85). IEEE.
45. Juneja A, Marefat M. 2018, Mar. Leveraging blockchain for retraining deep learning architecture in patient-specific arrhythmia classification. In *2018 Ieee Embs International Conference on Biomedical & Health Informatics (bhi)* (pp. 393–397). IEEE.
46. Ekblaw A, Azaria A, Halamka JD, Lippman A. 2016, Aug. A Case Study for Blockchain in Healthcare: "MedRec" prototype for electronic health records and medical research data. In *Proceedings of IEEE open & Big Data Conference* (Vol. 13, p. 13).
47. Yue X, Wang H, Jin D, Li M, Jiang W. 2016. Healthcare data gateways: Found healthcare intelligence on blockchain with novel privacy risk control. *J Med Syst. 40*, 1–8.
48. Dubovitskaya A, Xu Z, Ryu S, Schumacher M, Wang F. 2017. Secure and trustable electronic medical records sharing using blockchain. In *AMIA Annual Symposium Proceedings* (Vol. 2017, p. 650). American Medical Informatics Association.
49. Lai L, Suda N. 2018, Jun. Rethinking machine learning development and deployment for edge devices. arXiv preprint arXiv:1806.07846.
50. Dinh TT, Wang J, Chen G, Liu R, Ooi BC, Tan KL. 2017, May. Blockbench: A framework for analyzing private blockchains. In *Proceedings of the 2017 ACM International Conference on Management of Data* (pp. 1085–1100).
51. Li Z, Kang J, Yu R, Ye D, Deng Q, Zhang Y. 2017. Consortium blockchain for secure energy trading in industrial internet of things. *IEEE Trans Industr Inform. 14*(8), 3690–700.
52. Hwang GH, Chen PH, Lu CH, Chiu C, Lin HC, Jheng AJ. 2018. InfiniteChain: A multi-chain architecture with distributed auditing of sidechains for public blockchains. In *Blockchain–ICBC 2018: First International Conference, Held as Part of the Services Conference Federation, SCF 2018, Seattle, WA, USA, June 25–30, 2018, Proceedings* (pp. 47–60). Springer International Publishing.
53. King S, Nadal S. 2012. Ppcoin: Peer-to-peer crypto-currency with proof-of-stake. self-published paper, August. *19*(1).
54. Tschorsch F, Scheuermann B. 2016. Bitcoin and beyond: A technical survey on decentralized digital currencies. *IEEE Commun Surv Tutor. 18*(3), 2084–2123.
55. Zhang J, Xue N, Huang X. 2016. A secure system for pervasive social network-based healthcare. *IEEE Access 4*, 9239–9250.
56. Xia QI, Sifah EB, Asamoah KO, Gao J, Du X, Guizani M. 2017. MeDShare: Trust-less medical data sharing among cloud service providers via blockchain. *IEEE Access 5*, 14757–14767.
57. Jiang S, Cao J, Wu H, Yang Y, Ma M, He J. 2018, Jun. Blochie: A blockchain-based platform for healthcare information exchange. In *2018 Ieee International Conference on Smart Computing (smartcomp)* (pp. 49–56). IEEE.
58. Fan K, Wang S, Ren Y, Li H, Yang Y. 2018. Medblock: Efficient and secure medical data sharing via blockchain. *J Med Syst. 42*, 1–1.

59. Crosby M, Pattanayak P, Verma S, Kalyanaraman V. 2016. Blockchain technology: Beyond bitcoin. *Appl Innov*. *2*(6–10), 71.
60. Guo R, Shi H, Zhao Q, Zheng D. 2018. Secure attribute-based signature scheme with multiple authorities for blockchain in electronic health records systems. *IEEE Access 6*, 11676–11686.
61. Uddin MA, Stranieri A, Gondal I, Balasubramanian V. 2018. Continuous patient monitoring with a patient centric agent: A block architecture. *IEEE Access 6*, 32700–32726.
62. Zhang Y, Zeng D, Luo J, Xu Z, King I. 2023, Feb. A survey of trustworthy federated learning with perspectives on security, robustness, and privacy. arXiv preprint arXiv:2302.10637..
63. Wehbe Y, Al Zaabi M, Svetinovic D. 2018, Nov. Blockchain AI framework for healthcare records management: Constrained goal model. In *2018 26th Telecommunications forum (TELFOR)* (pp. 420–425). IEEE.
64. Yüksel B, Küpçü A, Özkasap Ö. 2017. Research issues for privacy and security of electronic health services. *Fut Gen Comput Syst. 68*, 1–3.
65. Houtan B, Hafid AS, Makrakis D. 2020. A survey on blockchain-based self-sovereign patient identity in healthcare. *IEEE Access 8*, 90478–90494.
66. Ferrag MA, Derdour M, Mukherjee M, Derhab A, Maglaras L, Janicke H. 2018. Blockchain technologies for the internet of things: Research issues and challenges. *IEEE IoT J. 6*(2), 2188–2204.
67. De Aguiar EJ, Faiçal BS, Krishnamachari B, Ueyama J. 2020. A survey of blockchain-based strategies for healthcare. *ACM Comput Surveys (CSUR) 53*(2), 1–27.
68. Rundo L, Pirrone R, Vitabile S, Sala E, Gambino O. 2020. Recent advances of HCI in decision-making tasks for optimized clinical workflows and precision medicine. *J Biomed Inform. 108*, 103479.
69. Kamel Boulos MN, Wilson JT, Clauson KA. 2018. Geospatial blockchain: Promises, challenges, and scenarios in health and healthcare. *Int J Health Geograph. 17*(1), 1–10.
70. Bhattacharya P, Tanwar S, Bodkhe U, Tyagi S, Kumar N. 2019. Bindaas: Blockchain-based deep-learning as-a-service in healthcare 4.0 applications. *IEEE Trans Netw Sci Engineer*. *8*(2), 1242–1255.
71. Corea F. 2017. The convergence of AI and Blockchain: What's the deal. (Accessed October 6, 2020).
72. Abdellatif AA, Samara L, Mohamed A, Erbad A, Chiasserini CF, Guizani M, O'Connor MD, Laughton J. 2021. Medge-chain: Leveraging edge computing and blockchain for efficient medical data exchange. *IEEE IoT J. 8*(21), 15762–15775.
73. Gai K, Wu Y, Zhu L, Xu L, Zhang Y. 2019. Permissioned blockchain and edge computing empowered privacy-preserving smart grid networks. *IEEE IoT J. 6*(5), 7992–8004.
74. Yang R, Yu FR, Si P, Yang Z, Zhang Y. 2019. Integrated blockchain and edge computing systems: A survey, some research issues and challenges. *IEEE Commun Surv Tutor*. *21*(2), 1508–1532.
75. De Filippi P. 2016. The interplay between decentralization and privacy: The case of blockchain technologies. *J Peer Prod Issue 14*(7).

76. Li C, Palanisamy B. 2019, Jun. Incentivized blockchain-based social media platforms: A case study of steemit. In *Proceedings of the 10th ACM Conference on Web Science* (pp. 145–154).
77. Mehta N, Devarakonda MV. 2018. Machine learning, natural language programming, and electronic health records: The next step in the artificial intelligence journey. *J Allergy Clin Immunol. 141*(6), 2019–2021.
78. Santosh KC, Gaur L, Santosh KC, Gaur L. 2021. Introduction to ai in public health. In *Artificial Intelligence and Machine Learning in Public Healthcare: Opportunities and Societal Impact* (pp. 1–10).
79. Stanfill MH, Marc DT. 2019. Health information management: Implications of artificial intelligence on healthcare data and information management. *Yearbook Med Inform. 28*(01), 56–64.
80. Hernandez Medrano I, Tello Guijarro J, Belda C, Ureña A, Salcedo I, Espinosa-Anke L, Saggion H. Savana: Re-using electronic health records with artificial intelligence.
81. Dinh-Le C, Chuang R, Chokshi S, Mann D. 2019. Wearable health technology and electronic health record integration: Scoping review and future directions. *JMIR Mhealth Uhealth 7*(9), e12861.
82. Reddy S, Allan S, Coghlan S, Cooper P. 2020. A governance model for the application of AI in health care. *J Am Med Inform Assoc. 27*(3), 491–497.
83. Jim HS, Hoogland AI, Brownstein NC, Barata A, Dicker AP, Knoop H, Gonzalez BD, Perkins R, Rollison D, Gilbert SM, Nanda R. 2020. Innovations in research and clinical care using patient-generated health data. *CA: Cancer J Clin. 70*(3), 182–199.
84. Neill DB. 2013. Using artificial intelligence to improve hospital inpatient care. *IEEE Intell Syst. 28*(2), 92–95.
85. Gerke S, Minssen T, Cohen G. 2020. Ethical and legal challenges of artificial intelligence-driven healthcare. In *Artificial Intelligence in Healthcare* (pp. 295–336). Academic Press.
86. Agatonovic-Kustrin S, Beresford R. 2000. Basic concepts of artificial neural network (ANN) modeling and its application in pharmaceutical research. *J Pharm Biomed Anal. 22*(5), 717–727.
87. Zupan J. 1994. Introduction to artificial neural network (ANN) methods: What they are and how to use them. *Acta Chimica Slovenica. 41*, 327-.
88. Bourquin J, Schmidli H, van Hoogevest P, Leuenberger H. 1997. Basic concepts of artificial neural networks (ANN) modeling in the application to pharmaceutical development. *Pharm Dev Technol. 2*(2), 95–109.
89. Mishra M, Srivastava M. 2014, Aug. A view of artificial neural network. In *2014 International Conference on Advances in Engineering & Technology Research (ICAETR-2014)* (pp. 1–3). IEEE.
90. Mettler M. 2016, Sep. Blockchain technology in healthcare: The revolution starts here. In *2016 IEEE 18th International Conference on e-health Networking, Applications and Services (Healthcom)* (pp. 1–3). IEEE.
91. Attaran M. 2022. Blockchain technology in healthcare: Challenges and opportunities. *Int J Healthc Manag. 15*(1), 70–83.
92. El-Gazzar R, Stendal K. 2020. Blockchain in health care: Hope or hype. *J Med Internet Res. 22*(7), e17199.

93. Schinckus C. 2022. A nuanced perspective on blockchain technology and healthcare. *Technol Soc. 71*, 102082.
94. Angraal S, Krumholz HM, Schulz WL. 2017. Blockchain technology: Applications in health care. *Circulation: Cardiovasc Qual Outcomes 10*(9), e003800.
95. Spanò R, Massaro M, Iacuzzi S. 2021. Blockchain for value creation in the healthcare sector. *Technovation 120*, 102440.
96. Sharma M, Joshi S. 2021. Barriers to blockchain adoption in health-care industry: An Indian perspective. *J Glob Oper Strateg Sourc. 14*(1), 134–169.

CHAPTER 7

Transforming Cardiovascular Health: AI-Driven Diagnostic and Therapeutic Strategies

*Corresponding author

ABSTRACT

Artificial intelligence (AI), the process of collecting data through intricate databases using advanced machine learning techniques, has become integrated into the field of medicine. AI methods have demonstrated the ability to expedite the advancement of diagnosing and treating cardiovascular disorders (CVDs), such as a condition known as heart failure (HF), atrial fibrillation, and heart rhythm disorders, such as hypertrophic cardiomyopathy or congenital cardiac defects. In medical applications, AI has demonstrated its effectiveness in diagnosing CVD, improving the performance of supplementary devices, stratifying and categorizing disorders, and predicting outcomes. It is anticipated that contemporary AI techniques, which are developed to discover complex sequences in massive healthcare records, will be able to perform more challenging tasks than previous approaches. This chapter provides a summary of the most recent uses of AI in the field of cardiology (CVDs). The purpose of this chapter is to provide practitioners, who have little experience in AI, a comprehensive overview of current advances in AI and the efficient incorporation of algorithms based on AI into medical procedures.

7.1 INTRODUCTION

Artificial intelligence (AI) is a subfield of computer science that focuses on the creation of sophisticated computers and systems that can imitate and

Computational Intelligence for Patient Care: Blockchain, AI, and ML in Healthcare.
Rishabha Malviya, Rishav Sharma, Sathvik Belagodu Sridhar, and Suraj Kumar (Authors)

DOI: 10.1201/9781779640819-7

improve individuals intellectual abilities to address challenging problems [1]. In the realm of medicine, AI is used to duplicate human cognitive functions to effectively manage and analyze massive volumes of therapeutic data. Activities that involve comprehending, interpreting, collaborating, and analyzing various types of therapeutic data, such as individual patient data, ultrasonography pictures, medication, and research discoveries, are included in this category [2]. Traditional algorithms for big data produce particular outcomes that medical professionals can utilize to enhance being diagnosed. For instance, AI algorithms are presently used for diagnosing cardiac failure, atrial fibrillation (AF), iron deficiency cardiomyopathy with hypertrophic remodeling, and pulmonary arterial hypertension by processing cardiac echocardiogram (ECG) data [3–9]. After being verified and evaluated, strategies may be used in healthcare facilities to decrease the mental strain on doctors. They can provide prediagnosis and rectify mistakes made by medical professionals while avoiding misinterpretation from happening [10].

AI utilizes machine learning (ML), which can capture intricate relationships from a set of information instead of being explicitly programmed. These minor findings have the potential to greatly impact the advancement of human illness in terms of predicting, diagnosing, prognosis, and recovering from them [11]. The branches associated with AI include neural networks and ML [12]. Assisted in teaching, unstructured guidance, and educational opportunities are the three general categories into which ML can be divided. There was a lack of external assessment throughout education and training [13]. Supervised instruction involves adjusting the characteristics of a classifier to reach the desired level of efficiency.

Supervised instruction encompasses several techniques such as neural network modeling, regression, statistical in nonlinear logic, Bayes naïve, reasoning trees, randomized plants, assisting vector algorithms, K-nearest neighbor, and neural networks [14]. The use of unstructured computational learning is a methodology used to classify specimens based on the statistical evaluation of an extensive number of specimens lacking any particular category information. It includes techniques such as clustering and associating rule-learning techniques [15]. A reinforcement learning approach may be seen as a fusion of unsupervised as well as supervised learning, using trial and error to enhance the precision of programs [16]. The methods mentioned above are not entirely autonomous. For instance, the deep learning (DL) algorithm may use an artificial neural network (ANN).

At present, some of the most often used technologies for healthcare applications are DL, ANNs, and assistance vector machines [17]. ANNs and support vector machines (SVMs) can effectively handle big and complex datasets, even when there are nonlinear relationships present [18]. ANNs excel in evaluating ECG data [19], while SVMs are effective in illness stratification [20]. However, ANNs and SVMs are unable to handle all circumstances identically due to the problems of overfitting, underfitting, and misspecification [21]. DL has a commendable level of proficiency when it comes to handling picture data. In the field of cardiopulmonary medical practice, the prevailing algorithmic approaches to DL encompass convolutional neural networks (CNNs), recurrent neuronal networks, and deep cognitive networks [22]. Despite the presence of both benefits and drawbacks, these techniques demonstrate effective performance in the evaluation, prognosis, and stratification of cardiovascular disorders (CVDs). The flowchart illustrating the implementation of AI in medical procedures is illustrated in Figure 7.1.

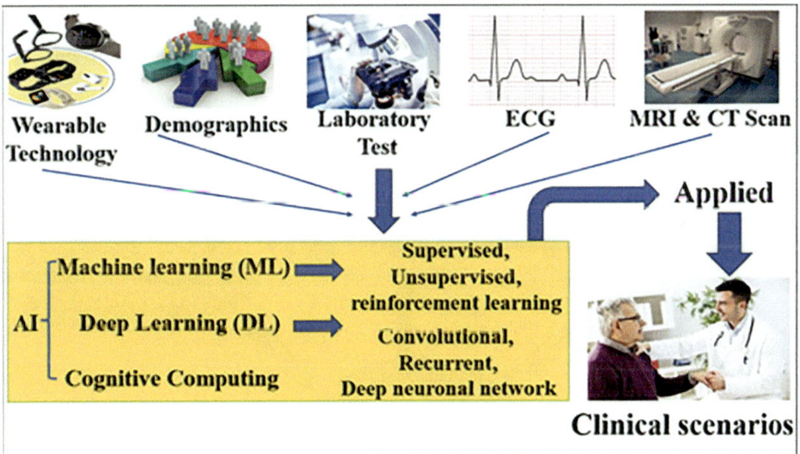

FIGURE 7.1 Implementation of AI in medical procedures is illustrated.

The recipient running essential for assessing a given approach is its distinctive curves and the region underneath the curve [23]. Generally, an area under the curve (AUC) larger than 0.70 is considered to have superior predictive ability [24]. In the field of cardiopulmonary medicine, numerous choices are based on electronic health records, such as electrocardiograms (ECGs) and cardiac ECGs. AI methods have demonstrated significant advantages in benefiting patients with various kinds of CVDs in diverse scenarios, as seen in Figures 7.2 and 7.3. This study is aimed at offering clinicians a thorough examination of the application of AI in CVDs from a clinician's viewpoint. The goal is to enhance medical professionals' awareness and AI in the field.

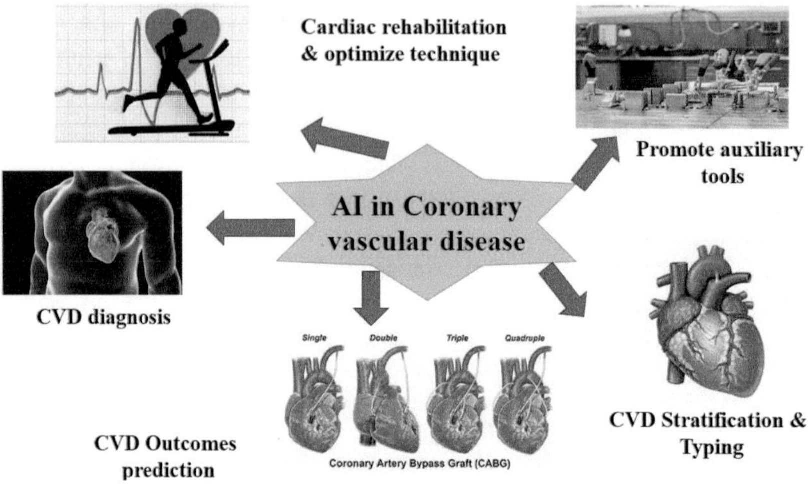

FIGURE 7.2 Situation of AI application in CV.

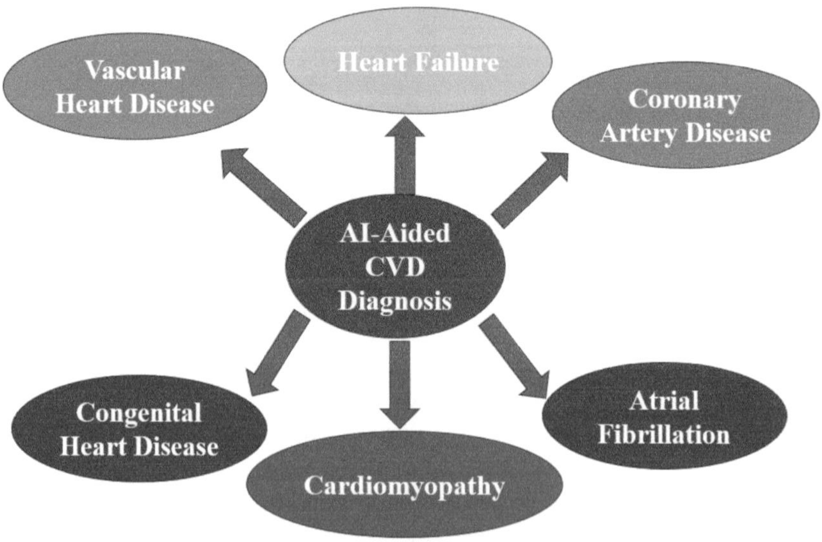

FIGURE 7.3 Types of diseases of AI application in CVD.

7.2 AI-AIDED CVD DIAGNOSIS

Prompt identification, assessment, and intervention play a crucial role in impeding the advancement of CVDs and enhancing general outcomes. It is generally agreed upon that ECGs and magnetic resonance imaging (MRIs) are particularly trustworthy methods for identifying specific CVDs. These include myocardial anomalies, heart valve stenosis, and cardiac dilation, among others [25–28]. On the other hand, these more sophisticated procedures are often saved for people experiencing ailments that are suggestive of these illnesses, as opposed to people who are asymptomatic yet might continue suffering from a medical condition [27]. As a result of the substantial cost and the need for specialized expertise, many diagnostic equipment have hindrances that make them impractical for broad prophylactic monitoring. Numerous constraints are a result of the fact that they are expensive. Because of this, attempts to diagnose cardiovascular conditions at an earlier stage are made more difficult [26, 29, 30] As a consequence of this, a significant number of people could not receive a diagnosis unless the illness has advanced to significantly more serious stages of development, which can result in negative health consequences, especially in more severe instances.

ECG is a straightforward and readily accessible therapy technique that is often used, especially in regions with scarce facilities [31]. ECG has long been a powerful tool for diagnosing CVDs, providing crucial diagnostic data. Nevertheless, the medical assessment of the ECG relies on their degree of knowledge and skill [31]. In addition, the initial ECG waveform consists of a large number of details, making it challenging for clinicians to analyze. This constraint hinders the full utilization of its benefits [30]. Due to its robust computational capabilities, graphical interpretation proficiency, and computational aptitude, AI can identify delicate and significant details within ECG waveforms that physicians are unable to see. This implies that AI can establish the correlation between ECG features and specific CVDs [31, 32]. We will thoroughly examine the most recent developments in using AI technology to analyze ordinary 12-lead ECGs to diagnose CVDs.

7.3 VALVULAR HEART DISEASE

Several valvular cardiac diseases have extended durations without symptoms [33]. Nevertheless, when signs manifest, the fatality rate experiences a significant surge [34]. Monitoring people with no symptoms and performing valve reconstruction in those with symptoms often lead to favorable results [33]. However, the task of identifying these individuals with no symptoms continues to be difficult. EKG is the definitive method for confirming identification of valvular cardiac disorders; however, it is not appropriate for use as a form of risk assessment [35]. Consequently, the question of the fact that an artificial intelligence-enhanced echocardiogram (AI-ECG) might be a practical way to evaluate people without symptoms has been widely discussed. Kwon et al. [35] created an algorithm for DL that combines a multilayered perceptron and CNN to identify mild to severe acute aortic stenosis (AS) using ECGs. The AUC values for detecting significant AS during both internal and external assessment were 0.88 and 0.86, respectively. A sensitivity analysis revealed that the technique that specifically targets the T-wave pattern of the precordial leads is utilized to identify the existence of AS. Remarkably, at the moment of operation when sensitivity is very substantial, the negative predictive accuracy exceeds 99%. This indicates that the methodology has the potential to serve as an assessment instrument for ruling out AS. This work has been corroborated by others. Shelly et al. [36] created a CNN model to examine adults who were treated for moderate to serious AS using ECG and echocardiography data. The study included a total of 129,788 individuals. The AI-ECG demonstrated excellent performance in its evaluation group, which included 102,926 people.

The overall precision of the data was 74%, and the negative value of prediction was 98.9%. Upon including age and gender in the model. The AUC was enhanced to 0.90. In addition, Elias and colleagues (30) created the Valve Nett DL model, which achieved an AUC of 0.88, 0.77, and 0.83 for the identification of mild to severe AS, aortic regurgitation AR, and mitral valve regurgitation, respectively, using an ECG. The AUC of the combination of any of them was 0.84. Subgroup studies demonstrated that the methodology performed equally well across all genders, ethnicities, and races. These findings suggest that the AI-ECG may have the ability to be used as a screening tool for HF with valvular disease.

7.4 ATRIAL FIBRILLATION

AF, particularly chaotic AF, is often without symptoms and difficult to detect [37]. Individuals diagnosed with AF often exhibit a regular cardiac rhythm known as a typical sinus pattern during ECG monitoring. However, this may sometimes result in the condition being overlooked or not diagnosed accurately [38]. Nevertheless, the configuration of the heart undergoes alterations after AF is established. Thus, normal sinus-rhythm ECGs can exhibit small alterations that may be detected by a well-trained neural system forecast AF [6]. Attia et al. [6] have used a CNN to detect individuals who have AF throughout regular sinus rhythm by analyzing a conventional 10-second, 12-lead ECG. The simulated heart underwent training using about 500,000 ECGs. The application of the framework to an evaluation set resulted in an AUC of 0.87 for the identification of AF from sinus-rhythm ECGs, with a total reliability of 79.4%. By evaluating the simulation model on all of the ECGs within the specified time frame that is relevant for each individual (from 31 days before the first observed AF ECG to the present day), the AUC elevated to 0.90, resulting in an enhanced overall precision of 88.3%. The results obtained demonstrate that this method can distinguish between people with AF from those with normal rhythms based on ECG data.

Subsequently, Khurshid et al. [39] conducted a comparison of the precision and association between AI-ECG and CHARGE-AF (Cohorts for Heart and Ageing Studies in Genetic Database of Medical Information—Atrial Fibrillation) ratings scores in forecasting the likelihood of subsequent AF risk in three distinct test groups. During a 5-year further investigation period, AI-ECG demonstrated prognostic utility for CHARGE-AF in forecasting the occurrence of AF. The AUC values for the model, Brigham and Women's Hospital, and the United Kingdom Biobank were 0.823 compared to 0.802, 0.747 compared to 0.752, and 0.705 compared to 0.732, respectively. Through the integration of AI-ECG and CHARGE-AF, the model demonstrated improved accuracy across many prognostic model parameters compared to CHARGE-AF alone. It appears that AI-ECGs have the potential to be an effective method for forecasting the possibility of recurrent atrial flutter. Furthermore, AI can predict future occurrences and evaluate risk categorization to comprehend the effects of AF. To analyze ECGs and categorize participants into vulnerable or minimal-risk groupings, AI was utilized in cohort research conducted by Noseworthy et al. [40], which included 1003 participants who had ischemic stroke markers but had a regular sinus rhythm. After that, mobile heart rhythm monitors were sent to each subject to identify AF over 30 days. Based on the results of the investigation, it was shown that persons with high risk had a much greater chance of suffering from infarction in contrast to people who were low risk (7.6% vs 1.6%). Over 9.9 months, the group of patients that was subjected to AI-guided monitoring had a greater rate of AF detection in comparison to the group that received normal therapy. This provides evidence that AI-based ECGs are capable of accurately identifying patients who are at a greater risk of developing AF, which might lead to improved outcomes using immediate intervention.

7.5 CORONARY ARTERY DISEASE (CAD)

Betancur et al. [41] attempted to construct a DL algorithm to forecast CAD using single-photon emission computed tomography (SPECT) imaging, coronary artery perfusion imaging (myocardial perfusion imaging (MPI)). A total of 1638 individuals who did not have CAD patients underwent anxiousness single-photon emissions computerized tomographic cardiac perfusion image processing, and pervasive myocardial angioplasty six months after the MPI. The model underwent evaluation using a stratified tenfold cross-validation procedure. The area under the receiver operating characteristic curve (AUC) for CAD prediction was 0.80 per individual and 0.76 per vessel, indicating that DL may assist in the interpretation of MPI and accurately forecast prospective CAD. There is a correlation between certain facial characteristics and a higher likelihood of developing certain illnesses [42]. DL also allows for illness screening based on face characteristics [43, 44]. Lin et al. [43] developed and tested a DL method to identify CAD by analyzing facial photographs of 5796 individuals. The DL algorithm achieved an AUC of 0.73 and a success rate of 68% in recognizing CAD in the specimen set, which consisted of 1013 individuals.

7.6 HEART FAILURE

Left ventricular ejection fraction (LVEF), a crucial indicator of the pumping efficiency of the left ventricle, is frequently assessed by ECG [26]. During the first phase of CAD, individuals may have unconsciously left ventricular dysfunction for a prolonged time due to a minor reduction in the LVEF [3, 5]. Effective therapy for individuals with HF is crucial for enhancing their respective left ventricle systolic functions, preventing future deterioration of LVEF and irreversible CAD, and improving both the likelihood of survival and the quality of life [45]. Nevertheless, an ECG is not feasible for patients who are asymptomatic due to its high cost and limited availability [5, 26]. Recent investigations have shown that AI-ECG has the potential to be used in the diagnosis of asymptomatic left ventricular dysfunction. A complete neuronal network was created by Attia and colleagues by using electrocardiography and ECG information gathered from 44,959 patients. The corresponding neural network was designed for patients with defective ventricular contractions purely based on ECG data. An AUC score of 0.93 was attained by the ML algorithm when it underwent evaluation on a group of 52,870 patients. This stage of achievement indicates that the algorithm is doing exceptionally well. In addition to that, the software exhibited an accuracy rate of 55.7%. Following a median of 3.4 decades of further investigation, individuals who tested optimistic for inappropriate AI-ECG but adverse for electrocardiography (false positive) were found to be four times more likely to construct a left ventricular defect contrasted to individuals who were identified to possess an adequate ejection fraction (EF) by both methods. This suggests that the network of machines not only detects individuals who have left ventricular dysfunction but also identifies inappropriate patterns of ECGs that become symptoms of ventricular dysfunction. Similarly, Yao et al. [5] created an AI system to detect individuals who had a low ejection fraction using their ECG. A total of 22,641 individuals suffering from HF and 120 healthcare professionals from 45 healthcare facilities were assigned at random to either the targeted group or control groups. The group that received the intervention was given the ability to view AI-ECG findings. This research discovered that the use of an AI ECG resulted in a 32% enhancement in the detection of poor EF, in contrast to the placebo arm, during 90 days following an ECG examination. In addition, the AI-ECG significantly enhanced the detection of low EF, particularly when used in ambulatory settings (or = 1.71). Based on this information, it could be concluded that AI-ECGs have the potential to dramatically boost the rapid recognition of persons who have inadequate EF in both traditional therapeutic contexts and those with a shortage of assets. On the other hand, right-sided cardiomyopathy is frequently misdiagnosed in healthcare settings. This is probably because there are no accurate techniques available to evaluate the level of functioning of the right ventricle. Nevertheless, there is a significant connection between the malfunction of the right ventricle, the malfunction of the left ventricle, and the total ailment of the cardiopulmonary system. Consequently, there is an immediate and pressing desire for equipment that is capable of reliably detecting and predicting heart function.

Through the use of ECG data, Vaid et al. [26] created a deep-learning model that was intended to anticipate both left and right ventricular performance. An AUC of 0.84 was achieved by an AI-ECG model, which displayed outstanding abilities in identifying right ventricular systolic dysfunction throughout inner as well as external databases. With an AUC of 0.94, it was also able to successfully identify individuals who had an LVEF of forty percent or below. Based on these results, it appears that the DL algorithm is capable of extracting beneficial details on the operation of the biventricular chambers from ECG data. A substantial amount of opportunity exists for the improvement of the detection and treatment of cardiac diseases with the use of AI-ECG.

7.7 CARDIOMYOPATHY

Dilated cardiomyopathy, often known as DC, is a medical condition that frequently leads to CAD and is characterized by a decreased LVEF. Those who have distant relatives who are afflicted with DC have a greater chance of having the ailment themself and are more susceptible to passing away unexpectedly [28]. As a consequence of this, certain members of the family require echocardiographic assessments regularly [29]. The performance of echocardiographic surveillance on unresponsive patients, on the other hand, is physically impossible. A CNN model was built by Shrivastava and his colleagues to identify DC at the beginning by utilizing ECG information [45]. This was done to solve the issue. In research that included 421 individuals who had DC and 16,025 persons with appropriate ventricle function, the AI-ECG approach was able to obtain an AUC of 0.955 for identifying a LVEF equal to or less than 45%, with an unacceptable probability ratio that exceeded 99% [25]. According to these results, AI-ECGs have the potential to act as a first assessment tool for DC, hence assisting in determining when additional echocardiographic assessment is required.

However, its utility as a means of screening for LVH is restricted due to its expensive nature and constrained accessibility. Khurshid et al. [46] used a CNN to develop an algorithm using ECGs from 32,239 people. The objective was to forecast the left ventricular mass (LVM), as assessed by cardiac magnetic resonance, utilizing a 12-lead ECG (LVM-AI).

During the evaluation process using two separate test sets, LVM-AI demonstrated a predictive accuracy of 0.653 and 0.621 for detecting LVH. These results indicate that LVM-AI had a modest capability to differentiate LVH. Hypertrophic cardiomyopathy (HCM) is a prominent contributor to the occurrence of unexpected death from CVD in adolescents [47]. Early detection of HCM may avoid a cardiac arrest caused by the condition. HCM may be diagnosed by ECGs, a technique that is challenging to employ in patients who do not show any symptoms [31]. While over 90% of individuals with HCM have ECG anomalies, these anomalies are nonspecific and cannot be differentiated from those seen in other disorders [48]. AI-ECG has the potential to be a very effective technique for diagnosing HCM. Ko et al. [8] conducted training and validation of an AI-ECG using a dataset of 2448 individuals diagnosed with HCM and 51,153 people lacking HCM who corresponded in terms of gender and years of age. When using this approach to identify HCM based on ECG data in an evaluation sample consisting of 612 individuals who had HCM and 12,788 placebo recipients, the AUC was 0.96. The precision of the data was 87% and the specificity was 90%. Remarkably, this model exhibited exceptional performance specifically for people under the age of 40, indicating that AI-ECG might be a viable method for evaluating HCM. In addition to ECG, AI also offers distinct benefits in computerized tomography [49], ultrasonography [50], SPECT MPI [41], and other areas. AI-powered DL algorithms can detect some illnesses only based on face characteristics. This enables the screening of a large number of individuals within an extended [43, 44].

7.8 CONGENITAL HEART DISEASE (CHD)

CHD is the most prevalent fetal condition, leading to significant postnatal death [51]. The identification of CHD while pregnant is often limited by the absence of specialized ultrasound technicians or the absence of essential frames for images necessary for reliable diagnosis. As a result, the rate of recognition of CHD in medical practice is typically rather low [52]. AI-ECG, with its developed AI models, can identify aberrant picture frames that may be challenging for clinicians to distinguish, hence enhancing the recognition of CHD [50]. Recent research conducted by Arnaout and colleagues utilized a machine-learning neural network to differentiate between hearts with normal function and those that were affected by CAD. During the training process, the equipment was educated using almost one hundred thousand pictures obtained from diagnostic ultrasonography and echocardiographic tests carried out during the ages of 18 and 24 weeks of pregnancy. In the simulation data set, the algorithm achieved an AUC of 0.99, indicating that it was able to differentiate between typical myocardial and diseased cardiomyopathy with an outstanding level of precision. Furthermore, it had an adverse predictive value of 100%. In addition to this, the model worked well on photographs that were obtained outside of medical environments as well as on visuals of lesser quality. This suggests that using DL-based screening ultrasonography might enhance the diagnosis of congenital heart defects in fetuses. AI algorithms may assist physicians in making more informed judgments [5, 29, 49]. Due to the widespread use of AI and technological advances, models based on AI have the potential to assist in disease identification and enhance the prompt identification and management of illnesses in resource-constrained environments [6, 29, 31].

7.9 AI IMPROVES THE EFFICIENCY OF SUPPLEMENTARY INSTRUMENTS

AI methods have the potential to enhance the efficiency of auxiliary technologies, including computed tomography, ECGs, and MRI. LVEF is a crucial factor in determining the long-term outcome of HF, as well as in guiding the use of resynchronization medication and defibrillators. Two-dimensional ultrasonography is commonly employed in healthcare settings as a precise method for evaluating EF. Typically, quantitative EF necessitates advanced abilities to carefully track end-diastolic and end-systolic frameworks, which is a laborious task. Autonomous EF is an AI-learned algorithm that efficiently computes the executive function. Asch et al. [53] introduced an ML system that could automate and precisely measure LVEF. The ML approach demonstrated similar precision to that of doctors in retrieving LVEF. The highly skilled, sophisticated methodology allowed nurses to continuously monitor patients' LVEF without the need for an experienced sonographer, hence enhancing clinical safety.

In addition, the emergence of AI has made it possible to track abnormalities in regional wall motion through the evaluation of cardiac ECGs.

Kusunose et al. [54] created an archive of data consisting of individuals regardless of whether they had a myocardial infarction. They subsequently developed and programmed a deep convolutional neural network (DCNN) to accurately detect ventricular rhythm wall articulation abnormalities. The DCNN attained an AUC of 0.99, which is similar to the accomplishments of heart specialists and ultrasound technologists (AUC = 0.98) and superior to that of trainee interpreters (AUC=0.90). Coronary artery disease computed tomographic angiogram (CCTA) is a very efficient and low-risk procedure technique used as the initial way for evaluating coronary artery stenosis. It is laborious, expensive, and necessitates a partially automatic subjective assessment. Choi et al. [55] employed an AI system to improve the outcome of CCTA. In addition to surpassing the degree of consensus of sophisticated readers at level 3, this approach made it possible to conduct an accurate and speedy examination of the constriction and arterial morphological concepts associated with CVD. Lin et al. [56] utilized a deep-learning approach to precisely measure the quantity of plaques and stiffness that were present in coronary computed tomography angiography. With the help of this DL system, it is also possible to anticipate the probable outcome of a heart CAD, which brings about therapeutic benefits.

By employing cardiac magnetic resonance imaging (CMR), Knott et al. were able to quantify the blood circulation of oxygenated blood in the heart muscle (also known as myocardial blood flow or MBF) and evaluate the blood vessel perfusion reserves of the heart (also known as myocardial perfusion reserve or MPR). Both of these measurements were accomplished with the use of an AI approach. An overall follow-up time of 605 days was utilized for this evaluation, which was carried out within the context of a cohort investigation that included 1049 total individuals [57]. A Cox proportional hazards model revealed that lower MBF and MPR, as evaluated by AI, were found to be distinct determinants of cardiovascular consequences. These findings were based on the findings of the model.

Despite being the gold-standard technique for detecting coronary stenosis, interventional fractionated flow reserve (FFR) is currently only used in around 70% of medical therapy choices, with the majority still relying on angiography. However, angiography lacks reliability in predicting stenosis for FFR < 0.80. Hae et al. [58] discovered that ML helps to overcome the discrepancy between the optical and operational aspects of FFR and angiogram. In addition, Cho et al. [59] conducted a study where they developed an AI model that employs a highly gradient-boosted (Boost) algorithm. The model they developed was able to accurately forecast specimens with an FFR value of 0.80 or below, reaching an AUC of 0.84.

7.10 AI-ASSISTED CVD CLASSIFICATION AND TAGGING

AI-based novel methodologies offer enhanced stratification and categorization for patients with CVD, potentially addressing the constraints of conventional techniques and optimizing personalized treatment. Improved Phen grouping might enhance choosing individuals for cardiac resynchronization therapy (CRT), as the conventional approach has yielded unsatisfactory results, and a significant number of individuals do not react to this treatment. Cikes et al. [60] utilized an autonomous ML system to classify participants into four different categories based on commonalities in medical characteristics, left ventricular volume, and deformation recordings at the beginning. Ultimately, four distinct phenogroups were discovered, and it was found that two of these phenogroups exhibited a significantly greater therapeutic effect when treated with CRT plus a defibrillator compared to an implanted cardioverter defibrillator. Despite advancements in treatments, those suffering from HF and decreasing LVEF still had restricted options available. Karwath et al. [61] employed neuronal network-based self-encoding algorithms to perform inconsistencies and hierarchy grouping techniques to analyze combined single information on patients using nine separates, randomized, trials with beta blockers that used placebos. The AI categorization methodology successfully differentiated the predictive responses of β-blockers in both individuals with sinus rhythm problems and those with concurrent AF.

AF is a heart problem that arises from multiple factors. The epidemiological evidence unambiguously shows that having many potential risk factors at the same time significantly enhances the likelihood of getting AF [62]. Proietti et al. [63] conducted a grouping technique with a hierarchy based on the European Society of Cardiology-EURObservational Research Program on Atrial Fibrillation Main Registrant to administer, which is part of the EU Observational Investigation Program in AF by the European Society of Cardiology-European Heart Rhythm Association. They identified three clusters. During an extension period of 22.5 months,

Cluster 3 exhibited the highest rates of HF incidents, all-cause death, and the combined outcome (which includes both). This indicates that ensemble assessment could be a useful tool for identifying the medical characteristics and forecasting events for individuals with AF. Applying attenuation to the aortic valve pressure throughout coronary angioplasty can prevent severe consequences and enable precise assessments of myocardial function. To precisely detect diminished artery waveform remnants, during the procedure of invasive myocardial coronary artery bypass, Howard et al. [64] employed a single-degree CNN to provide real-time data that had been taught on two previous data sets from individuals who underwent invasive coronary angioplasty at four heart rhythm centers in Europe. The algorithm demonstrates an accuracy rate for classification of 99.4% in distinguishing between regular beats, beating with dampness, and artefactual rhythms, as evaluated by the in-house core laboratories. When evaluated by an independent core laboratory not participating in the neuronal network education and training, the model achieves a precision of 98.7%.

The behavioral features of individuals with hypertension exhibit significant variability in terms of heart disease results, multiple medical conditions, and reactions to medications for hypertension. Therefore, it is crucial to categorize individuals with hypertension with clinically significant designations, optimize treatment approaches, and predict prognosis trajectories. Yang et al. [65] conducted an unattended, information clustering procedure on overall all initial factors associated with cardiovascular events as well as therapy responsiveness in participants from the Systolic Blood Pressure Interventions Trial. They were able to identify four categories that could be replicated. Cluster 4 exhibited the greatest propensity to experience primary CVD outcomes. The efficacy of rigorous antihypertensive therapy was observed only in Cluster 4 and Cluster 1, while it was found to be linked with a higher likelihood of serious side effects in Cluster 2. Despite contemporary therapeutic circumstances, endocrine hypertension (EHT) is often disregarded or incorrectly classified as primary arterial hypertension (PHT).

Reel et al. [66] employed a learning approach to differentiate several EHT subgroups from pulmonary hypertension. This characteristic set included plasma microRNAs, in particular, plasma catechol compounds, O-methylated metabolic products, plasma steroid hormones, urine corticosteroid compounds, and minuscule plasma therapy intermediates.

Out of the six ML models, the random forest approach achieved the highest performance in differentiating primary estrogenic deficiency (PA). It was successful in obtaining an AUC of 0.95 using 57 MOmics characteristics. The differentiation between EHT (PA + pheochromocytomas and paragangliomas + CS) and PHT was performed using a straightforward logistic classifier. The classifier attained an AUC of 0.96 using 37 MOmics characteristics. Over 1400 polymorphisms in genes that encode cartilage protein molecules have been identified in over 60% of individuals suffering from left ventricular hypertrophy [67]. Careful identification of individuals with a high likelihood of significant left ventricular hypertrophy, by optimizing the economic feasibility of genome testing, could allow the use of polymorphisms for screening.

Zhou and colleagues [68] developed a DL model using nonenhanced cine CMR images to investigate the possible utility of CMR in reflecting the familial inheritance of HCM. The effectiveness of the model was evaluated by doing a ten-time crossover validation on its internal database. The results showed an AUC value of 0.80 and a precision level of 78.43%. Furthermore, the integration of the DL model and the Toronto Diagnostic Centre score resulted in significantly improved diagnostic effectiveness compared to using a single score. The combination of the algorithms successfully obtained a region of AUC of 0.84 and a precision of 84.31%.

7.11 LIMITATIONS

However, prior to AI technology can be utilized in supplementary diagnostics, there are a few problems that need to be resolved: (1) Because people are unable to understand the intermediary stages of an AI network, the majority of investigations have not clarified what it is that conveys an algorithm the ability to identify disorders. The cause of this phenomenon needs to be investigated more thoroughly in order to increase the confidence of users in AI tools [6, 29, 32, 35]. (2) Present technique conclusions have been grounded on just a few study locations and the individuals they treat; therefore, further investigation could be necessary to verify the accuracy of such techniques to a more extensive extent with a greater number of patients [26, 29, 35]. (3) There is a need for additional research to be conducted to ascertain the cost-effectiveness of AI techniques for supplementary diagnostics and to quantify the influence that it has on the clinical setting [5, 32].

KEYWORDS

- **healthcare system**
- **blockchain**
- **digital signature**
- **artificial neural networks**

REFERENCES

1. Xu D, Liu R, Xu H, Zhang Z, Li W, Zhang Y, et al. 2022. Adoption of two-dimensional ultrasound gastrointestinal filling contrast on artificial intelligence algorithm in clinical diagnosis of gastric cancer. *Comput Math Methods Med. 2022*, 7385344.
2. Montull L, Slapsinskaite-Dackeviciene A, Kiely J, Hristovski R, Balague N. 2022. Integrative proposals of sports monitoring: Subjective outperforms objective monitoring. *Sports Med Open. 8*(1), 41.
3. Attia ZI, Kapa S, Lopez-Jimenez F, McKie PM, Ladewig DJ, Satam G, et al. 2019. Screening for cardiac contractile dysfunction using an artificial intelligence-enabled electrocardiogram. *Nat Med. 25*(1), 70–74.
4. Attia ZI, Kapa S, Noseworthy PA, Lopez-Jimenez F, Friedman PA. 2020. Artifcial intelligence ECG to detect left ventricular dysfunction in COVID-19: A case series. *Mayo Clin Proc. 95*(11), 2464–2466.
5. Yao X, Rushlow DR, Inselman JW, McCoy RG, Thacher TD, Behnken EM, et al. 2021. Artificial intelligence-enabled electrocardiograms for identification of patients with low ejection fraction: A pragmatic, randomized clinical trial. *Nat Med. 27*(5), 815–819.
6. Attia ZI, Noseworthy PA, Lopez-Jimenez F, Asirvatham SJ, Deshmukh AJ, Gersh BJ, et al. 2019. An artificial intelligence-enabled ECG algorithm for the identification of patients with atrial fibrillation during sinus rhythm: A retrospective analysis of outcome prediction. *Lancet 394*(10201), 861–867.
7. Kwon JM, Cho Y, Jeon KH, Cho S, Kim KH, Baek SD, et al. 2020. A deep learning algorithm to detect anemia with ECGs: A retrospective, multicentre study. *Lancet Digit Health 2*(7), e358–e367.
8. Ko WY, Siontis KC, Attia ZI, Carter RE, Kapa S, Ommen SR, et al. 2020. Detection of hypertrophic cardiomyopathy using a convolutional neural network-enabled electrocardiogram. *J Am Coll Cardiol. 75*(7), 722–733.
9. Kwon JM, Kim KH, Medina-Inojosa J, Jeon KH, Park J, Oh BH. 2020. Artificial intelligence for early prediction of pulmonary hypertension using electrocardiography. *J Heart Lung Transplant. 39*(8), 805–814.
10. Cho H, Keenan G, Madandola OO, Dos Santos FC, Macieira TGR, Bjarnadottir RI, et al. 2022. Assessing the usability of a clinical decision support system: Heuristic evaluation. *JMIR Hum Factors. 9*(2), e31758.

11. Emile SH, Hamid HKS. 2020. Fighting COVID-19, a place for artificial intelligence. *Transbound Emerg Dis. 67*(5), 1754–1755.
12. Dankwa-Mullan I, Rivo M, Sepulveda M, Park Y, Snowdon J, Rhee K. 2019. Transforming diabetes care through artificial intelligence: The future is here. *Popul Health Manag. 22*(3), 229–242.
13. Yan Y, Zhang JW, Zang GY, Pu J. 2019. The primary use of artificial intelligence in cardiovascular diseases: What kind of potential role does artificial intelligence play in future medicine? *J Geriatr Cardiol. 16*(8), 585–591.
14. Goodswen SJ, Barratt JLN, Kennedy PJ, Kaufer A, Calarco L, Ellis JT. 2021. Machine learning and applications in microbiology. *FEMS Microbiol Rev. 45*, 5.
15. Zhu R, Jiang C, Wang X, Wang S, Zheng H, Tang H. 2020. Privacy-preserving construction of generalized linear mixed model for biomedical computation. *Bioinformatics 36*(1), 128–135.
16. Yadav RS. 2020. Data analysis of COVID-2019 epidemic using machine learning methods: A case study of India. *Int J Inf Technol. 12*(4), 1321–1330.
17. Kahr M, Kovacs G, Loinig M, Bruckl H. 2022. Condition monitoring of ball bearings based on machine learning with synthetically generated data. *Sensors 22*, 7.
18. Ali A, Hu B, Ramahi O. 2015. Intelligent detection of cracks in metallic surfaces using a waveguide sensor loaded with metamaterial elements. *Sensors 15*(5), 11402–11416.
19. Muller E, Arnold E, Breitwieser O, Czierlinski M, Emmel A, Kaiser J, et al. 2022. A scalable approach to modeling on accelerated neuromorphic hardware. *Front Neurosci. 16*, 884128.
20. Yadav AK, Banerjee SK, Das B, Chaudhary K. 2022. Editorial: Systems biology and omics approaches for understanding complex disease biology. *Front Genet. 13*, 896818.
21. de Mattos Neto PSG, de Oliveira JFL, Bassetto P, Siqueira HV, Barbosa L, Alves EP, et al. 2021. Energy consumption forecasting for smart meters using extreme learning machine ensemble. *Sensors 21*, 23.
22. Krittanawong C, Zhang H, Wang Z, Aydar M, Kitai T. 2017. Artificial intelligence in precision cardiovascular medicine. *J Am Coll Cardiol. 69*(21), 2657–2664.
23. Chen L, Li N, Zheng Y, Gao L, Ge N, Xie D, et al. 2022. A novel semiautomatic Chinese keywords instrument screening delirium based on electronic medical records. *BMC Geriatr. 22*(1), 779.
24. Guan SY, Liu YY, Guo Y, Shen XX, Liu Y, Jin HX. 2022. Potential biomarkers for clinical outcomes of IVF cycles in women with/without PCOS: Searching with metabolomics. *Front Endocrinol. 13*, 982200.
25. Lenstrup M, Kjaergaard J, Petersen CL, Kjaer A, Hassager C. 2006. Evaluation of left ventricular mass measured by 3D echocardiography using magnetic resonance imaging as the gold standard. *Scand J Clin Lab Invest. 66*(8), 647–657.
26. Vaid A, Johnson KW, Badgeley MA, Somani SS, Bicak M, Landi I, et al. 2022. Using deep-learning algorithms to simultaneously identify right and left ventricular dysfunction from the electrocardiogram. *JACC Cardiovasc Imaging 15*(3), 395–410.
27. Saikrishnan N, Kumar G, Sawaya FJ, Lerakis S, Yoganathan AP. 2014. Accurate assessment of aortic stenosis: A review of diagnostic modalities and hemodynamic. *Circulation 129*(2), 244–253.

28. Japp AG, Gulati A, Cook SA, Cowie MR, Prasad SK. 2016. The diagnosis and evaluation of dilated cardiomyopathy. *J Am Coll Cardiol. 67*(25), 2996–3010.
29. Shrivastava S, Cohen-Shelly M, Attia ZI, Rosenbaum AN, Wang L, Giudicessi JR, et al. 2021. Artifcial intelligence-enabled electrocardiography to screen patients with dilated cardiomyopathy. *Am J Cardiol. 155*, 121–127.
30. Elias P, Poterucha TJ, Rajaram V, Moller LM, Rodriguez V, Bhave S, et al. 2022. Deep learning electrocardiographic analysis for detection of left-sided valvular heart disease. *J Am Coll Cardiol. 80*(6), 613–626.
31. Siontis KC, Noseworthy PA, Attia ZI, Friedman PA. 2021. Artificial intelligence enhanced electrocardiography in cardiovascular disease management. *Nat Rev Cardiol. 18*(7), 465–478.
32. Attia ZI, Harmon DM, Behr ER, Friedman PA. 2021. Application of artificial intelligence to the electrocardiogram. *Eur Heart J. 42*(46), 4717–4730.
33. Lancellotti P, Magne J, Dulgheru R, Clavel M-A, Donal E, Vannan MA, et al. 2018. Outcomes of patients with asymptomatic aortic stenosis followed up in heart valve clinics. *JAMA Cardiol. 3*(11), 1060–1068.
34. Leon MB, Smith CR, Mack M, Miller DC, Moses JW, Svensson LG, et al. 2010. Transcatheter aortic-valve implantation for aortic stenosis in patients who cannot undergo surgery. *N Engl J Med. 363*(17), 1597–1607.
35. Kwon JM, Lee SY, Jeon KH, Lee Y, Kim KH, Park J, et al. 2020. Deep learning-based algorithm for detecting aortic stenosis using electrocardiography. *J Am Heart Assoc. 9*(7), e014717.
36. Cohen-Shelly M, Attia ZI, Friedman PA, Ito S, Essayagh BA, Ko W-Y, et al. 2021. Electrocardiogram screening for aortic valve stenosis using artificial intelligence. *Eur Heart J. 42*(30), 2885–2896.
37. KC, Gersh BJ, Killian JM, Noseworthy PA, McCabe P, Weston SA, et al. 2016. Typical, atypical, and asymptomatic presentations of new-onset atrial fibrillation in the community: Characteristics and prognostic implications. *Heart Rhythm. 13*(7), 1418–1424.
38. Davidson KW, Barry MJ, Mangione CM, Cabana M, Caughey AB, Davis EM, et al. 2022. Screening for atrial fibrillation: US Preventive Services Task Force recommendation statement. *JAMA 327*(4), 360–367.
39. Khurshid S, Friedman S, Reeder C, Di Achille P, Diamant N, Singh P, et al. 2022. ECG-based deep learning and clinical risk factors to predict atrial fibrillation. *Circulation 145*(2), 122–133.
40. Noseworthy PA, Attia ZI, Behnken EM, Gibson RE, Bews KA, Liu S, et al. 2022. Artificial intelligence-guided screening for atrial fibrillation using electrocardiogram during sinus rhythm: A prospective non-randomized interventional trial. *Lancet 400*(10359), 1206–1212.
41. Betancur J, Commandeur F, Motlagh M, Sharir T, Einstein AJ, Bokhari S, et al. 2018. Deep learning for prediction of obstructive disease from fast myocardial perfusion SPECT: A multicenter study. *JACC Cardiovasc Imaging. 11*(11), 1654–1663.
42. Christofersen M, Tybjærg-Hansen A. 2016. Visible aging signs as risk markers for ischemic heart disease: Epidemiology, pathogenesis, and clinical implications. *Ageing Res Rev. 25*, 24–41.

43. Lin S, Li Z, Fu B, Chen S, Li X, Wang Y, et al. 2020. Feasibility of using deep learning to detect coronary artery disease based on facial photos. *Eur Heart J. 41*(46), 4400–4411.
44. Yan BP, Lai WHS, Chan CKY, Au ACK, Freedman B, Poh YC, et al. 2020. Highthroughput, contact-free detection of atrial fibrillation from video with deep learning. *JAMA Cardiol. 5*(1), 105–107.
45. de Couto G, Ouzounian M, Liu PP. 2010. Early detection of myocardial dysfunction and heart failure. *Nat Rev Cardiol. 7*(6), 334–344.
46. Khurshid S, Friedman S, Pirruccello JP, Di Achille P, Diamant N, Anderson CD, et al. 2021. Deep learning to predict cardiac magnetic resonance-derived left ventricular mass and hypertrophy from 12-lead ECGs. *Circ Cardiovasc Imaging 14*(6), e012281.
47. Maron BJ, Haas TS, Murphy CJ, Ahluwalia A, Rutten-Ramos S. 2014. Incidence and causes of sudden death in U.S. college athletes. *J Am Coll Cardiol. 63*(16), 1636–1643.
48. McLeod CJ, Ackerman MJ, Nishimura RA, Tajik AJ, Gersh BJ, Ommen SR. 2009. Outcome of patients with hypertrophic cardiomyopathy and a normal electrocardiogram. *J Am Coll Cardiol. 54*(3), 229–233.
49. Liu CM, Chang SL, Chen HH, Chen WS, Lin YJ, Lo LW, et al. 2020. The clinical application of the deep learning technique for predicting trigger origins in patients with paroxysmal atrial fibrillation with catheter ablation. *Circ Arrhythm Electrophysiol. 13*(11), e008518.
50. Arnaout R, Curran L, Zhao Y, Levine JC, Chinn E, Moon-Grady AJ. 2021. An ensemble of neural networks provides expert-level prenatal detection of complex congenital heart disease. *Nat Med. 27*(5), 882–891.
51. Donofrio MT, Moon-Grady AJ, Hornberger LK, Copel JA, Sklansky MS, Abuhamad A, et al. 2014. Diagnosis and treatment of fetal cardiac disease: A scientific statement from the American Heart Association. *Circulation 129*(21), 2183–2242.
52. Sun HY, Proudfoot JA, McCandless RT. 2018. Prenatal detection of critical cardiac outflow tract anomalies remains suboptimal despite revised obstetrical imaging guidelines. *Congenit Heart Dis. 13*(5), 748–756.
53. Asch FM, Mor-Avi V, Rubenson D, Goldstein S, Saric M, Mikati I, et al. 2021. Deep learning-based automated echocardiographic quantification of left ventricular ejection fraction: A point-of-care solution. *Circ Cardiovasc Imaging 14*(6), e012293.
54. Kusunose K, Abe T, Haga A, Fukuda D, Yamada H, Harada M, et al. 2020. A deep learning approach for assessment of regional wall motion abnormality from echocardiographic images. *JACC Cardiovasc Imaging 13*(2 Pt 1), 374–381.
55. Choi AD, Marques H, Kumar V, Grifn WF, Rahban H, Karlsberg RP, et al. 2021. CT evaluation by artificial intelligence for atherosclerosis, stenosis, and vascular morphology (CLARIFY): A multi-center, international study. *J Cardiovasc Comput Tomogr. 15*(6), 470–476.
56. Lin A, Manral N, McElhinney P, Killekar A, Matsumoto H, Kwiecinski J, et al. 2022. Deep learning-enabled coronary CT angiography for plaque and stenosis quantifcation and cardiac risk prediction: An international multicentre study. *Lancet Digit Health. 4*(4), e256–e265.
57. Knott KD, Seraphim A, Augusto JB, Xue H, Chacko L, Aung N, et al. 2020. The prognostic significance of quantitative myocardial perfusion: An artificial

intelligence-based approach using perfusion mapping. *Circulation 141*(16), 1282–1291.
58. Hae H, Kang SJ, Kim WJ, Choi SY, Lee JG, Bae Y, et al. 2018. Machine learning assessment of myocardial ischemia using angiography: Development and retrospective validation. *PLoS Med. 15*(11), e1002693.
59. Cho H, Lee JG, Kang SJ, Kim WJ, Choi SY, Ko J, et al. 2019. Angiography-based machine learning for predicting fractional flow reserve in intermediate coronary artery lesions. *J Am Heart Assoc. 8*(4), e011685.
60. Cikes M, Sanchez-Martinez S, Claggett B, Duchateau N, Piella G, Butakof C, et al. 2019. Machine learning-based Phen grouping in heart failure to identify responders to cardiac resynchronization therapy. *Eur J Heart Fail. 21*(1), 74–85.
61. Karwath A, Bunting KV, Gill SK, Tica O, Pendleton S, Aziz F, et al. 2021. Redefining beta-blocker response in heart failure patients with sinus rhythm and atrial fibrillation: A machine learning cluster analysis. *Lancet 398*(10309), 1427–1435.
62. Boriani G, Vitolo M, Diemberger I, Proietti M, Valenti AC, Malavasi VL, et al. 2021. Optimizing indices of atrial fibrillation susceptibility and burden to evaluate atrial fibrillation severity, risk, and outcomes. *Cardiovasc Res. 117*(7), 1–21.
63. Proietti M, Vitolo M, Harrison SL, Lane DA, Fauchier L, Marin F, et al. 2021. Impact of clinical phenotypes on management and outcomes in European atrial fibrillation patients: A report from the ESC-EHRA EU Observational research program in AF (EORP-AF) general long-term registry. *BMC Med. 19*(1), 256.
64. Howard JP, Cook CM, van de Hoef TP, Meuwissen M, de Waard GA, van Lavieren MA, et al. 2019. Artificial intelligence for aortic pressure waveform analysis during coronary angiography: Machine learning for patient safety. *JACC Cardiovasc Interv. 12*(20), 2093–2101.
65. Yang DY, Nie ZQ, Liao LZ, Zhang SZ, Zhou HM, Sun XT, et al. 2019. Phenomapping of subgroups in hypertensive patients using unsupervised data-driven cluster analysis: An exploratory study of the SPRINT trial. *Eur J Prev Cardiol. 26*(16), 1693–1706.
66. Reel PS, Reel S, van Kralingen JC, Langton K, Lang K, Erlic Z, et al. 2022. Machine learning for classification of hypertension subtypes using multi-omics: A multi-center, retrospective, data-driven study. *eBioMedicine 84*, 104276.
67. Maron BJ, Maron MS, Semsarian C. 2012. Genetics of hypertrophic cardiomyopathy after 20 years: Clinical perspectives. *J Am Coll Cardiol. 60*(8), 705–715.
68. Zhou H, Li L, Liu Z, Zhao K, Chen X, Lu M, et al. 2021. Deep learning algorithm to improve hypertrophic cardiomyopathy mutation prediction using cardiac cine images. *Eur Radiol. 31*(6), 3931–3940.

CHAPTER 8

Revolutionizing Ophthalmology with AI and Deep Learning

*Corresponding author

ABSTRACT

Artificial intelligence (AI) that relies on deep learning (DL) has generated significant worldwide attention in the past few decades. DL has been extensively used in the fields of recognizing images, voice recognition, and language processing. However, its influence on health services is only starting to emerge. DL has been utilized in eye care to analyze fundus images, optical coherence tomographic imaging, and visual fields. It has demonstrated strong reliability for classification in identifying diabetes-associated retinopathy, retinopathy of prematurity, glaucoma-like disc, macular edema, and age-associated macular degeneration. DL in ophthalmic images may be used with telecommunication as a potential approach for screening, diagnosing, and tracking significant eye conditions for patients in healthcare and community-based environments. However, some difficulties may arise when using DL in the field of ophthalmology. These obstacles include both clinical and technological aspects, as well as concerns over the interpretability of algorithmic outcomes, legal matters related to medical practice, and the willingness of physicians and patients to accept the use of AI algorithms that operate as "black boxes." DL has the potential to fundamentally transform the practice of ophthalmic in the decades to come. This chapter presents an overview of the most advanced DL systems used in ophthalmology applications. It also discusses probable difficulties in using these systems in a clinical setting and suggests possible solutions for the future.

Computational Intelligence for Patient Care: Blockchain, AI, and ML in Healthcare.
Rishabha Malviya, Rishav Sharma, Sathvik Belagodu Sridhar, and Suraj Kumar (Authors)

DOI: 10.1201/9781779640819-8

8.1 INTRODUCTION

The advent of artificial intelligence (AI) marks the beginning of the fourth industrial revolution that humans have experienced [1]. Deep learning (DL) is a group of innovative approaches to machine learning (ML) that have gotten a lot of attention around the world in the past few years [2]. DL processes raw data despite requiring human feature generation because it utilizes representation-learning methodologies with numerous degrees of generalization. It does this by projecting the complex patterns in large quantities of data onto small quantities of manifold [2]. When contrast to traditional methods, DL has been demonstrated to attain much greater levels of accuracy in a variety of fields, such as natural-language processing, computational perception [3–5], and speech detection [6, 7]. In the health sector, DL is mostly used for medical image interpretation. DL systems have been very good at diagnosing a wide range of illnesses, such as tuberculosis from chest ultrasounds, malignant melanoma from skin photos, and lymphoma metastases from breast carcinoma from biopsy specimens [8–10]. DL has also been used for studying the eyes, mostly fundus photos and imaging using optical coherence tomography (OCT) [11–15]. Diabetes-related retinopathy (DR), cataracts, macular degeneration caused by age, and retinal degeneration of premature growth are some of the eye diseases that DL methods have been used to treat [16–19]. DL has also been used to figure out refractive error and heart disease-associated variables like age, cholesterol levels, cigarette smoking, and overweight or obese status [20–21]. One of the main benefits of DL in the eyes could be assessment, like for DR and retinopathy of prematurity (ROP), for which there are clear standards. Some other diseases, like cataracts and age-related macular degeneration (AMD), may also need to be checked for and followed up on over time. On the other hand, screening needs a lot of people and money from healthcare systems, both in developed and developing countries with low and middle incomes. DL along with online could be a long-term way to screen and keep surveillance on patients in basic eye care situations. This study outlines new DL systems for ophthalmic uses, future obstacles in clinical usage, and potential routes onward.

8.2 APPLICATIONS OF DL IN THE FIELD OF OPHTHALMOLOGY

8.2.1 DIABETIC RETINOPATHY

By 2040, the global population is anticipated to reach 600 million inhabitants, who will be diagnosed with insulin resistance, and about one-third of them will also have DR [22]. An aggregated examination of 22,896 individuals diagnosed with insulin-dependent diabetes from 35 population-based research studies conducted in the United States of America, Australia, the European Union, and Asia between 1980 and 2008 revealed that the average occurrence of any form of diabetic cataracts (which is, in type 1 and type 2 diabetic) was 34.6%, including 7% of cases classified as vision-threatening [22]. Conducting tests to detect DR, together with promptly referring and treating the condition, is a well-recognized approach to avert eyesight loss [23]. DR screening may be conducted by many medical professionals, such as eye surgeons, optical professionals, medical professionals, diagnostic professionals, and professional photographers [24, 25]. The screening techniques include govern ophthalmology, prolonged slit-lamp biomicroscope with a handheld device camera (90 D or 78 D), optical photography (mydriatic or nonmydriatic), tele retinal evaluation, and archiving of optical video [26]. Nonetheless, screening programs for DR have difficulties regarding execution, the accessibility of individual evaluation specialists, and their financial sustainability [27].

In recent years, DL has significantly transformed its diagnostic reliability in identifying DR [2]. By using this method, several organizations have demonstrated exceptional proficiency in diagnosing [14]. A study conducted by Abràmoff et al. (2014) showed a DL model. The system achieved a region beneath the receiver's operational characteristic curve of 0.980, with an effective sensitivity of 96.8% and an accuracy of 87.0% in detecting accessible DR, which is defined as mild noninvasive DR or worse, analyzing diabetic macular edema (DMO) using the Messidor-2 data set. Comparably, Gargeya and Leng [15] achieved an area under the curve (AUC) of 0.97 for validation purposes on the identical information. They also obtained AUC values of 0.94 and 0.95 in two other test sets, namely, Messidor-2 and E-Ophtha.

In recent years, Gulshan and colleagues [12] from Google AI Healthcare announced a new DL system that demonstrated exceptional diagnosis efficiency. The DL system was created utilizing a data set of 128 retinal pictures. These representations were evaluated for DR and DMO by a group of 54 licensed eye specialists and ophthalmologists, its residents from the United States. The evaluations were conducted between May and December 2015, with each image being assessed between 3 and 7 times. The test set included over 10,000 photos obtained from two publicly accessible data sets (EyePACS-1 and Messidor-2). These images were evaluated by a minimum of seven eye specialists who are qualified by the United States Medical Board and have shown a high level of reliability in their evaluations.

While some organizations have shown promising outcomes by using DL algorithms on publicly accessible data sets, these approaches have not yet undergone evaluation in real-world drug screening initiatives. Adding more, the extent to which a DL system can be used for diverse ethnic groups and retinal pictures obtained from various webcams remains questionable. Ting et al. [11] demonstrated a satisfactory diagnostic accuracy of a DL system. The system was constructed and assessed using the Singapore Integrating DR Curriculum over 5 years. The DL system, constructed using the DL framework VGG-19 (Visual Geometry Group-19), achieved an AUC of 0.936, a degree of sensitivity of 90.5%, and an accuracy of 91.6% in accurately identifying referable DR [28]. The number of cases diagnosed for vision-threatening DR was as follows: 0.958, 100%, and 91.1%. Throughout the 10 further details sets, which included a total of 47,052 photographs, the area underneath the receiver operating characteristic curve (AUC) fluctuated between 0.889 and 0.983 [28]. The DL technique, which was developed by Abramoff and colleagues, has just been granted approval by the Food and Drug Administration of the United States of America for the purpose of identifying DR. The evaluation was placed in a potential, prospective context and resulted in an accuracy of 87.2% and a precision of 90.7%.

8.2.2 AGE-RELATED MACULAR DEGENERATION

Among the world's elderly population, AMD accounts for a disproportionate share of blindness. None, early, medium, and late were the stages of AMD identified by the age-dependent ocular disease investigation (AREDS) [29]. An extensive visual examination should be scheduled at least twice annually for those with mild to severe AMD, according to the American Academy of Ophthalmology. Several forms of age-associated macular degeneration, also known as AMD, may impact more than 288 million people by the year 2040, with around 10% of them experiencing moderate AMD or a more severe stage [29]. Due to the increasing number of elderly individuals, there is a pressing medical requirement for a strong DL system to assess these individuals for additional analysis at specialized eye care facilities.

Ting et al. [11] demonstrated that their DL method achieved a clinically reasonable level of diagnostic reliability in diagnosing referable AMD. DL was designed and evaluated utilizing a total of 108,558 retinal pictures obtained from 38,189 individuals. This research used pictures that were centered on the fovea and did not include macula delineation. Considering that this cohort consisted of individuals undergoing DR screening, there were a limited number of individuals diagnosed with AMD who required referral. Two more studies [17, 18] used the AREDS data set to create DL algorithms specifically designed for detecting a significant proportion of cases with accessible AMD, which includes intermediate AMD or worse. Burlina et al. [17] achieved a diagnosis efficiency ranging from 88.4% to 91.6% and an AUC ranging from 0.94 to 0.96 utilizing fivefold cross-validation. In contrast to Ting et al., the authors performed a presentation of the macular area before conducting both testing and training. The data were divided into an 80/20, separated with 80% used for training and 20% used for testing in each fold. Regarding the DL designs, additionally, AlexNet and OverFeat have been employed, with AlexNet demonstrating greater efficiency. Grassmann et al. [18] found that using the identical AREDS data set, they were able to identify any AMD with a specificity of 84.2%. Six different architectures of convolutional neural networks (CNNs) were used in the training process by the authors: the AlexNet website, Google's search engine, VGG, Inception-V3, ResNet, and Inception-ResNet-V2, to multiple neural networks in this research [30]. The data enhancement technique was used to enhance the diversity of the collected information and mitigate the potential for excess fitting. The photos in the AREDS data collection were first recorded as analog photographs and then digitized. The impact of this on the DL system's effectiveness is yet unknown. Furthermore, none of the three aforementioned experiments provided any external validation data for the various DL systems.

8.2.3 DIABETES MELLITUS, CHOROIDAL NEOVASCULARIZATION (CNV), AND OTHER MACULAR DISEASES

When it comes to treating macular illnesses, such as DMO and neovascular AMD, OCT has been a game-changer. OCT offers an up-close examination of the retina in living organisms, allowing for the detection of structural characteristics that are not visible with conventional ocular diagnostic methods. The prevalence of macula OCTs in the United States in the Medicare program demographic has only increased from 4.3 million in 2012 to 6.4 million in 2016. It is expected that this amount will continue to expand globally [31]. From a DL standpoint, macular OCT provides many appealing characteristics as a medium for DL. The first factor is the rapid and significant increase in the number of maculae OCTs that are regularly gathered globally. A substantial quantity of OCTs is necessary to train DL frameworks, since an enormous amount of training examples may facilitate the convergence of intricate networks with thousands of variables. Moreover, macular OCT consistently gathers voluminous structural data in three dimensions. Contrary to real-life photos or even color fundus images, the area that can be seen in the macula and the foveal convergence remains generally the same across different volume scans (Table 8.1).

By substantially decreasing the level of difficulty of the computer vision challenge, networks can accomplish substantial results with reduced information. In addition, OCT conveys characteristics of structures that are not readily discernible by standard imaging methods, therefore presenting an opportunity to discover novel biochemical markers for the disease. DL was first used on macular OCTs to automate the categorization of AMD, roughly 100,000 OCT. The DL classifier based on VGG-16 was trained using B-scans, resulting in an AUC of 0.97 (Table 8.2) [32]. Only a small number of research studies used the method of transfer learning, a technique in which a deep neural network first receives training in order to categorize retinal diseases using ImageNet, with additional training applied using optical coherence reconstruction to B-scans [30–35]. It is important to mention that these early investigations use two-dimensional DL models that are constructed using three-dimensional representations based on optical coherence measurements to amounts, instead of those developed on individual OCT B-scans. This might hinder their potential for practical use in a therapeutic setting. DL has significantly influenced the field of boundaries and feature-level recognition by using neural network algorithms specifically designed for semantic segmentation, such as the U-Net [36]. More precisely, these networks have undergone training to accurately identify and separate intraretinal edema cysts and subretinal fluid on OCT B-scans [13, 37, 38]. Deep CNN models have outperformed standard approaches in accurately segmenting the limits of

TABLE 8.1 Summarizing Several DL Algorithms Used for the Identification of Ocular Disorders Utilizing OCT

Disease	OCT Machines	Test Images	CNN	AUC	Ref
Age-related macular degeneration	Spectralis	20,613	VGG-16	0.928	13, 32
Age-related macular degeneration	Spectralis	100	Inception-v3	0.980	33
CNN	Spectralis	1000	Inception-v3	-	34
DMO	–	–	–	–	–
Multiclass comparison	–	–	–	0.999	-
Limited mode	–	–	–	0.988	-
Binary model	–	–	–	–	–
CNV vs normal	–	–	–	1	–
DMO vs norma	–	–	–	0.999	–
Drusen vs Norma	–	–	–	0.999	–
Immediate, somewhat immediate, regular, and only for monitoring purposes	Tapcon	997	Deep segmentation network using U-Net	Urgent referral 0.992	35, 43
Commonly seen retinal conditions include normal retinal function, CNV, macular edema, central serous retinopathy, full-thickness macular holes, partial-thickness macular holes, central serous retinopathy, vitreomacular traction, geographic atrophy, drusen, and the epiretinal membrane.	Spectralis	116	A deep classification network is implemented utilizing a proprietary architecture consisting of 29 CNN layers and five pooling layers.	Urgent referral 0.999	43

the retina's anatomy [39–41]. The foveal avascular region was segmented from en-face Optical Coherence Tomography Angiography photos using identical methods [42].

In recent years, DL and the Moorfields Eye Hospital in London have collaborated to use artificial neural networks in a unique AI platform for both category and segmentation tasks. This method first uses an algorithm for segmentation to accurately identify and outline 15 distinct retinal morphological characteristics and OCT acquisition errors. The neural network produces an output that is subsequently fed into an automatic classification network. The resulting classification network then renders recommendation-sorted decisions into four groups: critical, semicritical, prevalent, and observational. The Moorfields–DeepMind system demonstrates comparable results to professionals for various tasks related to classification, however, in a retroactive environment. Furthermore, the first segmentation network generates intermediary tissue participation, allowing the structure to be used for OCT devices from various manufacturers without the need for extensive rehabilitation. In the short term, this DL system will be integrated into an already established clinical route known as the immediate access "virtual" clinics, which are now being extensively used in the United Kingdom for the assessment and prioritization of macular disease cases [43, 44]. In the future, the approach might be used for prioritizing patients in nonhospital environments, especially since optometrists in the community are increasingly using OCT devices [45].

8.2.4 GLAUCOMA

The worldwide occurrence of glaucoma among those aged 40–80 is estimated to be 3.4%. It is expected that by the year 2040, there will be around 112 million people afflicted by this condition globally [46]. Both healthcare professionals and patients would appreciate advancements in illness diagnosis, evaluation of growing structural as well as operational harm, optimization of therapy to avoid vision handicaps, and precise forecasting of the future. Damage to the neuroretinal rim and subsequent excavation are hallmarks of the ocular neurological disorder glaucoma. This condition is clinically identified by an upsurge in the curving of the head of the optical nerve (ONH). However, due to the significant variation in the ONH area, it is difficult to establish a specific cup-to-disc ratio (CDR) that can be used to identify pathologic embracing, which makes it challenging to diagnose diseases [47]. Li et al. [16] and Ting et al. [11] developed ML models to identify the disc that is similar to conjunctivitis and is distinguished by a raised CDR of 0.7 and 0.8, respectively. For routine scans, researchers used 9 × 12 mm broad-spectrum OCT equipment, and they have used ML algorithms to identify damage to the glaucomatous brain fiber barrier [48]. One of the possible opportunities that might arise in the near future is the creation of neural networks that can precisely detect the optic disc that is related to fields of vision loss, regardless of the size of the disc. This is important since our present methods for detecting and treating the illness focus on stopping its progression. Moreover, DL might be used to identify gradual anatomical alterations in the optic nerve originating and caused by glaucoma. Glaucoma causes the nerve endings of retinal ganglion cells to shrink in a limited area inside the ONH. Ophthalmic surgeons usually use to determine the tangible consequences of this impairment, and low-dimensional psychophysical data will be used. This is the outcome of these tests usually includes measures of dependability, matched for age comparisons to norms, and overall summation indexes. However, there is a dearth of in-depth studies of this operational information.

Elze et al. [49] created an automated program that operates without human supervision and analyses visual field data. This program is capable of identifying clinically significant trends in visual field loss and assigning an approximate weight component to each trend. This approach has shown efficacy in identifying early visual field loss caused by glaucoma [50]. In addition, there are several computer programs available for detecting the evolution of visual field. These programs vary in their methods, ranging from evaluating overall indices over time to analyzing individual points and sectors of visual field. However, these techniques frequently do not correspond with the reality of clinical practice or with each other [51, 52]. Yousefi et al. [53–56] devised an equipment-based approach that was able to identify ventricular fibrillation (VF) development at an earlier phase compared to traditional techniques. Additional ML techniques that provide quantitative data on the advancement of the regional VF may be anticipated in the future.

While reducing intraocular pressure (IOP) has previously been proven to effectively delay the development of cataracts, some studies have indicated that the disease will still progress regardless. This suggests that we have not yet developed optimal therapies for the different types of glaucoma.

Kazemian et al. [57] created a medical prediction algorithm to use tonometric and VF data to estimate the progression of disease at various goal IOPs. Additional enhancement of this device, which incorporates information from both ophthalmologists and nonophthalmologists, could potentially be useful in calculating the IOPs that should be targeted and developing optimal tactics to attain them on an individualized basis. It has been recorded that individuals who have just been diagnosed with glaucoma have concerns about losing their vision. By utilizing ML that takes into account genomic data, patterns of behavior, and personal healthcare information, including a broad range of information, it may be possible to develop an automated estimating algorithm that can predict the potential likelihood of needing invasive procedures or experiencing functional vision loss due to glaucoma. With the advancement of ML algorithms, ophthalmologists will have a wide range of tools at their disposal to reliably identify cataracts, track the evolution of the condition, and develop customized therapeutic strategies utilizing precision healthcare techniques. In an idealistic situation, there may also exist therapeutic prognostic tools that provide patients with information on their comprehensive outlook and anticipated clinical progression, regardless of whether they get therapy or not.

8.2.5 RETINOPATHY OF PREMATURITY

ROP is a primary factor in causing vision loss in children globally, with a yearly occurrence of ROP-related vision affecting 32,000 individuals globally [58, 59]. The disease's geographical etiology differs depending on many circumstances, such as the prevalence of premature deliveries, the death rate of premature babies, and the ability to measure levels of oxygen. Screening for ROP may be done either by immediate assessment utilizing computerized fundus photography. These methods can detect the early indications of severe computerized ROP. By providing immediate assistance, most occurrences of vision loss caused by ROP can be prevented [60, 61]. The prevalence of blinding ROP is greatest in countries with low or middle incomes because of the significant number of preterm births, improvements in newborn survival rates, and the lack of resources for oxygen monitoring and ROP screenings [62, 63].

Two primary challenges affect the successful execution of ROP screening: (1) the determination of ROP is personal, resulting in incompatible application of evidence-based treatments due to substantial variation among examiners; and (2) there is a shortage of trained examiners in numerous regions worldwide [64]. Videoconferencing has become a practical solution to tackle this issue, particularly in regions where the cost of a fundus webcam footage is prohibitive. It enables one medical professional to remotely assess newborns throughout a wide geographic territory. Nevertheless, videoconferencing alone does not resolve the issue of impartiality in determining the presence of ROP. The acute-phase ROP research revealed that about 25% of videoconferencing evaluations conducted by qualified graders need arbitration because of disagreements among the evaluators regarding a therapeutically important ROP, one of the three indicators [65]. Several first efforts have been made to use computerized detection methods for ROP, and the application of DL order offers a potential solution to the problem. These are both obstacles that hinder the adoption of ROP screening. In their most recent study, Brown et al. [19] presented the findings of a fully computerized DL system. This system was able to reliably identify plus disease, which is the most critical characteristic of severe ROP. The system achieved an AUC of 0.98, outperforming the unanimous benchmark diagnosis that was combined based on photograph diagnosis and ophthalmology [66]. When compared directly with the eight professionals from across the globe who specialize in ROP in order evaluation, the i-ROP DL approach corresponded with the consensus assessment more frequently than six out of the eight doctors. The i-ROP DL system is capable of providing an intensity assessment for ROP, according to further study, which shows potential for objectively tracking the advancement, regression analysis, and response to therapy of the illness [67]. When the system was assessed against experts' rankings of the same set of 100 photos according to illness severity, it demonstrated 100% accuracy and 94% precision in detecting preplus or more serious diseases.

8.3 POTENTIAL CHALLENGES

Although based on AI computational models for ophthalmology have achieved a high degree of reliability in diagnosing various illnesses, there are still several therapeutic and technological issues that need to be addressed before these models can be effectively implemented and deployed in instantaneous fashion in clinical situations (Table 8.2).

TABLE 8.2 The Clinical and Technological Difficulties Involved in Developing and Implementing DL Methods from the Research Stage to Practical Use in Healthcare Settings

Steps	Potential challenges
Locating groups of data for training purposes	1. Matters about patients giving permission and the protection of their sensitive information. 2. Divergent norms and rules across the various organizational review bodies. 3. Limited data sets for training are available for uncommon illnesses such as ophthalmic malignancies or prevalent ailments like glaucoma that are not often included in normal data collection.
Data collections used for verification and evaluation	1. Insufficient sample size—lacking statistical power. 2. Limited generalizability—has not been extensively tested on other demographics or data obtained from various devices.
Elucidation of the outcomes	1. Displaying the locations identified as anomalous by DL. 2. Heat maps may be generated using numerous techniques such as assessments of impingement, stimulation of classes, combined gradients method, and soft responsiveness map.
Implementation of DL Algorithms in a medical environment	1. Suggestion of suitable locations for the implementation of therapeutic services. 2. Submission of regulatory consent applications to medical organizations like the U.S. Food and Drug Administration and EU medicinal product regulators for CE marking. 3. Carrying out future clinical research studies. 4. Implementation of a healthcare rebate program and adherence to medicolegal obligations. 5. Moral dilemmas

These obstacles may occur at different intervals throughout both investigative and medical settings. First, a significant number of researchers have used data sets for training from highly homogenous demographics [12, 14, 15]. AI instruction and evaluation, utilizing retinal pictures, is susceptible to several factors that introduce variability, such as the breadth of the field, the field of vision, the resolution of the image, the overall quality of the appearance, and the ethnic backgrounds of the participants. To tackle this difficulty, it would be beneficial to diversify the data set by including a wider range of nationalities and using different types of image-capture technology [11].

A significant obstacle in the advancement of AI algorithms in ophthalmology is the scarcity of extensive data sets for both uncommon conditions like ophthalmic tumors and prevalent diseases like glaucoma, which are not frequently captured in clinical imaging. In addition, there are disorders such as conjunctivitis and ROP that exhibit uncertainty and diversity among observers in defining the characteristics of the condition. The ML system acquires knowledge from the information it is provided with. The software's ability to provide precise results is doubtful if its initial data set is inadequate. The images that were provided to the AI program are either insufficiently large or not indicative of actual patient groups. Additional evidence about methods of obtaining numerous photographic techniques need ground-truth labels that are precise and trustworthy in order to function properly. Researchers Krause et al. [68] discovered that the evaluation ratings provided by retinal specialists were a greater stringent benchmark acceptable for detecting aberrations and missing tiny blood vessels in DR compared to a majority decision. This led to an improvement in the effectiveness of the algorithm. Furthermore, several AI organizations have shown strong diagnostic accuracy for their DL systems. However, certain articles failed to provide the methodology used for calculating the statistical power of the distinct information sets. When doing a power calculation, it is important to take into account factors such as the illness incidence, type 1 and type 2 errors, confidence intervals, and required accuracy. Before analyzing the metrics that measure the effectiveness of the algorithm, it is crucial to establish the appropriate operational barrier on the set used for training. This may be followed by evaluating the calibration process of the algorithm by assessing both the specificity and sensitivity of the test set.

Furthermore, the widespread use of AI in healthcare is not yet imminent due to concerns among healthcare professionals and patients about the opacity of AI and DL algorithms. In the field of medical care, enhancing practitioner acceptability relies not only on the statistical algorithmic performance but also on the fundamental characteristics that the algorithm uses to classify diseases. Producing thermal maps that indicate the areas of impact on the image that influenced the procedure's conclusion could be an initial approach. However, interpreting such visualizations can be difficult (for instance, what does it signify if a map emphasizes a vitreous area on an OCT scan of an individual with drusen?) [69]. They might additionally discover it challenging to handle negations (such as determining how to emphasize the most crucial aspect of an ophthalmology scan that indicates the absence of any illness) [70, 71]. An alternative approach is used by the system that decides that was developed by the researchers at Moorfields

Eye Hospital in Massachusetts and DeepMind Technologies. It employs an array of segments to generate a placeholder tissue representation, which serves to emphasize and quantify the appropriate regions for the clinician. This approach recognizes that the concept of "interpretability" in DL systems may have different implications for healthcare professionals compared to ML experts. While it is probable that eye specialists will be more inclined to embrace procedures that can be easily understood, additional clinical investigation is needed to confirm this and assess whether it results in demonstrable improvements in clinical efficacy for patients.

Furthermore, the existing intelligence screening methods for DR have been created and verified using 2-D pictures that lack panoramic qualities. The outcome is that increased lesion identification, including macular tractions, becomes more challenging. Integrating data from comprehensive neuroimaging into future AI has the potential to tackle this difficulty. Furthermore, the regulatory and legal needs change among nations and circumstances, necessitating additional efforts in these domains. A significant obstacle to the widespread use of AI technology in clinical settings is the issue of people placing their faith in computers to provide their medical treatment. Keel et al. [72] assessed the level of patient satisfaction based on AI DR assessment in an endocrinologist outpatient environment. They found that 96% of the respondents expressed satisfaction or high satisfaction with the automated screening model [72]. However, the general acceptance of AI screening for retinal disease may vary across various demographics and locations, which might provide challenges during its implementation.

8.3 CONCLUSIONS

DL is an advanced AI ML technology that has significantly transformed the AI sector. In the field of ophthalmology, DL has proven clinically satisfactory diagnostic accuracy in identifying several retinal disorders, namely, DR and ROP. Conducting further studies is essential to assess the implementation and affordability of various DL systems in healthcare settings. To enhance the adoption of DL techniques in clinical settings, it is crucial to elucidate the opaque nature of DL by using both current and forthcoming techniques. Despite the obstacles that lie ahead, DL will probably have a significant influence on the field of healthcare and specifically ophthalmology in the decades to follow.

KEYWORDS

- **artificial intelligence**
- **deep learning**
- **ophthalmology**
- **retinopathy**
- **macular edema**

REFERENCES

1. World Economic Forum, 2016. The fourth industrial revolution: What it means, how to respond. https://www.weforum.org/agenda/2016/01/the-fourth-industrial-revolutionwhat-it-means-and-how-to-respond/ (accessed 18 Aug 2018).
2. LeCun Y, Bengio Y, Hinton G. 2015. Deep learning. *Nature*. *521*, 436–44.
3. Zhang X, Zou J, He K, et al. 2016. Accelerating very deep convolutional networks for classification and detection. *IEEE Trans Pattern Anal Mach Intell*. *38*, 1943–55.
4. Shin HC, Roth HR, Gao M, et al. 2016. Deep convolutional neural networks for computer-aided detection: CNN architectures, dataset characteristics, and transfer learning. *IEEE Trans Med Imaging*. *35*, 1285–98.
5. Tompson J, Jain A, LeCun Y. 2014. Joint training of a convolutional network and a graphical model for human pose estimation. *Adv Neural Inf Process Syst*. *27*, 1799–807.
6. Hinton G, Deng L, Yu D. 2012. Deep neural networks for acoustic modeling in speech recognition. *IEEE Signal Process. Mag*. *29*, 82–97.
7. Lakhani P, Sundaram B. 2017. Deep learning at chest radiography: Automated classification of pulmonary tuberculosis by using convolutional neural networks. *Radiology*. *284*, 574–82.
8. [8]. Ting DSW, Yi PH, Hui F. 2018. Clinical applicability of deep learning system in detecting tuberculosis with chest radiography. *Radiology*. *286*, 729–31.
9. [9]. Esteva A, Kuprel B, Novoa RA, et al. 2017. Dermatologist-level classification of skin cancer with deep neural networks. *Nature*. *542*, 115–8.
10. Ehtisham Bejnordi B, Veta M, Johannes van Diest P, et al. 2017. Diagnostic assessment of deep learning algorithms for detection of lymph node metastases in women with breast cancer. *JAMA*. *318*, *21*99–210.
11. Ting DSW, Cheung CY, Lim G, et al. 2017. Development and validation of a deep learning system for diabetic retinopathy and related eye diseases using retinal images from multiethnic populations with diabetes. *JAMA*. *318*, *22*11–23.
12. Gulshan V, Peng L, Coram M, et al. 2016. Development and validation of a deep learning algorithm for the detection of diabetic retinopathy in retinal fundus photographs. *JAMA*. *316*, 2402–10.

13. Lee CS, Tyring AJ, Deruyter NP, et al. 2017. Deep-learning based, automated segmentation of macular edema in optical coherence tomography. *Biomed Opt Express*. *8*, 3440–8.
14. Abràmoff MD, Lou Y, Erginay A, et al. 2016. Improved automated detection of diabetic retinopathy on a publicly available dataset through integration of deep learning. *Invest Ophthalmol Vis Sci*. *57*, 5200–6.
15. Gargeya R, Leng T. 2017. Automated identification of diabetic retinopathy using deep learning. *Ophthalmol*. *124*, 962–9.
16. Li Z, He Y, Keel S, et al. 2018. Efficacy of a deep learning system for detecting glaucomatous optic neuropathy based on color fundus photographs. *Ophthalmology*. *125*, 1199–206.
17. Burlina PM, Joshi N, Pekala M, et al. 2017. Automated grading of age-related macular degeneration from color fundus images using deep convolutional neural networks. *JAMA Ophthalmol*. *135*, 1170–6.
18. Grassmann F, Mengelkamp J, Brandl C, et al. 2018. A deep learning algorithm for prediction of age-related eye disease study severity scale for age-related macular degeneration from color fundus photography. *Ophthalmology*. *125*, 1410–20.
19. Brown JM, Campbell JP, Beers A, et al. 2018. Automated diagnosis of plus disease in retinopathy of prematurity using deep convolutional neural networks. *JAMA Ophthalmol*. *136*, 803–10.
20. Poplin R, Varadarajan AV, Blumer K, et al. 2018. Prediction of cardiovascular risk factors from retinal fundus photographs via deep learning. *Nat Biomed Eng*. *2*, 158–64.
21. Varadarajan AV, Poplin R, Blumer K, et al. 2018. Deep learning for predicting refractive error from retinal fundus images. *Invest Ophthalmol Vis Sci*. *59*, 2861–8.
22. Yau JW, Rogers SL, Kawasaki R, et al. 2012. Global prevalence and major risk factors of diabetic retinopathy. *Diabetes Care*. *35*, 556–64. on May 31, 2024, by guest. Protected by copyright. http://bjo.bmj.com/ Br J Ophthalmol: First published as 10.1136/bjophthalmol-2018-313173 on 25 October 2018. Downloaded from Ting DSW, et al. Br J Ophthalmol 2019;103:167–175. doi:10.1136/bjophthalmol-2018-313173 175 Review
23. Hutchinson A, McIntosh A, Peters J, et al. 2000. Effectiveness of screening and monitoring tests for diabetic retinopathy—a systematic review. *Diabetes Med*. *17*, 495–506.
24. Scanlon PH, Malhotra R, Greenwood RH, et al. 2003. Comparison of two reference standards in validating two fields of mydriatic digital photography as a method of screening for diabetic retinopathy. *Br J Ophthalmol*. *87*, 1258–63.
25. Murray R, Metcalf SM, Lewis PM. 2005. Sustaining remote-area programs: retinal camera use by aboriginal health workers and nurses in a Kimberley partnership. *Med J Aust*. *182*, 520–3.
26. Ting DS, Tay-Kearney ML, Constable I, et al. 2011. Retinal video recording is a new way to image and diagnose diabetic retinopathy. *Ophthalmology*. *118*, 1588–93.
27. Ting DS, Cheung GC, Wong TY. 2016. Diabetic retinopathy: Global prevalence, major risk factors, screening practices, and public health challenges: A review. *Clin Exp Ophthalmol*. *44*, 260–77.

28. Abramoff MD, Lavin PT, Birch M, et al. 2018. Pivotal trial of an autonomous ai-based diagnostic system for detection of diabetic retinopathy in primary care offices. *NPJ Digit Med. 1*, 1–8.
29. Chew EY, Clemons TE, Agrón E, et al. 2015. Effect of omega-3 fatty acids, lutein/zeaxanthin, or other nutrient supplementation on cognitive function: The areds2 randomized clinical trial. *JAMA. 314*, 791–801.
30. Wong WL, Su X, Li X, et al. 2014. Global prevalence of age-related macular degeneration and disease burden projection for 2020 and 2040: A systematic review and meta-analysis. *Lancet Glob Health. 2*, e106–16.
31. Centers for Medicare & Medicaid Services, 2018. CMS Medicare provider utilization and payment data. https://www.cms.gov/Research-Statistics-Data-and-Systems/Statistics-Trends-and-Reports/Medicare-Provider-Charge-Data/index.html (accessed 4 Sep 2018).
32. Lee CS, Baughman DM, Lee AY. 2017. Deep learning is effective for classifying normal versus age-related macular degeneration oct images. *Ophthalmol Retina. 1*, 322–7.
33. Treder M, Lauermann JL, Eter N. 2018. Automated detection of exudative age-related macular degeneration in spectral domain optical coherence tomography using deep learning. *Graefes Arch Clin Exp Ophthalmol. 256*, 259–65.
34. Kermany DS, Goldbaum M, Cai W. 2018. Identifying medical diagnoses and treatable diseases by image-based deep learning. *Cell. 172*, 1122–31.
35. Ting DSW, Liu Y, Burlina P, et al. 2018. AI for medical imaging goes deep. *Nat Med. 24*, 539–40.
36. Ronneberger O, Fischer P, Brox T. 2015. U-net: Convolutional networks for biomedical image segmentation. *Medical Image Computing and Computer-Assisted Intervention—MICCAI.*
37. Roy AG, Conjeti S, Karri SPK, et al. 2017. Relaynet: Retinal layer and fluid segmentation of macular optical coherence tomography using fully convolutional networks. *Biomed Opt Express. 8*, 3627–42.
38. Venhuizen FG, van Ginneken B, Liefers B, et al. 2018. Deep learning approach for the detection and quantification of intraretinal cystoid fluid in multivendor optical coherence tomography. *Biomed Opt Express. 9*, 1545–69.
39. Hamwood J, Alonso-Caneiro D, Read SA, et al. 2018. Effect of patch size and network architecture on a convolutional neural network approach for automatic segmentation of oct retinal layers. *Biomed Opt Express. 9*, 3049–66.
40. Fang L, Cunefare D, Wang C, et al. 2017. Automatic segmentation of nine retinal layer boundaries in OCT images of non-exudative AMD patients using deep learning and graph search. *Biomed Opt Express. 8*, 2732–44.
41. Chen M, Wang J, Oguz I, et al. 2017. Automated segmentation of the choroid in EDI-OCT images with retinal pathology using convolution neural networks. *Fetal Infant Ophthalmic Med Image Anal. 10554*, 177–84.
42. Prentašic P, Heisler M, Mammo Z, et al. 2016. Segmentation of the foveal microvasculature using deep learning networks. *J Biomed Opt. 21*, 75008.
43. De Fauw J, Ledsam JR, Romera-Paredes B, et al. 2018. Clinically applicable deep learning for diagnosis and referral in retinal disease. *Nat Med. 24*, 1342–50.

44. Buchan JC, Amoaku W, Barnes B, et al. 2017. How to defuse a demographic time bomb: The way forward? *Eye. 31*, 1519–22.
45. 2018. OCT rollout in every specsavers announced. https://www.aop.org.uk/ot/industry/high-street/2017/05/22/oct-rollout-in-every-specsavers-announced (accessed 4 Sep 2018).
46. Tham YC, Li X, Wong TY, et al. 2014. Global prevalence of glaucoma and projections of glaucoma burden through 2040: A systematic review and meta-analysis. *Ophthalmology. 121*, 2081–90.
47. Jonas JB, Gusek GC, Guggenmoos-Holzmann I, et al. 1988. Size of the optic nerve scleral canal and comparison with intravital determination of optic disc dimensions. *Graefes Arch Clin Exp Ophthalmol. 226*, 213–5.
48. Christopher M, Belghith A, Weinreb RN, et al. 2018. Retinal nerve fiber layer features identified by unsupervised machine learning on optical coherence tomography scans predict glaucoma progression. *Invest Ophthalmol Vis Sci. 59*, 2748–56.
49. Elze T, Pasquale LR, Shen LQ, et al. 2015. Patterns of functional vision loss in glaucoma determined with archetypal analysis. *J R Soc Interface. 12*, 20141118.
50. Wang M, Pasquale LR, Shen LQ, et al. 2018. Reversal of glaucoma hemifield test results and visual field features in glaucoma. *Ophthalmology. 125*, 352–60.
51. Tanna AP, Bandi JR, Budenz DL, et al. 2011. Interobserver agreement and intraobserver reproducibility of the subjective determination of glaucomatous visual field progression. *Ophthalmology. 118*, 60–5.
52. Viswanathan AC, Crabb DP, McNaught AI, et al. 2003. Interobserver agreement on visual field progression in glaucoma: A comparison of methods. *Br J Ophthalmol. 87*, 726–30.
53. Yousefi S, Kiwaki T, Zheng Y, et al. 2018. Detection of longitudinal visual field progression in glaucoma using machine learning. *Am J Ophthalmol. 193*, 71–9.
54. Kass MA, Heuer DK, Higginbotham EJ, et al. 2002. The ocular hypertension treatment study: A randomized trial determines that topical ocular hypotensive medication delays or prevents the onset of primary open-angle glaucoma. *Arch Ophthalmol. 120*, 701–13.
55. Heijl A, Leske MC, Bengtsson B, et al. 2002. Reduction of intraocular pressure and glaucoma progression: results from the early manifest glaucoma trial. *Arch Ophthalmol. 120*, 1268–79.
56. Comparison of glaucomatous progression between untreated patients with normal-tension glaucoma and patients with therapeutically reduced intraocular pressures. Collaborative Normal-Tension Glaucoma Study Group. 1998, *Am J Ophthalmol. 126*, 487–97.
57. Kazemian P, Lavieri MS, Van Oyen MP, et al. 2018. Personalized prediction of glaucoma progression under different target intraocular pressure levels using filtered forecasting methods. *Ophthalmology. 125*, 569–77.
58. Lichter PR, Musch DC, Gillespie BW, et al. 2001. Interim clinical outcomes in the collaborative initial glaucoma treatment study comparing initial treatment randomized to medications or surgery. *Ophthalmology. 108*, 1943–53.
59. Blencowe H, Moxon S, Gilbert C. 2016. Update on blindness due to retinopathy of prematurity globally and in India. *Indian Pediatr. 53*(Suppl 2), S89–92.

60. Robinson R, O'Keefe M. 1992. Cryotherapy for retinopathy of prematurity--a prospective study. *Br J Ophthalmol. 76*, 289–91.
61. Cryotherapy for Retinopathy of Prematurity Cooperative Group. 2001. Multicenter trial of cryotherapy for retinopathy of prematurity: Ophthalmological outcomes at 10 years. *Arch Ophthalmol. 119*, 1110–8.
62. Gilbert C, Rahi J, Eckstein M, et al. 1997. Retinopathy of prematurity in middle-income countries. *Lancet. 350*, 12–14.
63. Fleck BW, Williams C, Juszczak E, et al. 2018. An international comparison of retinopathy of prematurity grading performance within the benefits of oxygen saturation targeting II trials. *Eye (Lond). 32*, 74–80.
64. Campbell JP, Swan R, Jonas K, et al. implementation and evaluation of a tele education system for the diagnosis of ophthalmic disease by international trainees. *AMIA Annu Symp Proc. 2015*, 366–75.
65. Daniel E, Quinn GE, Hildebrand PL, et al. 2015. Validated system for centralized grading of retinopathy of prematurity: Telemedicine approaches to evaluating acute-phase retinopathy of prematurity (e-ROP) study. *JAMA Ophthalmol. 133*, 675–82.
66. Worrall D, Wilson CM, Brostow GJ. 2016. Automated retinopathy of prematurity case detection with convolutional neural networks. In: Carneiro, G., et al. Deep Learning and Data Labeling for Medical Applications. DLMIA LABELS 2016 2016. Lecture Notes in Computer Science, vol 10008. Springer, Cham. https://doi.org/10.1007/978-3-319-46976-8_8
67. Brown JM, Campbell JP, Beers A. 2018. Fully automated disease severity assessment and treatment monitoring in retinopathy of prematurity using deep learning. Proc. SPIE 10579, Medical Imaging 2018: Imaging Informatics for Healthcare, Research, and Applications, 105790Q (6 March 2018); https://doi.org/10.1117/12.2295942
68. Krause J, Gulshan V, Rahimy E, et al. 2018. Grader variability and the importance of reference standards for evaluating machine learning models for diabetic retinopathy. *Ophthalmology. 125*, 1264–72.
69. Ramanishka V, Das A, Zhang J, 2016. Top-down visual saliency guided by captions. https://arxiv.org/abs/1612.07360
70. Lam C, Yu C, Huang L, et al. 2018. Retinal lesion detection with deep learning using image patches. Invest. *Ophthalmol Vis Sci. 59*, 590–6.
71. Quellec G, Charrière K, Boudi Y, et al. 2017. Deep image mining for diabetic retinopathy screening. *Med Image Anal. 39*, 178–93.
72. Keel S, Lee PY, Scheetz J, et al. 2018. Feasibility and patient acceptability of a novel artificial intelligence-based screening model for diabetic retinopathy at endocrinology outpatient services: A pilot study. *Sci Rep. 8*, 43–30

CHAPTER 9

Advancement of Artificial Intelligence and Machine Learning in Drug Discovery for the Central Nervous System Diseases

*Corresponding author

ABSTRACT

Neurological diseases often extend beyond the scope of various therapy fields. The development of treatments for brain and spinal cord diseases is a challenging field in drug discovery due to long timelines and high turnover rates. Artificial intelligence (AI) and machine learning (ML) have become essential tools for extracting valuable insights and enhancing governance in creating new medications. AI/ML-driven systems currently offer an exceptional capacity to expedite pharmaceutical research for the central nervous system (CNS) with a higher percentage of success. This chapter provides a detailed summary of ML and AI-enhanced pharmacological discovery efforts and their application in the CNS domain. AI and ML can be used in various stages of pharmaceutical discovery, including recognition, compound screening, hit/lead creation and optimization, medication reaction and synergistic forecasting *de novo* drug design, and drug repurposing. The latest advancements in AI/ML-guided CNS drug development focus on predicting cerebral blood vessel permeability and incorporating it into the development of treatments for neurological disorders.

Computational Intelligence for Patient Care: Blockchain, AI, and ML in Healthcare.
Rishabha Malviya, Rishav Sharma, Sathvik Belagodu Sridhar, and Suraj Kumar (Authors)

DOI: 10.1201/9781779640819-9

9.1 INTRODUCTION

Pathologies impacting the brain and spinal cord contribute to a variety of medical conditions that have a substantial influence on the economy and society. Although significant advancements have been made in comprehending the organization and operations of the brain and its neural pathways, the creation of novel medications for central nervous system (CNS) illnesses presents distinct obstacles. The brain and its neural pathways medications exhibit a smaller probability of being effective compared with different categories of drugs due to various factors, such as an inadequate comprehension of the pathology of intricate CNS conditions, suboptimal selection and involvement of objectives, limited effectiveness in the initial phases of growth and development, and the existence of a blood–brain barrier (BBB). These difficulties have resulted in a substantial increase in the amount of time it takes to create medications for the CNS. On average, it now takes 15–19 years for a medication to proceed from the discovery stage phase to receiving Food and Drug Administration (FDA) approval [1, 2]. The entire procedure of medication development produces a substantial amount of data. In recent years, the progress in "omics" innovations, rapid screening (high-throughput screening [HTS]), and chemical synthesis has resulted in a significant rise in the volume of information on chemical reactions and genome functioning [3, 4]. Efficiently integrating, correlating, and analyzing current massive quantities of data has become a critical challenge in CNS drug development.

Artificial intelligence (AI) technologies, such as machine learning (ML), may expedite pharmaceutical studies by retrieving novel and essential details from the extensive and intricate data produced throughout the drug development process. Recently, AI and ML techniques have been extensively used in several therapeutic fields and have shown outstanding effectiveness in solving a broad range of difficulties related to drug development.

Algorithms using AI and ML learning have demonstrated potential in advancing CNS therapies, which is considered an especially difficult field in drug discovery. Nevertheless, we are still in the early stages of investigating the capabilities of these advancements in uncovering new treatments and redesigning existing ones for CNS disorders. This study will specifically examine the uses of ML and AI in drug development, which show promise in this field.

In this chapter, we convey a summary of the latest advancements and uses of ML and AL technology in the field of drug discovery, with a specific focus on CNS illnesses. This overview is aimed at medical professionals who are interested in the prospect of AI and ML to enhance CNS drug development. It is meant for those who are considering using AI-based methods in their study. Initially, we convey a comprehensive outline of AI and ML methods in drug development. Subsequently, this study investigates the application of ML and AI in tackling the special difficulties associated with neurological diseases in the field of medication development. The chapter offers a succinct summary of AI techniques and the chemical characteristics they use as data. It provides a concise overview of AI/ML-based techniques employed during different stages of drug development, such as determining targets and assessment, simulation-based screening, lead discovery, and forecasting physicochemical and pharmacokinetic properties. We will explore current applications of AI and ML in pharmacokinetics and medication layout, encompassing the creation of novel medicines, responsiveness and responsiveness assessment, forecasting of medication cooperation, and drug repurposing. Using AI and ML to overcome substantial challenges, such as the barrier's blood permeation, is our most important goal in facilitating the development of medications for disorders affecting the brain and its functions. In conclusion, we will emphasize the difficulties, restrictions, and potential future paths of AI/ML-assisted drug development, with a particular focus on CNS illnesses.

9.2 ARTIFICIAL INTELLIGENCE AND MACHINE LEARNING APPLICATIONS IN THE FIELD OF DRUG DISCOVERY

AI and ML have been used in three separate phases of the initial drug discovery procedure: target identification, generating leads, and optimization, and preliminary research and development (as shown in Figure 9.1). Target discovery involves the use of AI techniques to combine different types of information to detect trends and gain insights into the molecular processes that drive illnesses and therapeutic effects.

Algorithms based on ML and AI enhance the assessment mechanisms and quantitatively structure–activity relationship (QSAR) models in simulated screening procedures to increase potential leads and optimization.

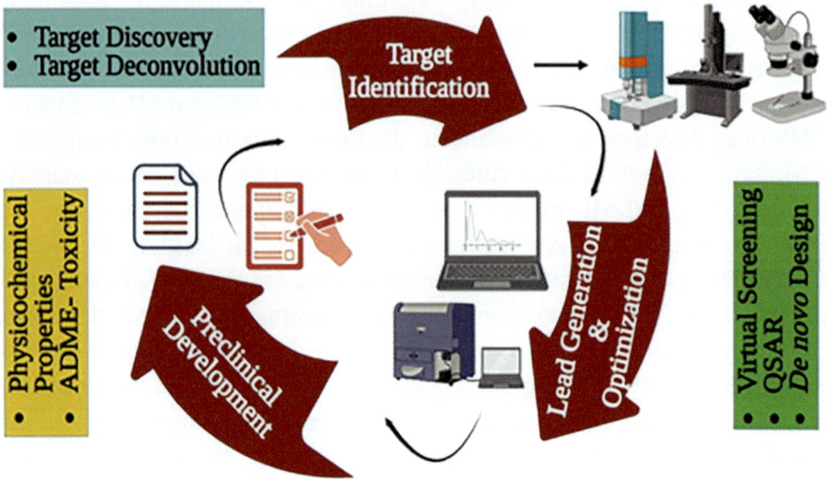

FIGURE 9.1 Artificial intelligence and machine learning are used at several stages of the drug development process.

They also facilitate the automated execution and evaluation of the newly developed drug-creation procedures. During the preliminary stage, AI and ML techniques are used to create models that forecast physicochemical qualities. These algorithms analyze enormous quantities of molecule-level data and are then used to optimize the absorption, distribution, metabolism, excretion, and toxicity (ADME-T) characteristics.

9.2.1 SUMMARY OF THE ALGORITHMS FOR ARTIFICIAL INTELLIGENCE AND MACHINE LEARNING

To enhance the viewer's comprehension of ML and AI implementations for CNS drug discovery, we present a concise overview of algorithms using AI that are extensively utilized in the field of drug discovery. AI employs a diverse range of models to construct autonomous machines, which can be categorized based on their learning processes. AI is often used to refer to ML algorithms, although it is important to remember that they are not identical. Therefore, it is advisable to provide clear definitions for both terms initially. This overview adheres to the precise description of AI provided by the FDA. AI is defined as the field of study and practice that involves developing machines with intelligence. On the other hand, ML is a specific approach within AI that involves designing and training software algorithms to gather information from data and make decisions based on that knowledge [5]. It is important to note that while all ML techniques fall under the general heading of AI, not all AI techniques involve ML. AI learning techniques can be classified into several categories, including autonomous, supervised, semisupervised, underway reassurance, relocation, and multitask learning. Various algorithms are employed in these learning architectures to carry out particular assignments, such as categorization or grouping. Nevertheless, achieving success in the field of AI necessitates more than just training an AI model. An effective AI workflow consists of the following steps: (1) defining the problem, (2) organizing the data, (3) obtaining relevant features, (4) choosing appropriate training and assessment datasets, (5) creating a model, (6) using the framework for validating data while implementing improvements, and (7) retraining the algorithm and assessing its efficacy using cross-validating. Figure 9.2 illustrates the fundamental stages involved in constructing an AI framework.

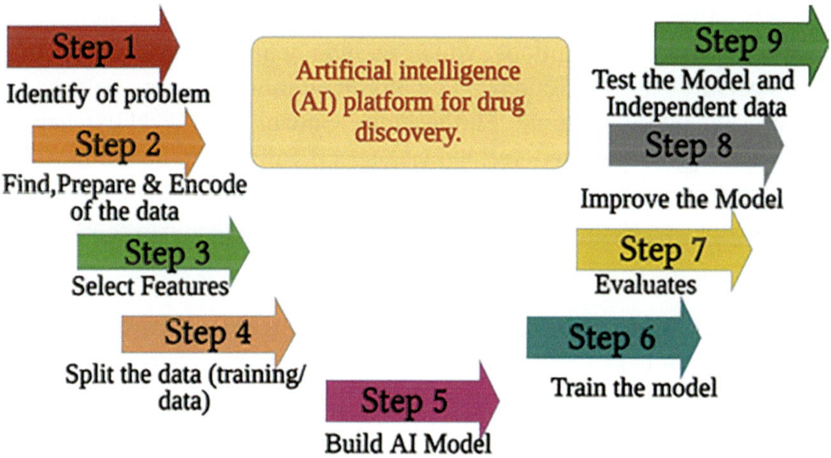

FIGURE 9.2 The fundamental procedures for constructing an artificial intelligence (AI) platform dedicated to the process of discovering new drugs.

9.2.2 MOLECULAR FINGERPRINTS AND DESCRIPTORS FOR INPUT DATA PREPARATION

An important factor in the preliminary phases of uncovering potential new medications is that they possess the desired preliminary characteristics.

Such possibilities are then refined into chemical arrangements that exhibit the desired effectiveness toward the intended target molecule. Biochemical descriptions and fingerprinting are utilized to measure the physical and biochemical characteristics that molecular targets and the material instances that use them in biology. Quantitative fingerprints are attributes of a molecule that can be measured or described conceptually. They reflect the physical, chemical, or combinatorial features of the molecules. On the other hand, molecular fingerprints are more intricate descriptions that are represented as discrete byte sequences [6, 7]. The use of biological identifiers and fingerprinting in drug identification procedures that employ ML is crucial, including the order of preference of target molecules. These include similarity-based compound search, simulation-based screening, QSAR analysis, and ADME-T for predicting leading compounds [8–10]. Several techniques exist for the computation of biological descriptors and fingerprints, each possessing a distinct array of characteristics. In this section, we explain biochemical descriptors, which include target protein descriptors and compound descriptions, as well as complex fingerprinting. Additionally, we present the commonly used programs for producing these descriptions, which include sequence-based techniques and structure-based techniques. The aforementioned data can be found in the accompanying material. Furthermore, Chuang et al. [11] extensively examined how AI-based techniques, specifically deep learning (DL), can overcome the constraints of molecule descriptors and fingerprints to enhance the accuracy of predicting compound biological activities.

9.3 ARTIFICIAL INTELLIGENCE AND MACHINE LEARNING ARE USED IN THE FIELD OF RECOGNIZING TARGETS

An influential strategy in the field of drug development involves the creation of molecules containing drugs that can effectively alter the progression of a health condition by controlling the functioning of a specific target [12]. The process of drug development typically starts by identifying an innovative target that, when manipulated, can result in a curative advantage while maintaining a reasonable degree of safety. Next, the significance of the chosen target in the disease is confirmed through validation *in vivo* models and, eventually, in clinical investigations. Hence, the ultimate resurgence of a drug development endeavor relies on the timely recognition of auspicious therapeutic targets. An effective drug target must be both responsive to medical therapy and associated with disease phenotype (considered "druggable"). The emergence of biological and technological advances has been consistently propelled. High-throughput processes and biomedical information offer novel possibilities for the swift finding of possible objectives for drugs. Nevertheless, the examination of extensive multimodal biomedical information necessitates efficient methodologies capable of generating precise forecasts for recognizing targets. AI and ML have emerged as highly influential technologies. The use of sophisticated equipment to analyze the quickly expanding multiomics data helps identify possible targets for therapy [13]. The primary objective is the identification of a novel disease target whose manipulation would result in therapeutic advantages. The second approach involves determining the existence of a target using a known active compound, commonly referred to as "target fishing." To prevent any misunderstandings, we will utilize terminology that is particular to the context of target discovery and deconvolution techniques, instead of using general terms for recognizing targets.

9.3.1 IDENTIFICATION OF A SPECIFIC TARGET

The drug discovery process commences with the identification of a novel prospective target. Following this, the objective is assessed through experimental verification and conceptual evaluation to ascertain the potential candidate's potential to coexist with small molecules (drug ability) [14]. The intended research process entails identifying key areas that contribute to the pathological evolution of diseases, assessing whether they are appropriate for pharmaceutical development, and assessing possible targets for targeting [15]. To understand the biological mechanisms underlying phenotypes of disease and identify particular modifications in every human being, a more comprehensive approach is often required due to the intricate nature of distinct disorders. This approach entails the incorporation of various evidence and information sources [16]. To tackle these obstacles, scientists have employed strategies for predicting dependable pharmacological targets using ML and AL. The following sections will show how various parts of the process might benefit from AI and ML's intended discovery process (as shown in Figure 9.3).

To comprehend the underlying mechanisms of intricately heterogeneous disorders and create effective subtype-specific procedures, it is essential to categorize individuals into clinical and biologically identical subgroups. Scientists recently developed AI and ML algorithms that can combine data from multiple scales to distinguish various causes of complex diseases. Shen et al. [17] created iCluster, a framework that combines implicit variables to analyze clusters. They used this framework to study carcinoma of the breast and lung cancer and found subgroups that shared similar modifications in Genomic copy numbers and gene transcription.

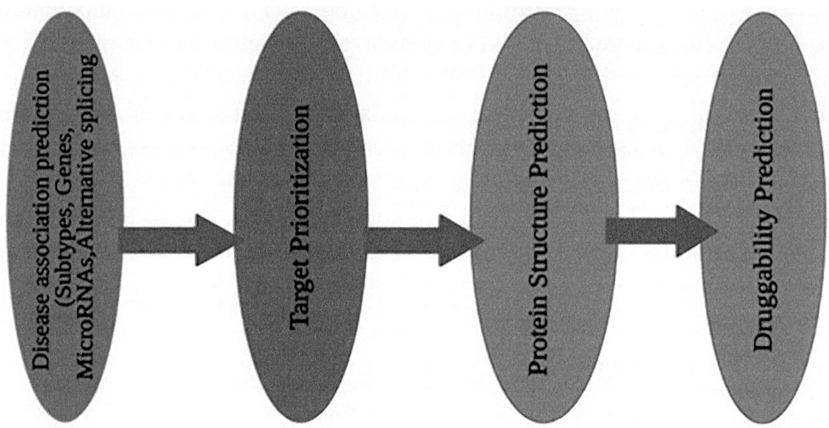

FIGURE 9.3 Target finding facilitated by artificial intelligence. Artificial intelligence and machine learning techniques can effectively analyze all accessible information to accelerate the identification of therapeutic targets associated with diseases.

Yuan et al. [18] employed a multivariate Bayesian model to combine variation in copy numbers and gene manifestation data, leading to the identification of predictive subgroups in prostate tumors and breast carcinoma. Zhang et al. [19] uncovered the melanoma prognosis categories by integrating numerous omics data sets using DL and analyzing them with K-means clustering. Gao et al. [20] recently introduced an oncology approach for classification called deep cancer subtype classification (DeepCC). This approach utilizes DL to analyze the operational spectrum, which are vectors of gene set enriched values that are associated with biological activities for each individual's specimen. ML and AI have been used recently to analyze extensive genetic and other biological profiling information related to malignancy [21]. The purpose is to identify specific molecular disease subtypes. Nevertheless, the utilization of AI categorizing assessment for different intricate diseases has not been extensively implemented. Employing reliable and adaptable methods using AI and ML for identifying disease subtypes allows for the creation of more effective remedies [22]. Predicting disease-causing genes from large volumes of inherited and operational genetic information is a highly demanding challenge in targeted discovery. To anticipate these genes that are linked to diseases using multiomics data, scientists have utilized different ML classification algorithms, such as randomly generated forests, support vector machines (SVMs) , and decision tree (DT)-based classifiers. DriverML, a supervised AI-guided device for targeted discoveries, has been utilized to effectively analyze all accessible data to expedite the identification of therapeutic targets associated with diseases [23]. ML and AI approaches are employed in particular for disease subtyping, discovering microRNAs as therapeutic and disease-causing genomes, forecasting splice alternatives, prioritizing newly discovered drug targets, modeling three-dimensional (3D) targeted frameworks, and assessing druggability. The utilization of concurrent learning has also been applied to forecast malignancy-driving genes [24].

The LOTUS algorithm, which relies on ML, accurately forecasts carcinoma driver genes in both all types of cancer contexts and for individual categories of cancer [25]. It achieves this by employing a multimodal learning approach that allows for the exchange of data across numerous kinds of cancer. To gain a deeper understanding of the possibilities and obstacles in forecasting for multiomics data sources, viewers are encouraged to consult the peer-reviewed paper authored by Kim and Tagkopoulos [26, 27]. BeFree was created to discover connections among genes and diseases through text analysis. Medline's summary data extracts connections between genes and diseases using ML and natural language processing Kernels techniques [27].

The emphasis in addressing disordered proteins is currently leaning toward disease microRNAs as therapeutics (miRNAs), which are diminutive, noncoding RNAs that control gene activity by particularly concentrating on messenger genomes [28]. Since miRNAs are involved in a variety of diseases, they are thought to represent interesting candidates for therapeutics. Approaches for ML, or ML, are being used to detect associations among microRNAs (miRNAs) and diseases, with recent approaches leveraging neural networks (NN). Zeng et al. devised an NN approach called NNMDA, which demonstrates outstanding results compared with other existing algorithms in predicting miRNA-disease connections.

Zheng et al. [29] recently introduced a novel ML approach called MLMDA. This approach combines various factors to forecast correlations between miRNAs and diseases. However, MLMDA exhibits somewhat inferior efficiency compared with NNMDA.

Alternative splicing (AS) is a crucial process in regulating transcription and creating polypeptide variation [30]. It involves producing multiple transcripts from a single gene. AI/ML-based models can uncover potential therapies and identify novel targets by comprehending variations in genes in cutting signals. A web-based tool called AVISPA has been created to facilitate the forecasting and analysis of cutting [31]. Leung et al. [31] achieved better results than the Bayesian NN approach in identifying AS by creating a deep neural network (DNN) model based on mouse RNA sequencing data [32]. Jha et al. [32] conducted a comparative analysis of two modeling approaches, namely Bayesian and Deep NN, to examine the potential obscuring implications of information sets and target functions [33]. Stanescu et al. [33] utilized semisupervised ML techniques to predict AS [34]. Xiong et al. [34] developed a DL model that underwent training to forecast splicing patterns solely based on DNA sequence data [35]. This model was able to successfully identify previously unknown genes that are associated with autism. AI and ML techniques have been employed to assist in determining the most favorable target candidates for future operations. Jeon et al. [35] constructed a SVMs classifier that utilizes features from various kinds of information to identify pharmaceutical targets that are particular to the breast, pancreas, and ovarian tumors [36]. Valentini et al. [36] integrated various functional genome networks and utilized a kernel-based approach to rank genes based on ailment MeSH terms [37]. Ferrero et al. [38] utilized publicly accessible target-disease correlation information obtained from the open targets platform to train an NN classifier using semisupervised learning techniques. They then made predictions for new therapeutic targets. ML and AI designs have been utilized in predicting protein structures for more than 30 years, and numerous organizations have conducted thorough evaluations of these strategies [39].

The Comprehensive Assessing of Protein Structure Prediction contests have been held every two years since 1994. The contests aim to evaluate the most advanced techniques that forecast protein sequences may be used to determine the 3D configurations of amino acids without prior knowledge of the actual structures. The AlphaFold system, created by

DeepMind, an AI company owned by Google, has achieved an unparalleled level of precision in predicting outcomes using *ab initio* methods. Scientists have devised multiple approaches to enhance the accuracy of protein structure prediction, drawing inspiration from AlphaFold and previous effective implementations of DL in predicting residue contacts [40]. The approaches encompass an extensive recurrent network model, a fragment library constructed using deeper context learning techniques known as DeepFragLib, and a community-developed, open-source version of AlphaFold called ProSPr [41]. DL has spurred the development of novel methods to tackle the issue of protein structure. One such method is the recurring geometric shape Network (RGN) model, which is a fully distinguishable simulation that requires an ordered set of amino acid sequences and position-specific achieving matrices as inputs and generates a 3D structure as output [42].

The RGN has been created by the same laboratory that also released a series of data sets. This collection of data serves as a standardized resource for developing and accessing ML algorithms that anticipate structural features of proteins. ProteinNet incorporates a particular order, framework, and chronological data into preformatted input/output records, which can be accessed in a publicly available repository [82]. Scientists have utilized ML not only for predicting protein composition but also for predicting protein dynamics. This is because target proteins are dynamic and can exist in various configurations. Ung et al. [43] employed random forest (RF) to categorize pharmaceutically significant configurations associated with protein kinases. In contrast, Okuno et al. devised DEFMap, a method that extracts concealed dynamical data from a provided cryo-EM density map, thereby offering important insights into the functioning of proteins. ML and AI frameworks have demonstrated their usefulness in accurately predicting protein structural characteristics solely based on sequence information [44]. Rost et al. [45] examined the utility of ML algorithms in elucidating the impact of amino acid sequence variations on the function of proteins and pathways. Structural biologists have easy access to ML and AI techniques that allow them to rapidly predict protein structures. Assessing the druggability of a target is a vital step in drug design during target discovery. ML-based models typically assess the druggability of a target by leveraging various characteristics associated with it [46]. SVMs were utilized to forecast potential drug targets by analyzing diverse chemical and physical characteristics derived from amino acid sequences [47]. Costa et al. [48]

developed a metaclassifier using a DT algorithm. The classification algorithm was trained on multiple characteristics such as Subatomic localization of operations regional transcriptional description, and network arrangement features are all important factors to consider. These characteristics were considered for both druggable and nondruggable genes.

9.3.2 TARGET DECONVOLUTION

Target deconvolution, also known as targeting fishing, is a crucial process that follows the identification of components that induce an appealing alteration in phenotypes. Understanding the binding target of compounds derived from phenotypic screens can help with better analogy development and the detection of potential undesirable effects. However, existing methods of experimentation for focused deconvolution techniques require significant amounts of labor, resources, and time. Scientists have utilized computational techniques to address deconvolution techniques challenges, thereby decreasing the number of necessary variables for the tests. Multiple studies have incorporated AI and ML techniques into computational techniques for targeting deconvolution, resulting in an improved ability to forecast. For instance, Schneider and other scientists have extensively utilized self-organizing maps (SOMs) to forecast the macromolecular objectives of pharmaceuticals [49–52]. The authors decided to utilize a "fuzzy" molecular approach. They utilize pharmacophoric attribute descriptors as illustrations, as these fuzzy molecular models have shown to have greater potential for scaffold-hopping in comparison searches compared with fragmented approaches. The unconstrained SOM methodology grouped the input molecules with uncertain targets and molecules resembling drugs with recognized targets based on the resemblance of their pharmacophoric characteristics. Therefore, the well-trained SOM successfully transferred the information about annotation drug targets for querying compounds that most closely resemble recognized medications [49].

The SOM approach has been utilized to determine the macromolecular precursors of newly created fragments, advanced chemical intermediates, fragment-like compounds found in nature, and a naturally occurring chemotherapeutic drug [52]. Furthermore, to the SOM models, a multi-category inexperienced Bayesian model was created to quickly identify possible targets for substances using only knowledge of the arrangement of atoms and bonds in a chemical compound. This information is derived from the association fingerprints of compounds belonging to 964 target categories in the World of Molecular BioAcTivity [53]. Additionally, a server called RF-QSAR was constructed to specifically identify target compounds using a SAR model generated by an RF algorithm. This website ranks possible candidates for a given query compound [54]. The target-identifying technique called Bayesian analysis to find drug interaction targets utilizes a Bayesian approach to combine six different types of data: pharmaceutical effectiveness, subsequent assessments of transcriptomic responses, chemical configurations, known side effects, biological assay outcomes, and recognized target. There is growing enthusiasm for forecasting drug–target interactions (DTI) to identify novel candidates for drugs. This is important for anticipating side effects and exploring therapeutic repurposing [55–61]. The presence of diverse biological information on known DTI has helped improve ML and AI applications approaches to uncover unknown DTI. AI/ML-driven data integration strategies surpass conventional approaches in accurately categorizing both beneficial and detrimental interactions, enhancing the accuracy of forecasted interactions, and accelerating the discovery of novel DTI.

9.4 APPLICATIONS OF ARTIFICIAL INTELLIGENCE AND MACHINE LEARNING IN CENTRAL NERVOUS SYSTEM DRUG DISCOVERY

Disorders of the CNS refer to a collection of brain disorders that have a substantial socioeconomic influence. The research and development of novel medications for CNS disorders presents distinct obstacles in comparison with other illnesses. The complexity of the NN, the lack of understanding of the causes of disorders affecting the brain and spinal cord, and the presence of a BBB all contribute to these issues. The following part offers a thorough overview of the AI and ML methods that have been used to address the problem of the neuroscience drug development of blood-brain vulnerability. You can see the data in Figure 9.4.

9.4.1 PREDICTING THE VULNERABILITY OF THE BLOOD-BRAIN BARRIER

Developing innovative therapeutics for illnesses of the brain and spinal cord is fraught with considerable problems, one of which is the complexity

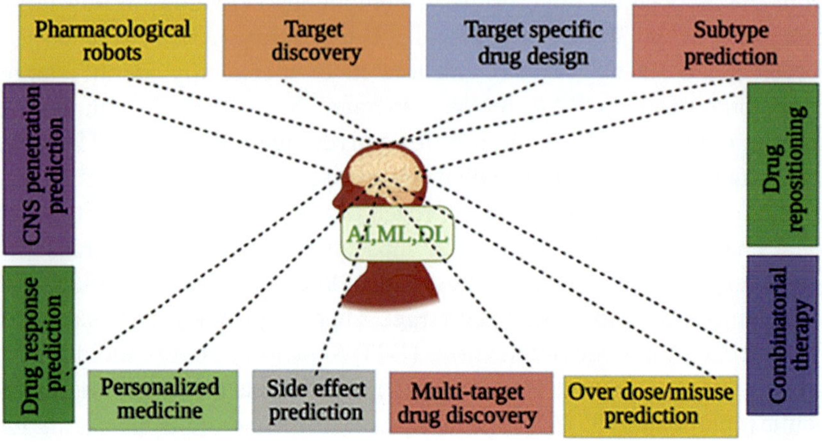

FIGURE 9.4 Advancements in the treatment of central nervous system (CNS) illnesses facilitated by artificial intelligence (AI) and machine learning (ML).

of determining the target compounds and developing novel compounds that are capable of penetrating the BBB. With the help of the BBB, the cognitive system is shielded against the effects of circulatory viruses and fluctuations in bloodstream content. Microglial cells, pericytes, astrocytic end feet, and endothelial cells of capillary vessels are the components that make up this structure [62].

The basal lamina, which is composed of protein scaffolding, also plays a role. This biological membrane can facilitate the intake of fluid, sugar levels, and necessary amino acids, as well as the expulsion of small particles and amino acids that are not required from the nervous system to the bloodstream, and the passive diffusion of certain molecules [63]. Earlier in the procedure of medication development, the availability of possible treatments for the brain's bloodstream (also known as the BBB) is an important factor that must be considered to increase the likelihood of neurological drug discovery. The amount of tedious, costly, and tedious permeability of the BBB studies that are required for CNS drug development has been suggested to be reduced by the application of forecasting algorithms that are based on AI. To create BBB permeability forecasting algorithms, scientists have used a variety of methods based on supervised learning, including SVMs, recurrent partitioning (RP), Stochastic procedure, deep NNs (DT), K-nearest neighbor, linear discriminant analysis, a compromise classification algorithm, and artificial NNs (ANN).

These approaches, on the other hand, are restricted to passively diffusional reception and include the use of just a few molecular descriptors [64–78]. Numerous chemicals, including glucose and insulin, can cross the BBB via intricate procedures that include specific reactions between drug transporters and drug receptors [79, 80]. Gao et al. [81] created a technique for predicting the openness of the BBB by making use of pharmacological clinical characteristics, which include therapeutic contraindications and drug side effects. However, there is still room for growth in terms of the degree of precision of their SVM approach. Architectures that employ DL have the capability of extracting appropriate details from complicated data structures that contain several abstract associations. To predict the BBB permeability of medications by considering clinical characteristics, Miao et al. [82] developed a DL model, which produced outstanding results compared to other approaches that are currently in use.

9.4.2 ARTIFICIAL INTELLIGENCE/MACHINE LEARNING USES WITHIN MEDICATION DEVELOPMENT FOR NEUROLOGICAL DISORDERS

9.4.2.1 ARTIFICIAL INTELLIGENCE/MACHINE LEARNING UTILIZATION IN THE PROCESS OF FINDING NEW DRUGS FOR NEUROLOGICAL DEVELOPMENT DISEASES

The multifaceted neurological complications known as schizophrenia have an overall prevalence ranging from 0.30% to 0.66%, putting it as one of the top contributors to the epidemic of illness on a worldwide scale. Even after more than a century of study, the intricate pathogenesis of schizophrenia is still a mystery, and no medication is presently successful in addressing the condition [83–88]. In the field of schizophrenic assessment, recognition, variation, subtyping, and therapy, AI and ML, and ML have been seen as potentially useful technologies. AI and ML techniques have been used by scientists in the process of drug discovery for schizophrenics. These techniques include therapeutic targeting recognition, the development of QSAR models, the prediction of tracking dose compliance, the prediction of G protein coupled receptors targeting compounds, and medication repositioning [89–93]. Based on microarray information sets that were accessible to the general public, a technique for choosing features known as SVM-RFE (recursive feature elimination) was employed to find genes that are associated with schizophrenia [94]. A further use of SVM classifiers was the identification of optimum biological indicators of presynaptic dopaminergic excessive stimulation, which has been linked to the development of schizophrenia. While trained on drug expression characteristics, SVMs fared better than other ML approaches for forecasting the repositioning of medicines for schizophrenia. The subdividing of schizophrenics was accomplished by the use of multiview grouping [95].

In Phase 2 clinical studies involving schizophrenia patients, a revolutionary AI framework called AiCure was implemented on smartphones and tablets to evaluate patients' adherence to treatment. When it comes to creating algorithms using AI and ML for the development of drugs for schizophrenia; however, the accessibility of information is a significant impediment. There is a significant dearth of details that are readily accessible to the public, on a wide scale, and that are properly organized about brain phenotypes, genomes, and clinical stages. This absence of knowledge raises problems regarding the ability to generalize ML and AI algorithms across diverse types of data without compromising efficiency. Even though there are not many applications of ML in the field of medication development for autism spectrum disorder (ASD), ML techniques have been used in ASD studies to enhance diagnostic and prognostic prediction [96–98]. It was shown that ML-based cluster analysis of clinical data performed well in predicting the therapeutic outcome of ASD patients. Bayesian ML techniques, derived from HTS data, have identified the possible use of nicardipine or additional dihydropyridine calcium channel stimulants for the treatment of Pitt-Hopkins Condition. This neurological condition is an extremely uncommon genetic condition that exhibits traits similar to ASDs.

9.4.2.2 ARTIFICIAL INTELLIGENCE AND MACHINE LEARNING TO IDENTIFY NEW ANTIDEPRESSANTS

AI and ML methods in the area of psychotropic drug development, specifically for assisting in making pharmaceutical decisions [100,101]. In an investigation on depressive disorders, scientists created gradient-enhancing equipment employing elastic network classifiers to forecast whether a patient on citalopram would experience symptomatic remission [102]. This model was effectively used in a separate clinical investigation group to evaluate the effectiveness of escitalopram therapy. An online tool was developed to offer decision help for physicians in choosing the most effective medications for a certain set of symptoms. Nevertheless, the Chekroud et al. [106] model is limited in that it just forecasts the likelihood a person with depression might respond to an antipsychotic despite measuring the depressed reaction. To overcome these constraints, Chang et al. [107] devised an Antidepressant Response Prediction Network (ARPANET) model using an NN design [103]. ARPNet accurately forecasts the level of response to antidepressant treatment, including the likelihood of achieving clinical respite from depressive disorders, as well as the patient's reaction to a combination consisting of one or more antidepressant medications. Zhdanov et al. [108] used an SVM classifier to make precise predictions about the effectiveness of escitalopram therapy [104]. They achieved this by analyzing patients' electroencephalogram (EEG) scans both before therapy and after the first two weeks of medication. Wu et al. [109] developed a comprehensive prediction system using an implicit space model to detect a strong pattern from resting-state EEG data that accurately forecasts the response to antidepressant drugs [105]. Although AI and ML have quickly progressed to clinical trials, they have not yet been extensively used in clinical settings. To bridge the divide between research and clinical practice, it is necessary to make advancements in diagnosis and predicting labeling, the capacity to accurately describe characteristics, and the capacity for generalization of models [106].

9.4.2.3 ARTIFICIAL INTELLIGENCE AND MACHINE LEARNING FOR PARKINSON'S DISORDER MEDICATION DISCOVERY

Parkinson's disease (PD) is the second prevalent neurological ailment associated with aging, impacting more than 1% of persons aged 60 and older and rising to 5% in those aged 85 and above [106]. PD is an exemplary instance of a complex ailment, involving a wide array of rhythmic and nonmotor manifestations, with potential involvement of hereditary and contextual risk elements [107] At present, there is no known therapy to halt the gradual reduction of dopamine-producing neurons in the brain region called the substantia nigra, which is responsible for regulating mobility and mental function. This degeneration leads to symptoms such as tremors and cognitive loss [108, 109]. The current medication therapies include the use of levodopa (L-dopa) and antagonists of catechol-*O*-methyltransferase or the enzyme monoamine oxidase B. However, these therapies only provide a temporary alleviation of symptoms for individuals [108]. Previous uses of AI in studies on PD have primarily concentrated on the identification of biomarkers that are diagnostic in cerebrospinal fluid and blood [110–113] and evaluating response to therapy remotely via the use of smart devices [114–118]. In contrast, ML and AI have lately garnered little interest in the field of PD drug research. Shao et al. [119] developed SVM models to efficiently identify elements with the indole–piperazine–pyrimidine scaffolding from extensive chemically based databases. They then discovered innovative substances that can bind to two types of channels that have a role in the development of movement disorders, such as PD: adenosine A2A and dopaminergic D2. Sebastián-Pérez [120] used numerous ML approaches in a separate investigation to deduce QSAR predictions for the detection of potential. These articles focus on substances that hinder the activity of the LRRK2 protein, a significant hereditary risk component for both familial and spontaneous PD. In addition, AI-based techniques have successfully addressed the issue of pharmacological side effects in the treatment of PD. Although L-dopa has been the primary treatment for PD in lowering manifestations caused by a lack of dopamine, almost half of those with PD who get this treatment ultimately have levodopa-induced dyskinesia (LID), which is an undesirable adverse reaction characterized by aberrant uncontrolled movements. Johnston et al. [121] conducted a review article where they examined the application of AI platforms for identifying viable drugs for the management of LID. They also emphasized the effectiveness of AI techniques by presenting a case study on medication repositioning. To discover novel prospective drugs that might potentially lower LID, the researchers used an existing literature-mining strategy using an IBM Watson engine. One way to do this was to evaluate and rank all of the potential medicines employing semantic comparisons and a "plot diffusing" approach.

In addition to identifying new and repurposed prospective employees, using AI and ML techniques has resulted in the development of *in vitro* and *in vivo* models of PD for medication assessment. Monzel et al. [122] developed a model of PD using human midbrain organoids. This model was used as an experimental toxicity experiment to assess the neurotoxic consequences of several chemicals. The researchers also constructed an RF classifier to predict the neurotoxicity of these compounds based on cellular characteristics. Hughes et al. [123] devised a zebrafish-based model of PD and used an AI/ML approach to accurately categorize movement-related issues seen in this model. This was achieved by analyzing high-resolution images and video footage, thereby establishing a reliable and effective drug-testing pathway. The positive outcomes of the aforementioned research emphasize the possible benefits of using ML and AI technologies in identifying effective and multitargeting medications for new targets in PD (as well as in evaluating the impact of pharmaceuticals on PD models.

9.4.2.4 ALZHEIMER'S MEDICATION DISCOVERY USING ARTIFICIAL INTELLIGENCE/MACHINE LEARNING

The rise in average lifespan has resulted in a substantial surge in disorders associated with aging, with Alzheimer's disease (AD) constituting a particularly common neurological disease among older individuals. AD is defined by a gradual decline in behavioral and cognitive abilities, specifically affecting memory. Existing medications for AD focus on enhancing the functioning of acetylcholine and neurotransmitter glut neurotransmitters, resulting in symptom improvement [124]. However, these treatments provide minimal advantages to the majority of patients. There is a pressing need for the development of new medicines that may either avoid or postpone the start of diseases, slow down their course, or ameliorate the symptoms experienced by patients.

The process of developing drugs for AD has proven to be very challenging, with an abandonment rate above 99% and no new treatment receiving approval since 2003 [125]. The failure may be attributed to insufficient targeting and toxic effects, in addition to an imperfect knowl edge of the causes, origins, and mechanisms of AD. AI and ML models are widely employed in AD research, namely for diagnosing and predicting the progression of the disease using electronic health data and photographs. Nevertheless, the use of AI and ML approaches in AD medication development has not been extensively adopted. Several studies indicate the potential advantages of using the application of AI and ML in the discovery of new cognitive impairment medications. For example, Cordax is a new method that utilizes ML to identify areas in proteins that are susceptible to accumulation and anticipate the configuration, perspective, and general layout of the leading to the amyloid core [126]. heterogeneous network-based data set for Alzheimer's disease is a data collection that combines several forms of data using Graph Convolutional Networks to identify genes related to AD.

Scientists have created ML algorithms to forecast the ability of medicines to interfere with AD-related protein molecules, including histone deacetylase (HDAC), acetylcholinesterase, and S100 calcium-binding protein A9 [127–129]. Nevertheless, a significant degree of dependability is important for determining the priority of substances that will eventually be transformed into tests. Jamal et al. [131] encompassed the unpredictable properties of chemicals and interactions between molecules to create highly predictive ML models [130]. The researchers obtained dynamic descriptors using molecular dynamics simulations of caspase-8 ligand complexes. These descriptors were used to train ANN and RF models. The simulations were subsequently used to forecast active medications targeting the caspase enzyme-8, a pivotal enzyme involved in the pathogenesis of cognitive impairment (AD). Miyazaki et al. [135] devised a graph-driven convolutional NN to address the problem of inadequate data on true-negative compound-protein interactions [131]. This framework was designed to investigate compounds that precisely target particular proteins, without relying on knowledge about the true-negative interactions. This framework was used to find antagonists of the beta-secretase enzyme, which is a primary target for AD.

The identification of single-target inhibitors has been significantly advanced by ML approaches; nonetheless, the complex properties of these antagonists continue to be a challenge of AD and necessitate the development of multitarget medications that can target many pathways involved in the progression of the illness. Scientists have used ML algorithms to forecast chemicals that target many aspects of AD. Kleandrova et al. [136] developed a set of seven compounds that act as inhibitors for three proteins associated with AD: GSK3B, HDAC1, and HDAC6. This was achieved by using perturbation theories and in the field of ML, NNs based on AI (ANN) are used. [132]. Concur et al. made predictions about the antagonists of each of the monoamine-A and monoamine-B enzymes, which are two distinct variants of the MAO. Enzymes like this play a part in the progression of AD, PD, and other neurological conditions, as well as other neuropsychiatric disorders [133]. Gupta et al. [138] combined a number of different virtual screening and ML techniques to categorize the HDAC inhibitors [134]. Through this approach, they discovered a new molecule with the ability to impede both the variants of HDAC belonging to classes I and IIb, making it a promising candidate for AD treatment. Fang et al. constructed a set of 100 binary classifiers using naïve Bayesian and RP methods. These classifiers were designed to forecast the activity of small medicines against 25 significant targets related to AD. ML methods have been used in medication repositioning initiatives, including the identification of telmisartan as being linked to a network-based classification approach used in the study of AD. There has also been the application of methods, including AI and ML, in medication response studies for the treatment of AD patients in a more accurate and tailored manner.

9.4.2.5 ARTIFICIAL INTELLIGENCE/MACHINE LEARNING IMPLICATIONS FOR ANESTHESIA AND PAIN THERAPY

The CNS medicines involve both generalized anesthetics and analgesia. Over the last several years, there has been a notable rise in the number of instances in which independence and AI have been implemented in recommendation algorithms in the field of anesthesia and pain alleviation to assist with therapeutic decisions. Pharmacological robotics are now essential in the area of anesthesia since they provide personalized doses of anesthetic drugs to preserve individual homeostasis throughout general unconsciousness and drowsiness [135]. The aforementioned robots employ sophisticated ML algorithms that analyze patient data, such as EEG monitoring, cardiovascular activity, blood pressure, and other factors, together with pharmacokinetic characteristics of medications, to determine the most effective dose. Cédrick et al. have provided a detailed review of the function of pharmacological robotics and advanced autonomous machines, such as cognition robots capable of identifying critical clinical conditions that need human assistance in the area of anesthesia [136]. In addition to the use of automated equipment, MI applications aided physicians in monitoring the individual anesthetic states of patients and predicting any potential negative consequences in anesthesia patients [137–139]. AI models have mostly been used in pain treatment for therapeutic decision assistance, reminiscent of the use of anesthesia in the medical industry. The growing volume of data gathered by sophisticated surveillance sensors and the ubiquitous Internet of Things presents a significant opportunity for AI-assisted analgesia administered by patients to revolutionize personalized pain management [140].

AI systems in alleviating pain have various therapeutic uses. These involve predicting the degree of discomfort and kind of pain, as well as determining the necessary dosage of pain relievers. AI can also assist in making decisions for personalized healthcare in analgesic therapy and anticipate the efficacy of numerous analgesic medications. Furthermore, AI can predict cases of medication overuse [141–143]. In addition to its use in clinical settings, scientists have also used ML techniques in the first phases of analgesics development. This includes tasks such as finding new genes and pathways that are linked to chronic and acute pain, as well as forecasting possible antagonists of a specific therapeutic; the specific focus on discomfort is the NaV1.7 sodium levels module [144]. To enhance the ability to anticipate new pain medications or a variety of drugs for pain management, scientists have created a thorough database of knowledge specific to the field of pain, known as pain-domain-specific chemogenomics. This information database contains information on currently used pain medications, as well as 3D structures of pain-related targets and chemical compounds that have been stated to interact with these protein targets [145–149].

9.5 CONCLUSIONS AND FUTURE DIRECTIONS

The intricate nature of mental health conditions renders the creation of pharmaceuticals targeting the brain and spinal cord a protracted, costly, ineffective, and arduous endeavor, characterized by an inadequate proportion of successful identification of novel treatment options. To address these difficulties, scientists have used AI/ML-driven techniques, which have shown great potential in every phase of medication development for different ailments. The quantity of new businesses in this region has had a remarkable increase, reaching a total of 230 by June 2020. Several healthcare companies have allocated resources to develop in-house studies using AI technology. Additionally, they have formed partnerships with AI startups and university institutions to further their research efforts. In light of the COVID-19 epidemic, there has been a significant joint effort between academics and industry. Laboratories and AI companies have made their information and processes available on open-source platforms, such as Google DeepMind's AlphaFold system. The algorithm has revealed projected 3D structures of SARS-CoV-2 proteins. Nevertheless, the application of AI technology to enhance CNS medication development is now in its nascent phase. The primary constraint in integrating ML and AI into pharmaceutical compounds targeting the brain and spinal cord research is the absence of superior-quality, well-structured datasets required for training effective NNs. The data obtained from public databases are often derived from various biological tests, procedures, or settings, making them noncomparable. Before doing certain ML and AI operations, it is essential to filter the raw inputs to get data of superior quality. The inherent opacity of most advanced AI poses an extra hurdle within the domain of the neurological framework of medication research. The absence of comprehension in AI/ML-generated outcomes restricts their potential uses. While simple ML algorithms such as Boost, TensorFlow, Lasso, Ridge, and Elastic Net do not have this issue, the fundamental mechanisms of more powerful ML models like DNN are yet unknown.

Researchers are unable to elucidate the process by which the theoretical framework reaches its conclusion and comprehend the fundamental biological systems involved.

The quantity of readily available information has a direct impact on the efficiency of AI and ML models since the effective learning of algorithms depends on having a sufficiently large volume of information for training. Identifying novel targets or medications for brain conditions that currently have no effective therapy is an exclusive challenge. Transfer learning technology may provide an alternative in cases when there are insufficient instructional resources to conduct a drug discovery assignment. One specific constraint for AI and ML use in the CNS drug development is the lack of knowledge about the underlying causes of many nervous system ailments, which makes it very difficult to determine possible objectives. To investigate the intricate causes of diseases and identify the appropriate biological targets, it is necessary to develop more advanced AI and ML algorithms capable of extracting information from the diverse data sets created across several biological layers, such as transcriptomics, the field of proteomics, and metabolomics. The use of AI and ML models in CNS drug development encounters the obstacle of incorporating diverse data types, such as genome-wide data obtained from patients, multiomics data derived from pharmaceutical therapies, and chemical data acquired from biological activity and toxicological experiments. For these sorts of applications, multitasking instruction, which includes simultaneously learning several tasks, might be appropriate. By using multiomics data sets, physicochemical features, HTS, and biological activity tests, multifunctional NNs have the potential to simultaneously forecast the impact of a medicine and its BBB permeability. Recently, advanced neuroimaging technologies, including pharmaceutical functional MRI and pharmaceutically influenced operational ultrasonography, exist. These techniques allow researchers to see the effects of medications on the neurological system in real time. Nevertheless, the preclinical application of these techniques is restricted due to problems such as reduced factors like sensibility, the necessity for anesthesia, and constraints in hemoglobin oxygenation-level reliant tomography that might impact the results.

Pharmaco-functional ultrasound (fUS) is a recently developed technology that allows for the surveillance of neurons by monitoring changes in cerebral blood volume dynamics. This method provides very detailed and precise spatial and temporal resolution and does not suffer from the limitations of anesthesia-induced bias. Recent research has shown that fUS imaging can analyze the changing patterns of CNS medicines. This involves researching the impact of a medication conjunction consisting of administered donepezil and mefloquine on dementia and AD, as well as atomoxetine on attention-deficient/hyperactivity disorder. AI and ML algorithms can analyze and categorize the effects of therapy using new neuroscience information sets, therefore enhancing our comprehension of how medications work in the brain. However, it is sometimes disregarded that BBB serves not only as an anatomical barrier for transporting medications to the brain and spinal cord but also as an intricate and ever-changing interaction that can be influenced by many disorders. To enhance the accuracy of our forecasting algorithms for BBB permeability, it is crucial to include the alterations in the barrier that are associated with diseases. This also presents several distinctive prospects for the development of disease-specific AI and ML technology in the NN drug discovery. The process of discovering drugs concerns the CNS is characterized by its unpredictability. This is because neurology objectives include multiple pathways, and the resulting biological implications cannot be simply calculated by adding up the individual functionalities.

Many medications exhibit many actions by interacting with different biological targets, and the response to a drug is influenced by a variety of circumstances. AI and ML algorithms often struggle to identify context-dependent nonlinear correlations and several other undisclosed relevant elements. In CNS drug development, there will always be some level of dependability that is not fully understood owing to the limited representation of the domain. However, ML and AI systems may improve their understanding and provide the most effective scientific outcomes by acquiring information from human specialists. AI and ML techniques have already brought about significant changes in several industries. However, their use in the area of drug development is still in its early stages. The subject of therapeutic discovery offers several prospects for the development of unique and original algorithms. As a result, ML and AI approaches are becoming more crucial in both conventional pharmaceutical research and CNS drug discovery. In the realm of personalized brain-based medication development, ML and AI will play more vital roles in medicine. This includes tasks such as categorizing individuals into subgroups, identifying the main causes of diseases, predicting how particular cells will respond to drugs, independently creating new drugs, and testing the porousness of the BBB for particular conditions.

ACKNOWLEDGMENTS

Not applicable.

AUTHOR CONTRIBUTIONS

Suraj Kumar—contributed to major writing, original draft preparation, contributed writing and figures & tables; Dr. Rishabha Malviya—contributed to writing and contributed editing, and proofreading the manuscript.

FUNDING

Not applicable.

DATA AVAILABILITY

Not applicable.

CONFLICT OF INTEREST

The author does not have any conflict of interest.

KEYWORDS

- **Alzheimer's disease**
- **anesthesia**
- **artificial intelligence**
- **blood–brain barrier**
- **central nervous system**
- **depression**
- **machine learning**
- **drug development**
- **target recognition**
- **Parkinson's disease**
- **schizophrenia**
- **neurological disorders**

REFERENCES

1. Mohs RC, Greig NH. 2017. Drug discovery and development: Role of basic biological research. *Alzheimers Dement (N Y)*. *3*(4), 651–657.
2. Papadatos G, Gaulton A, Hersey A, Overington JP. 2015. Activity, assay, and target data curation and quality in the Chembl database. *J Comput Aided Mol Des*. *29*(9), 885–896.
3. Wilson BJ, Nicholls SG. 2015. The human genome project, and recent advances in personalized genomics. *Risk Manag Health Policy*. *8*, 9–20.
4. David L, Arús-Pous J, Karlsson J, et al. 2019. applications of deep-learning in exploiting large-scale and heterogeneous compound data in industrial pharmaceutical research. *Front Pharmacol*. *10*, 1303.
5. Administration USFD. 2020. Artificial intelligence and machine learning in software as a medical device. https://www.fda.gov/medical-devices/software-medical-device-samd/artificial-intelligence-and-machine-learningsoftware-medical-device. *Accessed October 26*
6. Todeschini R, Wiese M, Consonni V. 2001. Books—handbook of molecular descriptors. *Angew Chem*. *40*(10), 1977.

7. Dong J, Cao D-S, Miao H-Y, et al. 2015. Chemdes: An integrated web-based platform for molecular descriptor and fingerprint computation. *J Cheminform.* *7*(1), 60.
8. Viswanadhan VN, Rajesh H, Balaji VN. 2011. Atom type preferences, structural diversity, and property profiles of known drugs, leads, and nondrugs: A comparative assessment. *ACS Comb Sci.* *13*(3):327–336.
9. Khan MT. Predictions of the admet properties of candidate drug molecules utilizing different qsar/qspr modeling approaches. *Curr Drug Metab.* *11*(4), 285–295.
10. Cheng F, Li W, Zhou Y, et al. 2019. Correction to "admetSAR: A comprehensive source and free tool for assessment of chemical ADMET properties". *J Chem Inf Model.* *59*, 4959.
11. Maltarollo VG, Gertrudes JC, Oliveira PR, Honorio KM. 2015. Applying machine learning techniques for ADME-Tox prediction: A review. *Expert Opin Drug Metab Toxicol.* *11*(2), 259–271.
12. Chuang KV, Gunsalus LM, Keiser MJ. 2020. Learning molecular representations for medicinal chemistry. *J Med Chem.* *63*, 8705–8722.
13. Moffat JG, Vincent F, Lee JA, Eder J, Prunotto M. 2017. Opportunities and challenges In phenotypic drug discovery: An industry perspective. *Nat Rev Drug Discovery.* *16*(8), 531–543.
14. Van den Broeck WMM. 2015. Chapter 3. Drug targets, target identification, validation, and screening. In Wermuth CG, Aldous D, Raboisson P, Rognan D. (Eds.), *The Practice of Medicinal Chemistry.* 4th Ed. (pp. 45–70). San Diego, CA: Academic Press.
15. Gashaw I, Ellinghaus P, Sommer A, Asadullah K. 2011. What makes a good drug target? *Drug Discovery Today.* *16*(23–24), 1037–1043.
16. Gashaw I, Ellinghaus P, Sommer A, Asadullah K. 2003. What makes a good drug target? *Drug Discovery Today.* *17*(suppl), S24–S30.
17. Shen R, Olshen AB, Ladanyi M. 2009. Integrative clustering of multiple genomic data types using a joint latent variable model with application to breast and lung cancer subtype analysis. *Bioinformatics.* *25*(22), 2906–2912.
18. Yuan Y, Savage RS, Markowetz F. 2011. Patient-specific data fusion defines prognostic cancer subtypes. *PLOS Comput Biol.* 7(10), e1002227
19. Zhang L, Lv C, Jin Y, et al. 2018. Deep learning-based multi-omics data integration reveals two prognostic subtypes in high-risk neuroblastoma. *Front Genet.* 9, 477.
20. Gao F, Wang W, Tan M, et al. 2019. DeepCC: A novel deep learning-based framework for cancer molecular subtype classification. *Oncogenesis.* *8*(9), 44.
21. Singh A, Shannon CP, Gautier B, et al. 2019. Diablo: An integrative approach for identifying key molecular drivers from multi-omics assays. *Bioinformatics.* *35*(17), 3055–3062.
22. Tenenhaus A, Tenenhaus M. 2011. Regularized generalized canonical correlation analysis. *Psychometrika.* *76*(2), 257–284.
23. Argelaguet R, Velten B, Arnol D, et al. 2018. Multi-omics factor analysis—a framework for unsupervised integration of multi-omics data sets. *Mol Syst Biol.* *14*(6), e8124.
24. Lock EF, Hoadley KA, Marron JS, Nobel AB. 2013. Joint and individual variation explained (jive) for integrated analysis of multiple data types. *Ann Appl Stat.* *7*(1), 523–542.

25. Collier O, Stoven V, Vert JP. 2019. LOTUS: A single- and multitask machine learning algorithm for the prediction of cancer driver genes. *PLOS Comput Biol. 15*(9), e1007381.
26. Kim M, Tagkopoulos I. 2018. Data integration and predictive modeling methods for multi-omics datasets. *Mol Omics. 14*(1), 8–25.
27. Bravo A, Pinero J, Queralt-Rosinach N, Rautschka M, Furlong LI. 2015. Extraction of relations between genes and diseases from text and large-scale data analysis: Implications for translational research. *BMC Bioinformatics. 16*, 55.
28. Bartel DP. 2004. Micrornas: Genomics, biogenesis, mechanism, and function. *Cell. 116*(2), 281–297
29. [29]. Black DL. 2003. Mechanisms of alternative pre-messenger RNA splicing. *Annu Rev Biochim. 72*, 291–336.
30. Barash Y, Vaquero-Garcia J, González-Vallinas J, et al. 2013. Avispa: A web tool for the prediction and analysis of alternative splicing. *Genome Biol. 14*(10), R114.
31. Leung MK, Xiong HY, Lee LJ, Frey BJ. 2014. Deep learning of the tissue-regulated splicing code. Bioinformatics. *30*(12), i121–i129.
32. Jha A, Gazzara MR, Barash Y. 2017. Integrative deep models for alternative splicing. *Bioinformatics. 33*(14), i274–i282.
33. Stanescu A, Tangirala K, Caragea D. 2016. Predicting alternatively spliced exons using semi-supervised learning. *Int J Data Min Bioinform. 14*(1), 1–21.
34. Xiong HY, Alipanahi B, Lee LJ, et al. 2015. RNA splicing. the human splicing code reveals new insights into the genetic determinants of disease. *Science. 347*(6218), 1254806
35. Jeon J, Nim S, Teyra J, et al. 2014. A systematic approach to identify novel cancer drug targets using machine learning, inhibitor design, and high-throughput screening. *Genome Med.* 6, 57.
36. Valentini G, Paccanaro A, Caniza H, Romero AE, Re M. 2014. An extensive analysis of disease-gene associations using network integration and fast kernel-based gene prioritization methods. *Artif Intell Med. 61*(2), 63–78.
37. Feng Z, Chen M, Shen M, Liang T, Chen H, Xie XQ. 2020. Pain-CKB, a pain-domain-specific chemogenomics knowledgebase for target identification and systems pharmacology research. *J Chem Inf Model. 60*, 4429–4435
38. Ferrero E, Dunham I, Sanseau P. 2017. In silico prediction of novel therapeutic targets using gene-disease association data. *J Transl Med. 15*(1), 182.
39. Kim J, So S, Lee HJ, Park JC, Kim JJ, Lee H. 2013. DigSee: Disease gene search engine with evidence sentences (version cancer). *Nucleic Acids Res. 41*(Web Server issue), W510–W517.
40. Arabfard M, Ohadi M, Rezaei Tabar V, Delbari A, Kavousi K. 2019. Genome-wide prediction and prioritization of human aging genes by data fusion: A machine learning approach. *BMC Genomics. 20*(1), 832.
41. Holbrook SR, Muskal SM, Kim S-H. 1993. Predicting protein structural features with artificial neural networks. *Artif Intell Mol Biol.* 161–194.
42. Cheng J, Tegge AN, Baldi P. 2008. Machine learning methods for protein structure prediction. *IEEE Rev Biomed Eng.* 141–49.
43. PM, Rahman R, Schlessinger A. 2018. Redefining the protein kinase conformational space with machine learning. *Cell Chem Biol25*(7), 916–924.

44. Matsumoto S, Ishida S, Araki M, Kato T, Terayama K, Okuno Y. 2020. Extraction of protein dynamics information hidden in cryo-EM map using deep learning. bioRxiv. https://doi.org/10.1101/2020.02.17.951863
45. Rost B, Radivojac P, Bromberg Y. 2016. Protein function in precision medicine: Deep understanding with machine learning. *FEBS Lett. 590*(15), 2327–2341.
46. Owens J. 2007. Determining druggability. *Nat Rev Drug Discovery. 6*(3), 187.
47. Nayal M, Honig B. 2006. On the nature of cavities on protein surfaces: Application to the identification of drug-binding sites. *Proteins. 63*(4), 892–906
48. Costa PR, Acencio ML, Lemke N. 2010. A machine learning approach for genome-wide prediction of morbid and druggable human genes based on systems-level data. *BMC Genomics. 11*(suppl 5), S9.
49. Reker D, Perna AM, Rodrigues T, et al. 2014. Revealing the macromolecular targets of complex natural products. *Nat Chem. 6*(12), 1072–1078.
50. Reker D, Rodrigues T, Schneider P, Schneider G. 2014. Identifying the macromolecular targets of de novo-designed chemical entities through self-organizing map consensus. *Proc Natl Acad Sci USA. 111*(11).,4067–4072.
51. Rodrigues T, Reker D, Kunze J, Schneider P, Schneider G. 2015. Revealing the macromolecular targets of fragment-like natural products. *Angew Chem Int Ed. 54*(36), 10516–10520.
52. Schneider G, Reker D, Chen T, Hauenstein K, Schneider P, Altmann KH. 2016. Deorphaning the macromolecular targets of the natural anticancer compound doliculide. *Angew Chem Int Ed. 55*(40), 12408–12411
53. Nidhi Glick, M, Davies JW, Jenkins JL. 2006. Prediction of biological targets for compounds using multiple-category Bayesian models trained on chemogenomics databases. *J Chem Inf Model. 46*(3), 1124–1133.
54. Lee K, Lee M, Kim D. 2017. Utilizing random forest QSAR models with optimized parameters for target identification and its application to target-fishing server. *BMC Bioinformatics. 18*(suppl 16), 567.
55. Madhukar NS, Khade PK, Huang L, et al. 2019. A Bayesian machine learning approach for drug target identification using diverse data types. *Nat Commun. 10*(1), 5221.
56. D'Souza S, Prema KV, Balaji S. 2020. Machine learning models for drug–target interactions: current knowledge and future directions. *Drug Discovery Today. 25*(4), 748–756. https://doi.org/10.1016/j.drudis.2020.03.003
57. Perlman L, Gottlieb A, Atias N, Ruppin E, Sharan R. 2011. Combining drug and gene similarity measures for drug-target elucidation. *J Comput Biol. 18*(2), 133–45.
58. Wang YC, Zhang CH, Deng NY, Wang Y. 2011. Kernel-based data fusion improves the drug-protein interaction prediction. *Comput Biol Chem. 35*(6), 353–362.
59. Wang Y, Chen S, Deng N, Wang Y. 2013. Drug repositioning by kernel-based integration of molecular structure, molecular activity, and phenotype data. *PLoS One. 8*(11), e78518.
60. Yamanishi Y, Araki M, Gutteridge A, Honda W, Kanehisa M. 2008. Prediction of drug-target interaction networks from the integration of chemical and genomic spaces. *Bioinformatics. 24*(13), i232 –i240.
61. Nascimento AC, Prudencio RB, Costa IG. 2016. A multiple kernel learning algorithm for drug-target interaction prediction. *BMC Bioinformatics. 17,* 46

62. Feustel SM, Meissner M, Liesenfeld O. 2012. Toxoplasma gondii and the blood-brain barrier. *Virulence. 3*(2), 182–192.
63. Ballabh P, Braun A, Nedergaard M. 2004. The blood-brain barrier: An overview: structure, regulation, and clinical implications. *Neurobiol Dis. 16*(1), 1–13.
64. Doniger S, Hofmann T, Yeh J. 2002. Predicting CNS permeability of drug molecules: comparison of neural network and support vector machine algorithms. *J Comput Biol. 9*(6), 849–864.
65. Martins IF, Teixeira AL, Pinheiro L, Falcao AO. 2012. A bayesian approach to In silico blood-brain barrier penetration modeling. *J Chem Inf Model. 52*(6), 1686–1697.
66. Majumdar S, Basak SC, Lungu CN, Diudea MV, Grunwald GD. 2019. Finding needles in a haystack: Determining key molecular descriptors associated with the blood-brain barrier entry of chemical compounds using machine learning. *Mol Inf. 38,* 1800164.
67. Gol Mohammadi H, Dashtbozorgi Z, Acree WE Jr. 2012. Quantitative structure-activity relationship prediction of blood-to-brain partitioning behavior using support vector machine. *Eur J Pharm Sci. 47*(2)421–429.
68. Yuan Y, Zheng F, Zhan CG. 2018. Improved prediction of blood-brain barrier permeability through machine learning with combined use of molecular property-based descriptors and fingerprints. *AAPS J. 20*(3), 54.
69. Mente SR, Lombardo F. 2005. A recursive-partitioning model for blood-brain barrier permeation. *J Comput Aided Mol Des. 19*(7), 465–481.
70. Zhao YH, Abraham MH, Ibrahim A, et al. 2007. Predicting penetration across the blood-brain barrier from simple descriptors and fragmentation schemes. *J Chem Inf Model. 47*(1), 170–175.
71. Obrezanova O, Csanyi G, Gola JM, Segall MD. 2007. Gaussian processes: a method for automatic QSAR modeling of ADME properties. *J Chem Inf Model. 47*(5), 1847–1857.
72. Andres C, Hutter MC. 2006. Cns permeability of drugs predicted by a decision tree. *QSAR Comb Sci. 25*(4), 305–309.
73. Zhang L, Zhu H, Oprea TI, Golbraikh A, Tropsha A. 2008. Qsar modeling of the blood-brain barrier permeability for diverse organic compounds. *Pharm Res*. 25(8), 1902–1914.
74. Vilar S, Chakrabarti M, Costanzi S. 2010. Prediction of passive blood-brain partitioning: straightforward and effective classification models based on in silico derived physicochemical descriptors. *J Mol Graph Model. 28*(8), 899–903
75. Z, Yang H, Wu Z, et al. 2018. In silico prediction of blood-brain barrier permeability of compounds by machine learning and resampling methods. *Chem. Bio. Chem. 13*(20), 2189–2201.
76. Garg P, Verma J. 2006. In silico prediction of blood-brain barrier permeability: an Artificial Neural Network model. *J Chem Inf Model. 46*(1)289–297.
77. Garg P, Dhakne R, Belekar V. 2015. Role of breast cancer resistance protein (bcrp) as active efflux transporter on blood-brain barrier (BBB) permeability. *Mol Divers. 19*(1), 163–172.
78. Lingineni K, Belekar V, Tangadpalliwar SR, Garg P. 2017. The role of multidrug resistance protein (MRP-1) as an active efflux transporter on blood-brain barrier (BBB) permeability. *Mol Divers. 21*(2)355–365

79. Geier EG, Schlessinger A, Fan H, et al. 2013. Structure-based ligand discovery for the large-neutral amino acid transporter 1, lat-1. *Proc Natl Acad Sci USA. 110*(14), 5480–5485.
80. Dolphin E, Jacobson MP. 2013. Predicting efflux ratios and blood-brain barrier penetration from chemical structure: Combining passive permeability with active efflux by P-glycoprotein. *ACS Chem Neurosci. 4*(2), 361–367.
81. Gao Z, Chen Y, Cai X, Xu R. 2017. Predict drug permeability to blood-brain-barrier from clinical phenotypes: drug side effects and drug indications. *Bioinformatics. 33*(6), 901–908.
82. Miao R, Xia LY, Chen HH, Huang HH, Liang Y. 2019. Improved classification of blood-brain-barrier drugs using deep learning. *Sci Rep*. 9(1), 8802.
83. Sullivan PF. 2012. Puzzling over schizophrenia: schizophrenia as a pathway disease. *Nat Med. 18*(2)210–211.
84. Stachowiak MK, Kucinski A, Curl R, et al. 2013. Schizophrenia: A neurodevelopmental disorder—Integrative genomic hypothesis and therapeutic implications from a transgenic mouse model. *Schizophrenia Research. 143*(2), 367–376.
85. McGrath J, Saha S, Chant D, Welham J. 2008. Schizophrenia: a concise overview of incidence, prevalence, and mortality. *Epidemiol Rev. 30*, 67–76. Mathers C. The global burden of disease: 2004 update. World Health Organization; 2008.
86. Kambeitz J, Kambeitz-Ilankovic L, Leucht S, et al. 2015. Detecting neuroimaging biomarkers for schizophrenia: a meta-analysis of multivariate pattern recognition studies. *Neuropsychopharmacology. 40*(7), 1742–1751.
87. Hyman SE. 2012. Revolution stalled. *Sci Transl Med. 4*(155), 155cm111. 357. Palaniyappan L, Deshpande G, Lanka P, et al. 2019. Effective connectivity within a triple network brain system discriminates schizophrenia spectrum disorders from psychotic bipolar disorder at the single-subject level. *Schizophr Res. 214*24–33.
88. Schnack HG. 2019. Improving individual predictions: Machine learning approaches for detecting and attacking heterogeneity in schizophrenia (and other psychiatric diseases*). Schizophr Res. 214*, 34–42.
89. Honnorat N, Dong A, Meisenzahl-Lechner E, Koutsouleris N, Davatzikos C. 2019. Neuroanatomical heterogeneity of schizophrenia revealed by semi-supervised machine learning methods. *Schizophr Res. 214*, 43–50.
90. Tandon N, Tandon R. 2019. Using machine learning to explain the heterogeneity of schizophrenia. Realizing the promise and avoiding the hype. *Schizophr Res. 214,* 70–75.
91. Talpalaru A, Bhagwat N, Devenyi GA, Lepage M, Chakravarty MM. 2019. Identifying schizophrenia subgroups using clustering and supervised learning. *Schizophr Res. 214,* 51–59.
92. Mothi SS, Sudarshan M, Tandon N, et al. 2019. Machine learning improved classification of psychoses using clinical and biological stratification: Update from the bipolar-schizophrenia network for intermediate phenotypes (B-SNIP). *Schizophr Res. 214,* 60–69.
93. Hsu KC, Wang FS. 2017. Model-based optimization approaches for precision medicine: A case study in presynaptic dopamine overactivity. *PLoS One. 12*(6), e0179575.

94. Yang QX, Wang YX, Li FC, et al. 2019. Identification of the gene signature reflecting schizophrenia's etiology by constructing an artificial intelligence-based method of enhanced reproducibility. *CNS Neurosci Ther*. *25*(9), 1054–1063.
95. Marunnan SM, Pulikkal BP, Jabamalairaj A, et al. 2017. Development of MLR and SVM aided QSAR models to identify common SAR of GABA uptake herbal inhibitors used in the treatment of schizophrenia. *Curr Neuropharmacol*. *15*(8), 1085–1092.
96. Bain EE, Shafner L, Walling DP, et al. 2017. Use of a novel artificial intelligence platform on mobile devices to assess dosing compliance in phase 2 clinical trial in subjects with schizophrenia. *JMIR Mhealth Uhealth*. *5*(2), e18.
97. Zhao K, So HC. 2019. Drug Repositioning for schizophrenia and depression/anxiety disorders: A machine learning approach leveraging expression. *Data. IEEE J Biomed Health Inform*. *23*(3), 1304–1315
98. Yin L, Chau CKL, Sham PC, So HC. 2019. Integrating clinical data and imputed transcriptome from GWAS to uncover complex disease subtypes: applications in psychiatry and cardiology. *Am J Hum Genet*. *105*(6), 1193–1212.
99. Chakravarty MM. 2019. Guest editorial: Special issue on machine learning in schizophrenia. *Schizophr Res*. *214*1–2.
100. Fitzpatrick SE, Srivorakiat L, Wink LK, Pedapati EV, Erickson CA. 2016. Aggression in autism spectrum disorder: Presentation and treatment options. *Neuropsychiatr Dis Treat*. *12*1525–1538.
101. Anzulewicz A, Sobota K, Delafield-Butt JT. 2016. Toward the autism motor signature: Gesture patterns during smart tablet gameplay identify children with autism. *Sci Rep*. *6*31107.
102. Obara T, Ishikuro M, Tamiya G, et al. 2018. Potential identification of vitamin b6 responsiveness in autism spectrum disorder utilizing phenotype variables and machine learning methods. *Sci Rep*. *8*(1), 14840.
103. Ekins S, Gerlach J, Zorn KM, Antonio BM, Lin Z, Gerlach A. 2019. Repurposing approved drugs as inhibitors of kv7.1 and nav1.8 to treat Pitt Hopkins syndrome. Pharm Res. *36*(9), 137.
104. Tian S, Sun Y, Shao J, et al. 2019. Predicting escitalopram monotherapy response in depression: The role of the anterior cingulate cortex. *Hum Brain Mapp*. *41*(5), 1249–1260.
105. Koutsouleris N, Kahn RS, Chekroud AM, et al. 2016. Multisite prediction of 4-week and 52-week treatment outcomes in patients with first-episode psychosis: A machine learning approach. *Lancet Psychiatry*. *3*(10), 935–946.
106. Chekroud AM, Zotti RJ, Shehzad Z, et al. 2016. Cross-trial prediction of treatment outcome in depression: A machine learning approach. *Lancet Psychiatry*. *3*(3), 243–250
107. Chang B, Choi Y, Jeon M, et al). 2019. Arpnet: antidepressant response prediction network for major depressive disorder. *Genes (Basel)*. *10,* 11.
108. Zhdanov A, Atluri S, Wong W, et al. 2020. Use of machine learning for predicting escitalopram treatment outcome from electroencephalography recordings in adult patients with depression. *JAMA Netw Open*. *3*(1), e1918377.
109. Wu W, Zhang Y, Jiang J, et al. 2020. An electroencephalographic signature predicts antidepressant response in major depression. *Nat Biotechnol*. *38*(4), 439–447.

110. Reeve A, Simcox E, Turnbull D. 2014. Ageing and Parkinson's disease: Why is advancing age the biggest risk factor? Ageing Res Rev. *14,* 19–30.
111. Glaab E. 2018. Computational systems biology approaches for Parkinson's disease. *Cell Tissue Res*. *373*(1)91–109.
112. Pinto M, Fernandes C, Martins E, et al. 2019. Boosting drug discovery for Parkinson's: Enhancement of the delivery of a monoamine oxidase-B inhibitor by brain-targeted PEGylated polycaprolactone-based nanoparticles. *Pharmaceutics*. *11*(7), 331.
113. Taylor JP, Hardy J, Fischbeck KH. 2002. Toxic proteins in neurodegenerative disease. *Science*. *296*(5575), 1991–1995.
114. Varadi C, Nehez K, Hornyak O, Viskolcz B, Bones J. 2019. Serum n-glycosylation in Parkinson's disease: A novel approach for potential alterations. *Molecules (Basel, Switzerland*). *24*(12), 2220.
115. Ishigami N, Tokuda T, Ikegawa M, et al. 2012. Cerebrospinal fluid proteomic patterns discriminate Parkinson's disease and multiple system atrophy. *Mov Disord*. *27*(7), 851–857
116. Potashkin JA, Santiago JA, Ravina BM, Watts A, Leontovich AA. 2012. Biosignatures for Parkinson's disease and atypical parkinsonian disorders patients. *PLoS One*. *7*(8), e43595.
117. Abdi F, Quinn JF, Jankovic J, et al. 2006. Detection of biomarkers with a multiplex quantitative proteomic platform in cerebrospinal fluid of patients with neurodegenerative disorders. *J Alzheimers Dis*. *9*(3), 293–348.
118. Matarazzo M, Arroyo-Gallego T, Montero P, et al. 2019. Remote monitoring of treatment response in Parkinson's disease: The habit of typing on a computer. *Mov Disord*. *34*(10), 1488–1495.
119.]. Hssayeni MD, Burack MA, Ghoraani B. 2016. Automatic assessment of medication states of patients with Parkinson's disease using wearable sensors. *Conf Proc IEEE Eng Med Biol Soc*. *2016*6082–6085.
120. Nguyen V, Kunz H, Taylor P, Acosta D. 2018. Insights into pharmacotherapy management for Parkinson's disease patients using wearables activity data. *Stud Health Technol Inform*. *247*156–160.
121. Hssayeni MD, Burack MA, Jimenez-Shahed J, Ghoraani B. 2019. Assessment of response to medication in individuals with Parkinson's disease. *Med Eng Phys*. *67*33–4
122. Sakawa T, Sugiyama K, Nozaki T, et al). 2019. Can the latest computerized technologies revolutionize conventional assessment tools and therapies for neurological disease? the example of Parkinson's disease. *Neurol Med Chir (Tokyo)*. *59*(3)69–78
123. Shao YM, Ma X, Paira P, et al. 2018. Discovery of indolylpiperazinylpyrimidines with dual-target profiles at adenosine a2a and dopamine d2 receptors for Parkinson's disease treatment. *PLoS One*. 13(1), e0188212.
124. Sebastian-Perez V, Martinez MJ, Gil C, Campillo NE, Martinez A, Ponzoni I. 2019. Qsar modeling to identify lrrk2 inhibitors for Parkinson's disease. *J Integr Bioinform*. *16*(1), 20180063.
125. Johnston TH, Lacoste AMB, Visanji NP, Lang AE, Fox SH, Brotchie JM. 2019. Repurposing drugs to treat l-dopa-induced dyskinesia in Parkinson’s disease. *Neuropharmacology*. *147*11–27.

126. Monzel AS, Hemmer K, Kaoma T, et al. 2020. Machine learning-assisted neurotoxicity prediction in human midbrain organoids. *Parkinsonism Rel Disord. 75,* 105–109.
127. Hughes GL, Lones MA, Bedder M, Currie PD, Smith SL, Pownall ME. 2020. Machine learning discriminates a movement disorder in a zebrafish model of Parkinson's disease. *Dis Model Mech. 13*(10), dmm045815.
128. Goedert M, Spillantini MG. 2006. A century of Alzheimer's disease. *Science. 314*(5800), 777–781.
129. Cummings JL, Morstorf T, Zhong K. 2014. Alzheimer's disease drug-development pipeline: Few candidates, frequent failures. *Alzheimer's Res Ther. 6*(4), 37
130. Sügis E, Dauvillier J, Leontjeva A, et al. 2019. Hena, heterogeneous network-based data set for alzheimer's disease. *Sci Data. 6*(1), 151.
131.]. Hung TC, Lee WY, Chen KB, Chan YC, Lee CC, Chen CY. 2014. In silico investigation of traditional Chinese medicine compounds to inhibit human histone deacetylase 2 for patients with Alzheimer's disease. *BioMed Res Int.* 2014, 769867. https://doi.org/10.1155/2014/769867
132. Canvas L, Topcam G, Gundogdu-Hizliates C, Ergun Y. 2019. Neural network modeling of ache inhibition by new carbazole-bearing oxazolones. *Interdiscip Sci. 11*(1), 95–107.
133. Lee J, Kumar S, Lee SY, Park SJ, Kim MH. 2019. Development of predictive models for identifying potential S100A9 inhibitors based on machine learning methods. *Front Chem. 7,* 779.
134. Jamal S, Grover A, Grover S. 2019. Machine learning from molecular dynamics trajectories to predict caspase-8 inhibitors against Alzheimer's disease. *Front Pharmacol. 10,* 780.
135. Miyazaki Y, Ono N, Huang M, Altaf-Ul-Amin M, Kanaya S. 2020. Comprehensive exploration of target-specific ligands using a graph convolution neural network. *Mol Inf. 39*(1–2), e1900095.
136. Kleandrova VV, Speck-Planche A. 2020. Ptml modeling for alzheimer's disease: Design and prediction of virtual multi-target inhibitors of gsk3b, hdac1, and hdac6. *Curr Top Med Chem. 20*(19), 1661–1676.
137. Riccardo C, Michael G-D, Maria Natália DSC. 2020. Developing a multi-target model to predict the activity of monoamine oxidase a and b drugs. *Curr Top Med Chem. 20*(18), 1593–1600.
138. Gupta R, Ambasta RK, Kumar P. 2020. Identification of novel class I and class IIb histone deacetylase inhibitor for Alzheimer's disease therapeutics. *Life Sci. 256,* 117912
139. Hemmerling TM, Taddei R, Wehbe M, Morse J, Cyr S, Zaouter C. 2011. Robotic anesthesia—a vision for the future of anesthesia. *Transl Med UniSa. 1,* 1–20.
140. Zaouter C, Joosten A, Rinehart J, Struys MMRF, Hemmerling TM. 2020. Autonomous systems in anesthesia: where do we stand in 2020? a narrative review. *Anesth Analg. 130*(5), 1120–1132
141. Kang AR, Lee J, Jung W, et al. 2020. Development of a prediction model for hypotension after induction of anesthesia using machine learning. *PLoS One. 15*(4), e0231172.

142. Ermer SC, Farney RJ, Johnson KB, Orr JA, Egan TD, Brewer LM. 2020. An automated algorithm incorporating Poincare analysis can quantify the severity of opioid-induced ataxic breathing. *Anesth Analg. 130*(5), 1147–1156.
143. Moghadam MC, Abad EMK, Bagherzadeh N, Ramsingh D, Li GP, Kain ZN. 2020. A machine-learning approach to predicting hypotensive events in ICU settings. *Comput Biol Med. 118,* 103626.
144. Wang R, Wang S, Duan N, Wang Q. 2020. From patient-controlled analgesia to artificial intelligence-assisted patient-controlled analgesia: Practices and perspectives. *Front Med. 7*(145)
145. Ferroni P, Zanzotto FM, Scarpato N, et al. 2020. Machine learning approach to predict medication overuse in migraine patients. *Comput Struct Biotechnol J. 18,* 1487–1496.
146. Lee S, Wei S, White V, Bain P, Baker C, Li J. 2020. Classification of opioid usage through semi-supervised learning for total joint replacement patients. *IEEE J Biomed Health Inform*, 25(1), 189–200.
147. Zhang Y, Fatemi P, Medress Z, et al. 2020. A predictive-modeling-based screening tool for prolonged opioid use after surgical management of low back and lower extremity pain. *Spine J. 20*(8), 1184–1195.
148. Chidambaran V, Ashton M, Martin LJ, Jegga AG. 2020. Systems biology-based approaches to summarize and identify novel genes and pathways associated with acute and chronic postsurgical pain. *J Clin Anesth. 62*, 109738.
149. Kong W, Tu X, Huang W, Yang Y, Xie Z, Huang Z. 2020. Prediction and optimization of nav1.7 sodium channel inhibitors based on machine learning and simulated annealing. *J Chem Inf Model. 60*(6), 2739–2753.

CHAPTER 10

Navigating the Regulatory Landscape: Addressing Challenges in AI Integration within Healthcare

*Corresponding author

ABSTRACT

The oversight of medical equipment should be stringent, ensuring reliability and confidence across medical professionals and individuals. Ensuring effective management and monitoring of the expanding application of artificial intelligence (AI) within medical settings is of utmost significance. The chapter provides an overview of the potential applications of AI in the field of healthcare and identifies five significant difficulties that legislators must address when interacting with such cutting-edge technologies. Tackling the aforementioned challenges will be difficult to accomplish. Although patient advantages and quick advancements have already been demonstrated in AI utilization in medical services, there are undoubtedly tremendous possibilities for such applications to grow in future generations.

10.1 INTRODUCTION

The incorporation of artificial intelligence (AI) within healthcare organizations has ushered in an entirely novel era in pharmaceutical inventiveness, which holds the promise of better diagnoses, personalized therapies, and raised patient satisfaction [1]. Nevertheless, this fast growth additionally throws forth a wide variety of issues in terms of oversight by regulations.

Computational Intelligence for Patient Care: Blockchain, AI, and ML in Healthcare.
Rishabha Malviya, Rishav Sharma, Sathvik Belagodu Sridhar, and Suraj Kumar (Authors)

DOI: 10.1201/9781779640819-10

Regulating organizations and lawmakers are confronted with the onerous challenge of building broad frameworks to guarantee that patient confidentiality, confidentiality of information, and moral guidelines are maintained [2]. This is because AI technologies are becoming more powerful and prevalent inside medical facilities. Establishing a delicate equilibrium between encouraging invention and protecting against possible hazards is now of the utmost importance in this age of rapidly expanding uses of AI [3]. This overview delves into a variety of topics, including data integrity and prejudice, compatibility problems, accountability, and the moral consequences of based on AI choices, to investigate the multitude of obstacles that are associated with governing AI in the medical sector [4]. Participants may establish the path for the appropriate implementation of AI innovations by first gaining an awareness of these problems and then resolving them. This will eventually allow them to maximize the revolutionary possibilities of these innovations while lessening the negative impacts they have on patients as well as healthcare systems alike.

10.2 HEALTH PRODUCTS SUBJECT TO REGULATION

The regulations that govern medical equipment need to be stringent to inspire confidence not just among individuals but also among medical professionals. The rules and regulations have evolved, with advancements often occurring after the disclosure of flaws in the system of oversight. For example, the regulatory processes that permitted the potentially teratogenic medication thalidomide to be given in the 1960s are examples that demonstrate these inadequacies [5]. To regulate additional healthcare technology, the concepts that underpin the oversight of medicines have been translated. Legislators are currently figuring out ways to interact with apps that employ AI in the field of health care, as explained in the corresponding article written by Van Laere and colleagues on the implementation of systems that support clinical decisions [6].

The process of governing technology used in healthcare has an assortment of obstacles. Dealing with the appearance of negative consequences that were not recognized in the original studies is an obvious instance. These negative consequences may not have been discovered in the research studies since they are uncommon, they do not appear until some time has passed, or perhaps they have only been identified among individuals who had features that were not investigated in those trials [7]. Biological substances provide additional problems, such as the fact that even minute variations in the process of production may influence both the safety and the efficacy of the product, as well as the difficulties associated with enrolling sufficient patients for clinical studies of medications that treat uncommon disorders [8]. It may be argued that the difficulties associated with medical equipment are considerably more severe. Regulators can have different perspectives concerning what they consider to be under their purview, therefore has led to inadequate oversight and management of healthcare equipment in a variety of circumstances [9]. It is also possible for the functioning of the gadget to change depending on the level of expertise and experience of the person using it [9].

However, when contrasted with the challenges that pose themselves in controlling the increasing use of AI in the medical field, these obstacles are very modest. The conclusion that Van Laere and his co-authors reach in their opinion piece is that "it is exceedingly difficult to construct a framework for regulation that accomplishes an appropriate equilibrium between encouraging innovations and rapid access to markets on one side of the coin and assuring reliability and safety on the opposite side [6]." We concur, and the purpose of this chapter is to supplement their studies by taking a closer look at some of the challenges that are associated with governing the use of AI in the healthcare sector.

10.3 AI TECHNIQUE FOR MEDICAL TREATMENT

Initially, it could be beneficial to provide an overview of the potential applications of AI in the medical sector, since certain people might not be aware of the fundamental aspects of this field. Its primary objective is to enhance the procedure of decision-making that is carried out by individuals who are responsible for synthesizing and interpreting data while making choices. To deal with ambiguity, current advances have integrated reasoning based on probabilities. Additionally, machine learning (ML) has been used, which allows strategies to evolve with exposure. ML is now the foundation of the majority of contemporary AI systems. It is capable of being unattended, in which it searches for identifiable trends in the data set that is provided to it, or it can be monitored, in which it acquires from facts that are pumped into it by an individual who additionally has assigned a label it (for instance, by including an authoritative diagnosis to a package of clinical data). The majority of initial applications in the field of medical technology depended on imagery, such as those employed in radiation therapy (e.g., positron emission tomographic scans), pathological (for instance, pictures of living organisms and cells), or ophthalmologist (e.g., retina photographs) [10]. However, AI is capable of using a broad variety of information inputs [11]. Over some time, this has grown to include the evaluation of increasingly sophisticated three-dimensional pictures, including those produced during a bowel movement as well as a broad variety of physiological information, like as that generated by electrocardiograms, with the primary objective of reaching a diagnosis. Artistic connections are being made between the data in a few instances. To effectively identify pneumonia in the lungs, for instance, analysts have effectively combined information regarding symptoms with recordings of coughs [12]. Additionally, they have connected radiography and persistent clinical information to provide an outlook and advise future surveillance and therapy [13]. AI has the potential to not only enhance the standard of treatment but also, and this is of utmost importance, to enable growing activity in medical institutions that are frequently constrained by the quantity of experienced medical professionals [13]. Using portable technology, such as fitness monitors that are built into cellular phones or gadgets that repeatedly evaluate, for instance, blood glucose levels, there is a tremendous opportunity to make use of the enormous amount of information that is now accessible to individuals who participate in tasks that they engage in daily.

Similar to pharmaceuticals and healthcare equipment, it is impossible to draw broad conclusions regarding the effectiveness of AI-powered clinical decision-support platforms. Nevertheless, there is currently growing proof that, under specific conditions, certain platforms can match or surpass individual legislators [14–16]. Nevertheless, AI does not constitute a silver bullet, as the recent incidents that occurred throughout the global outbreak of coronavirus illness 2019 (COVID-19) have demonstrated [17]. When Weiner and his colleagues first coined the term "e-iatrogenesis" in 2007, they were referring to the damage that patients experienced as a consequence of technological advances [18]. Cabitza and his colleagues have determined that there are four major concerns [19]. AI could fail to take into consideration its proper context, which includes variations in individuals mixed among various circumstances; it might not succeed in taking into consideration unpredictability, for instance, in grouping the input information that is susceptible to interobserver fluctuation; and issues can result due to the transparency of the process. These constitute the potential drawbacks of AI. The effectiveness of healthcare providers may be diminished if the outcome is not accessible or becomes malfunctioning. The degree of transparency is broken down into three distinct properties by Burrell [20]. At a minimum, in principle, it is possible to circumvent two of these factors, notably the service's need to maintain corporate secrets and the client's absence of technical expertise. However, the third issue, which is the inherent difficulty of the strategy, is not something that can be simply remedied. Grote and Berens illustrate the issue by referring to the typical scenario in which two doctors on the cutting edge of their field disagree [21]. When a healthcare professional and equipment have a dispute, the communication will be biased toward the opposing side of the argument. However, they can explain the rationale behind their disagreement. In conclusion, AI is making important contributions to the field of medical care in other areas as well. In the process of developing new drugs, biosimulation, a process that includes analyzing the behavioral patterns associated with chemical entities in a computerized simulation, has evolved into a more significant technique [22]. In the field of transcriptomics, which is the investigation of messenger RNA to determine which of the genes in a living thing are active, AI is being used to evaluate genome and transcriptome information gathered from microbes to identify antibiotic resistance [23].

10.4 CHALLENGES FACING REGULATORS

The advancements in question have a likelihood of having significant repercussions for medical procedures; yet, they additionally provide regulations with highly challenging problems. These authorities are tasked with the responsibility of safeguarding people of all ages from harmful and inefficient technologies. A minimum of five of them are within our reach. First and foremost, a proposal that makes use of AI is just one aspect of a more complicated therapeutic platform. It will be essential for the information to be entered in an appropriate format. However, what would occur if the information provided by the source has not been calibrated properly, or if the pro was initially trained on excellent photographs but is greeted with mediocre photos? Will this be anything that can be taken into consideration by the governing process?

In the second scenario, the procedure of training the application could integrate preexisting prejudices and attitudes while explicitly stating those. One research, for instance, discovered that a white patient who was assigned an appropriate rating by an application that was supposed to evaluate vulnerability among patients receiving primary healthcare in the United States was considered to be in better condition than a black patient who received the same score [24]. The reason for this was that the resulting factor had been determined in part by the expenditure of medication, with black patients often getting service that was considered to be more affordable. Providing analysts with the ability to access larger sets of information that seem more comparable to the population could potentially lessen the amount of bias that is inherent in techniques; however, this would require merging data from several suppliers into just one application [24]. AI systems in healthcare might be significantly improved by enacting regulations that make this possible, while also putting protections in place to guarantee that it is carried out in an approach that is secure, and moral, and protects the confidentiality of individuals.

Furthermore, in cases when the program incorporates ML, the functionality of the application will evolve. According to this, authorization procedures for regulatory bodies need to be time-bound. Considering the compromise between danger, which may be very challenging to predict, and legislative burden, which can be measured, the question arises as to how often it should be repeated [25]. The FDA (Food and Drug Administration) of the United States has suggested an all-encompassing procedure, which would begin before the market opens innovation and end with postmarket performance. However, it is not apparent how this would be implemented in reality [25].

In the fourth place, the use of AI for medical purposes may be in contradiction with the laws governing data protection. The aforementioned legislation, which applies to numerous contexts (including those that are governed by the European Data Protection Regulation), mandates that only identifiable information that is necessary for the objective that is being pursued ought to be gathered [26]. Despite this, systems that use AI use a tremendous amount of data, and it is sometimes extremely challenging, if not unattainable, to establish which information is required for the computations to work and which knowledge is not required [26].

Additionally, it highlights concerns about the possibility of fraudulent activity: According to research that was published not too long ago by the World Health Organization (WHO), this risk has been brought to light. The report outlines how a questionnaire that was disseminated by the social network and was misrepresented as a psychiatric exam was used to build techniques that were subsequently utilized in influencing politics [27]. In connection with healthcare, if private health insurers were to be able to get access to sensitive information that may assist them in predicting the likelihood of persons needing medical treatment, then they would be able to use this knowledge, something they are not meant to be privy to, to make unauthorized adjustments to premiums. If carried out on a large scale, this may affect millions of people. Even though this was always a possible risk associated with any unauthorized possession of health-related data, the prospects that are provided by AI are enormous.

The fifth concern is that programs are collecting enormous amounts of data, which raises privacy concerns. There are certain aspects of the individual that they might not want to be included in their personal information, and it is feasible to detect such aspects. It is common knowledge that AI is capable of predicting characteristics such as age over time from nothing more than a relatively small privacy concerns amount of radiological data, which is not a revelation that comes as a surprise [28]. Nevertheless, Gichoya and colleagues have shown that deep learning algorithms are capable of accurately predicting ethnicity from a broad range of radiological scans. This might be a significant advancement in the field [29].

When it comes to evaluating AI as an aid to diagnosis, these are among a few of the most significant challenges that authorities must face. On the other hand, there is additionally one more domain that, even though in its early stages, must not be ignored. The application of this in the creation of drugs was discussed before. On the other hand, much as with other forms of technology, such as nuclear energy, things have the potential to be employed for both harmful and beneficial purposes. Even though techniques employed in this manner are normally intended to eliminate harmful substances, an ensemble of investigators decided to flip this concept on its head. According to the findings of preliminary proof of idea research, they demonstrated that they were able to build replicas of existing chemical agents that were anticipated to be more dangerous in a matter of hours [30]. They advocate for a better understanding of the prospects for multiple applications of AI, ethical training for individuals who are engaged, and the means by which allegations of possible abuses may be reported. To summarize, this presents an additional obstacle that has been largely overlooked until now for those who are responsible for governing AI [30]. The problem is on the periphery of the technological evaluation frameworks that are now in use.

In light of these concerns, it is frequently challenging to determine who is responsible for the event that anything goes wrong. Whenever a drug is granted permission, the approval is accompanied by certain guidelines. These encompass the guidelines for use, which refer to the ailment that the remedy is intended to treat, as well as individual factors, such as age or renal function, that ought to be taken into consideration while delivering a product [31]. Additionally, other drugs should not be administered with the medication due to the known interactions that may occur between the two. It is still possible for the healthcare professional to utilize it without a prescription if these circumstances are not satisfied; however, the practitioner will then be responsible for its usage. It has been observed that a medicine that has been supplied could continue to be harmful, even if it has been used correctly. This might be because there had been a possibility of harm that should have been discovered during development but was not, or because the medication was not kept in the appropriate circumstances. The accountability is quite evident in situations like this. The issue is far more complicated when it comes to technologies that rely on AI. While the computer program gives a result that opposes additional evidence that the provider can see but the algorithm's developers did not capture, who is accountable for deciding what proportion of weight to give to the software's answer? Is it the person who developed the algorithm, the person who enters data into the program (such as an echocardiograph operator), or the doctor who recommends treatment?

10.5 CAPABILITIES AND OBLIGATIONS OF REGULATORS

Van Laere and his fellow researchers have provided a comprehensive description of the regulatory processes that have been established by organizations in the United States and Europe to govern the use of AI systems for therapeutic decision assistance [2]. They described the challenges that arise when attempting to determine which items need to be susceptible to these kinds of regulations and when attempting to categorize the risk assessments of commodities. Maresova further commented on the regulations that pertain to healthcare equipment in the European Union in a remark that accompanied the previous statement [32]. It is hoped that the AI Act, which is being floated by the European Union, will bring in an era of change in the oversight of AI while setting an international standard for government agencies and companies. This act would not only be the initial exhaustive regulating initiative for AI globally, but it would additionally allocate merchandise through risk classifications [32].

We agree with Van Laere and his coworkers that neither group of authorities has yet provided resolutions to all of the problems that were originally brought up. Among the issues that people bring up, we recognize two of them as being particularly difficult to deal with. One of the initial concerns, as was additionally brought up by the FDA of the United States, is the desire to develop an enforcement procedure that covers the whole of the petition's potential life cycle [33]. The situation needs to encourage entrepreneurship while also maintaining the confidentiality of patients, which is a challenging equilibrium to pull off. To do the aforementioned, it will be necessary to create norms for every stage of this cycle. Beginning with the premarket authorization, this would entail the development of a procedure that is analogous to the stages of research studies that are carried out with drugs, but with modifications to match the specific circumstances of the situation. A prime instance of this would be the establishment of guidelines for ensuring the accuracy of algorithms; nevertheless, it is important to note that the difficulties associated with this endeavor ought to be taken seriously, considering the numerous uses that may be found for AI. At first glance, it could seem that having the capacity to describe the rationale would be good; yet, as the WHO research pointed out, this might potentially hinder invention [32]. On the other hand, there is a case to be made for the inclusion of a condition that techniques ought to be susceptible to being reviewed autonomously. In addition to that, it would involve an evaluation of patient benefits, which would exclude apps that are ultimately nothing more than data-gathering tools. Following the launch of the program, there have to be well-defined guidelines that specify the circumstances under which modifications to the system are deemed to be of enough significance to warrant another assessment to guarantee that no new dangers were introduced. Last but not least, there is the possibility that there will be a necessity for periodical inspections to be carried out at intervals that have been predetermined to discover possible adverse drift from the original functionality [33].

The second is regulating which is typical of the oversight of traditional healthcare products, including medicines. In this manner, assessments that have been employed to guide the regulatory procedure may be carried out in groups that are not comparable to the individuals on whom their findings will eventually be used. For instance, it is well known that numerous clinical studies of drugs do not include participants who are persons of advanced age or who have more than one illness [34]. In the process of assessing applications that use AI, this is of even greater significance. To add insult to injury, it is of utmost significance to foresee, examine, and prevent programs from duplicating or perpetuating biases that already exist. This is contingent upon a high degree of knowledge of the hazards, but it is possible to decrease the risks by the implementation of procedures such as the production of training data sets that have been validated as having a low risk of bias [35].

This is not going to be a simple endeavor. Although applications of AI in the medical field have already achieved significant headway, it is abundantly obvious that these kinds of applications have a great deal more opportunity for further growth in the future. Patients are in a better position to profit from the advancements that they have already provided. Nevertheless, to foresee and, to the greatest degree feasible, mitigate the dangers that could occur, the legal framework has had to keep up with the rapidly changing landscape of the medical sector [36].

10.6 CONCLUSION

Ultimately, the regulation of AI in healthcare is a challenging and intricate task that requires a careful equilibrium between fostering invention and guaranteeing patient confidentiality, confidentiality of information, and integrity of ethics. As AI techniques progress and become more widespread within the healthcare sector, regulatory frameworks must adapt to minimize dangers and maximize advantages. The endeavor of governing AI in healthcare necessitates a cooperative endeavor including legislators, healthcare practitioners, technicians, and ethical scholars. It is necessary to create strong and comprehensive regulatory structures to oversee the creation, implementation, and use of AI. These structures should include guidelines for ensuring the accuracy of statistics, accessibility of algorithms, compatibility across different systems, and responsibility for actions taken. Furthermore, continuous conversation and involvement with individuals or groups affected by AI-based decisions are crucial to address the moral ramifications, particularly regarding matters of prejudice, impartiality, and the possibility of unforeseen outcomes. Regulating organizations may cultivate confidence in AI technologies and encourage their appropriate incorporation into healthcare organizations by promoting a culture of transparency, ownership, and ongoing education. To effectively regulate AI in the medical field, it is crucial to adopt a proactive and versatile strategy that places the well-being of patients as the top priority, adheres to ethical principles, and leverages the revolutionary capabilities of AI to revolutionize the delivery of healthcare for the benefit of the community as a whole. As we traverse the intricacies of this legal environment, let us be resolute in our dedication to using the potential AI to progress healthcare while also protecting ourselves from its inherent dangers.

ACKNOWLEDGMENTS

Not applicable.

AUTHOR CONTRIBUTIONS

Suraj Kumar contributed to major writing, and original draft preparation, contributed writing and figures and tables, and contributed to writing and figures and tables; Dr. Rishabha Malviya contributed to writing and contributed editing and proofreading the manuscript.

FUNDING

Not applicable.

DATA AVAILABILITY

Not applicable.

CONFLICT OF INTEREST

The author does not have any conflict of interest.

KEYWORDS

- **regulation**
- **clinical decision support**
- **artificial intelligence**

REFERENCES

1. Haider R. 2023. The future of pharmaceuticals industry 2024. *J. Pharm Pharmacol Res*. *6*(6).
2. Seddon JJ, Currie WL. 2013. Cloud computing and trans-border health data: Unpacking US and EU healthcare regulation and compliance. *Health Policy Technol*. *2*(4), 229–241.
3. Barrat J. 2023. *Our Final Invention: Artificial Intelligence and the End of the Human Era*. Hachette: UK.
4. Rane N. 2023, Aug. Potential role and challenges of ChatGPT and similar generative artificial intelligence in architectural engineering. Available at SSRN 4607767.
5. Eichler HG, Abadie E, Baker M, Rasi G. 2012. Fifty years after thalidomide; what role for drug regulators? *Br J Clin Pharmacol. 74*(5), 731–733. https://doi.org/10.1111/j.1365-2125.2012.04255. x.
6. Van Laere S, Muylle KM, Cornu P. 2022. Clinical decision support and new regulatory frameworks for medical devices: Are we ready for it?—A viewpoint paper. *Int J Health Policy Manag. 11*(12), 3159–3163. https://doi.org/10.34172/ijhpm.2021.144.
7. Kirchhoff CF, Wang XM, Conlon HD, Anderson S, Ryan AM, Bose A. 2017. Biosimilars: Key regulatory considerations and similarity assessment tools. *Biotechnol Bioeng. 114*(12), 2696–2705. https://doi.org/10.1002/bit.26438.
8. Tudur Smith C, Williamson PR, Beresford MW. 2014. Methodology of clinical trials for rare diseases. *Best Pract Res Clin Rheumatol. 28*(2), 247–262. https://doi.org/10.1016/j.berh.2014.03.004.
9. World Health Organization. 2015. *World Report on Aging and Health*. World Health Organization.
10. Rajpurkar P, Chen E, Banerjee O, Topol EJ. 2022. AI in health and medicine. *Nat Med. 28*(1), 31–38. https://doi.org/10.1038/s41591-021-01614-0.
11. Gulshan V, Peng L, Coram M, et al. 2016. Development and validation of a deep learning algorithm for the detection of diabetic retinopathy in retinal fundus photographs. *JAMA 316*(22), 2402–2410. https://doi.org/10.1001/jama.2016.17216.

12. Porter P, Abeyratne U, Swarnkar V, et al. 2019. A prospective multicentre study testing the diagnostic accuracy of an automated cough sound centered analytic system for the identification of common respiratory disorders in children. *Respir Res. 20*(1), 81. https://doi.org/10.1186/s12931-019-1046-6.
13. Kehl KL, Elmarakeby H, Nishino M, et al. 2019. Assessment of deep natural language processing in ascertaining oncologic outcomes from radiology reports. *JAMA Oncol. 5*(10), 1421–1429. https://doi.org/10.1001/jamaoncol.2019.1800.
14. Esteva A, Kuprel B, Novoa RA, et al. 2017. Dermatologist-level classification of skin cancer with deep neural networks. *Nature 542*(7639), 115–118. https://doi.org/10.1038/nature21056.
15. Walsh CG, Ribeiro JD, Franklin JC. 2017. Predicting risk of suicide attempts over time through machine learning. *Clin Psychol Sci. 5*(3), 457–469. https://doi.org/10.1177/2167702617691560.
16. Topol EJ. 2019. High-performance medicine: The convergence of human and artificial intelligence. *Nat Med. 25*(1), 44–56. https://doi.org/10.1038/s41591-018-0300-7.
17. Heaven WD. Hundreds of AI tools have been built to catch covid. None of them helped. in 2021. https://www.technologyreview.com/2021/07/30/1030329/machine-learning-ai-failed-covid-hospital-diagnosis-pandemic/. (Accessed May 20, 2022).
18. Weiner JP, Kfuri T, Chan K, Fowles JB. 2007. "e-Iatrogenesis": The most critical unintended consequence of CPOE and other HIT. *J Am Med Inform Assoc. 14*(3), 387–388. https://doi.org/10.1197/jamia.M2338.
19. Cabitza F, Rasoini R, Gensini GF. 2017. Unintended consequences of machine learning in medicine. *JAMA. 318*(6), 517–518. https://doi.org/10.1001/jama.2017.7797.
20. Burrell J. 2016. How the machine 'thinks': Understanding opacity in machine learning algorithms. *Big Data Soc. 3*(1), 2053951715622512. https://doi.org/10.1177/2053951715622512.
21. Grote T, Berens P. 2020. On the ethics of algorithmic decision-making in healthcare. *J Med Ethics. 46*(3), 205–211. https://doi.org/10.1136/medethics-2019-105586.
22. Maharao N, Antontsev V, Wright M, Varshney J. 2020. Entering the era of computationally driven drug development. *Drug Metab Rev. 52*(2), 283–298. https://doi.org/10.1080/03602532.2020.1726944.
23. Bhattacharyya RP, Bandyopadhyay N, Ma P, et al. 2019. Simultaneous detection of genotype and phenotype enables rapid and accurate antibiotic susceptibility determination. *Nat Med. 25*(12), 1858–1864. https://doi.org/10.1038/s41591-019-0650-9.
24. Obermeyer Z, Powers B, Vogeli C, Mullainathan S. 2019. Dissecting racial bias in an algorithm used to manage the health of populations. *Science 366*(6464), 447–453. https://doi.org/10.1126/science. aax2342.
25. Food and Drug Administration. 2021. Artificial intelligence and machine learning in software as a medical device. https://www.fda.gov/medical-devices/software-medical-device-samd/artificial-intelligence-and-machine-learning-software-medical-device. (Accessed March 17, 2022).
26. van Kolfschooten H. 2022. EU regulation of artificial intelligence: Challenges for patients' rights. *Common Mark Law Rev. 59*(1), 81–112. https://doi.org/10.54648/cola2022005.

27. World Health Organization (WHO). 2021. *Ethics and Governance of Artificial Intelligence for Health: WHO Guidance*. WHO: Geneva.
28. Eng DK, Khandwala NB, Long J, et al. 2021. Artificial intelligence algorithm improves radiologist performance in skeletal age assessment: A prospective multicenter randomized controlled trial. *Radiology 301*(3), 692–699. https://doi.org/10.1148/radiol.2021204021.
29. Gichoya JW, Banerjee I, Bhimireddy AR, et al. 2022. AI recognition of patient race in medical imaging: A modeling study. *Lancet Digit Health 4*(6), e406–e414. https://doi.org/10.1016/s2589-7500(22)00063-2.
30. rbina F, Lentzos F, Invernizzi C, Ekins S. 2022. Dual use of artificial-intelligence-powered drug discovery. *Nat Mach Intell. 4*(3), 189–191. https://doi.org/10.1038/s42256-022-00465-9.
31. Maresova P. 2022. Impact of regulatory changes on innovations in the medical device industry: Comment on "clinical decision support and new regulatory frameworks for medical devices: Are we ready for it?—viewpoint paper." *Int J Health Policy Manag. 12*, 7262. https://doi.org/10.34172/ijhpm.2022.7262.
32. Heikkilä M. A quick guide to the most important AI law you've never heard of. 2022.
33. Hwang TJ, Kesselheim AS, Vokinger KN. 2019. Lifecycle regulation of artificial intelligence- and machine learning-based software devices in medicine. *JAMA 322*(23), 2285–2286. https://doi.org/10.1001/jama.2019.16842
34. Britton A, McKee M, Black N, McPherson K, Sanderson C, Bain C. 1999. Threats to the applicability of randomized trials: Exclusions and selective participation. *J Health Serv Res Policy. 4*(2), 112–121. https://doi.org/10.1177/135581969900400210.
35. Vayena E, Blasimme A, Cohen IG. 2018. Machine learning in medicine: Addressing ethical challenges. *PLoS Med. 15*(11), e1002689. https://doi.org/10.1371/journal.pmed.1002689
36. Patel KR. 2023. Enhancing global supply chain resilience: Effective strategies for mitigating disruptions in an interconnected world. *BULLET: J Multidiscipline Ilmu. 2*(1), 257–264.

Index

C

D

E

M

N

O

For Product Safety Concerns and Information please contact our EU representative GPSR@taylorandfrancis.com Taylor & Francis Verlag GmbH, Kaufingerstraße 24, 80331 München, Germany